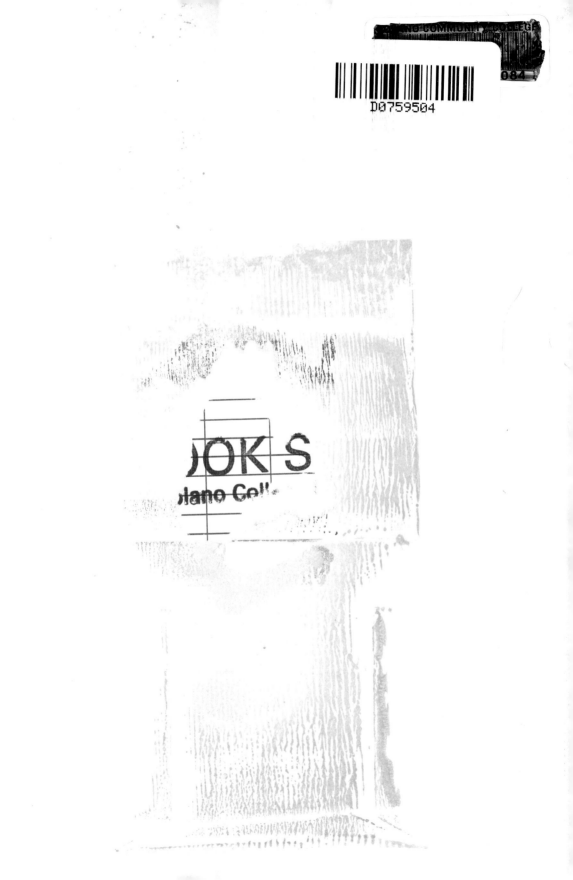
D0759504

OOK S
olano Coll

LIBRARY
SOLANO COMMUNITY COLLEGE
P. O. BOX 246
SUISUN CITY, CALIFORNIA 94585
(707) 864-7000

MIGRANT

Agricultural Workers in America's Northeast

MIGRANT

Agricultural Workers in America's Northeast

by

WILLIAM H. FRIEDLAND

and

DOROTHY NELKIN

LIBRARY
SOLANO COMMUNITY COLLEGE
P. O. BOX 246
SUISUN CITY, CALIFORNIA 94585
(707) 864-7000

HOLT, RINEHART AND WINSTON

NEW YORK   CHICAGO   SAN FRANCISCO

Copyright © 1971 by Holt, Rinehart and Winston, Inc.
All rights reserved
Library of Congress Catalog Card Number: 77–162649
ISBN: 0–03–085767–8 (Paper)
ISBN: 0–03–086706–1 (Cloth)
Printed in the United States of America
1 2 3 4   0 9 0   9 8 7 6 5 4 3 2 1

HD
1527
A 125
F 74
50590

For

LIAM, FIONA, NICOLE

and

LISA AND LAURIE

So that, by the time they can all read about it,
this blight will be gone.

Foreword

For too many farmworkers life is poor, nasty, brutish, and short. Too many farmworkers are present-day slaves, subservient to and dependent upon the fluctuations of economics, the whims of growers, the vagaries of weather, the march of technology, and the decisions of government. This condition is the predictable consequence of economic and political powerlessness.

This study presents a grim reminder of the exploitation, poverty, and hopelessness which characterizes one of the hardest working yet most essential elements of our nation's work force—migrant agricultural workers.

The firsthand accounts of the lives of east coast migrants presented in this book point out the glaring contrast between the nation of plenty which most of us take for granted, and the demeaned, undignified, impoverished, and joyless existence of the harvesters on whom we depend for our daily food. Except for an occasional television documentary, we seem oblivious to the hundreds of thousands of uneducated, unemployable, sick, malnourished, poorly housed, and hopeless victims who are living in the shadows of the economic and political system of the most affluent society in history. The findings of the students who investigated the living and working environments of east coast migrants make clear the reasons for their hopelessness and powerlessness.

The erratic nature of their work opportunities offers no assurance that migrants will have work from one day to the next. When there is no field work to be done, migrants have no income, a situation which forces them to suffer hunger and malnutrition at worst, or at best, to become indebted to a contractor or crew leader who more often than not has long been known for exploitation and abuses. Indebtedness to a crew leader often makes many workers captives so that they cannot leave to seek work elsewhere.

Poor working conditions are matched by horrible living conditions. Labor camps frequently fail to meet even minimal housing code standards. Migrants are all too often housed in cramped, squalid quarters which allow virtually no privacy—vermin-infested firetraps with no screens or windowpanes, no running water, no drainage system, inadequate sanitation facilities, and housing inspectors who either do their work superficially or do not come at all. As the situation is now, there are few effective ways of enforcing even weak housing code requirements.

For all practical purposes, farmworkers are either specifically excluded from, or at best only minimally included under, every major federal or state social or worker benefit program, such as collective bargaining, minimum wage, workmen's compensation, unemployment insurance, child labor laws, social security, welfare, and housing programs. Even when migrants are covered, enforcement is inadequate or nonexistent. Thus those benefits which most U.S. workers take for granted have been explicitly denied to farmworkers.

Where legislation makes social and worker benefits available to farmworkers, and this availability is known, the farmworkers are still effectively excluded by their inability to meet invidious conditions precedent for receiving benefits, conditions such as income standards and residence requirements. Not unexpectedly, even special programs that have been designed to benefit farmworkers, like the Farm Labor Contractor Registration Act, the Migrant Health Act, food and nutrition programs, specific programs within OEO (with the possible exception of rural legal-service programs) and the Office of Education, have often been rendered useless to farmworkers because of lack of adequate enforcement, lack of awareness, apathy, discrimination, absence of outreach, poor program design, or lack of funds. Even when migrants are eligible for such assistance, they often cannot afford to spend the extravagant amounts of time and energy demanded by the red-tape procedures associated with aid programs. Many programs, by holding out false hopes and promises, virtually become negative influences on the lives of the people.

Finally, both legal and motivational obstacles, residence requirements, and high illiteracy rates all limit farmworker registration and voting participation in the political process.

A special tragedy of the farmworkers' situation is that children particularly are the victims of the family's powerlessness and constant mobility. Children of migrant workers never receive an education comparable to that of the rest of the U.S. population. They are too often treated as outcasts in schools, and many toil beside their parents in the fields for extra income where protective child labor laws are inapplicable or ignored.

Equal in significance to the material harm suffered by neglected children is the psychological and emotional injury to the individuals and families which results from their situation. Migrant workers never become part of any community in which they work since they are mistrusted, feared, or disdained by permanent residents of any community through which they pass as temporary visitors. Thus they suffer not only from the rootlessness and homelessness of their life-style, but also from the constant exposure to rejection by the rest of society.

The hopelessness of the migrant worker's outlook, as described in these pages, rises from his inability to foresee any possible way of breaking loose from the pattern of political, social, and economic vulnerability, which in turn results from society's unwillingness to guarantee equal protections and rights to a group of our fellow citizens. How long will we tolerate this unjust double standard?

How long can we continue to turn our backs on the migrant workers? How long can we ignore—and tacitly accept—the poverty, hunger and malnutrition, and miserable living and working conditions which migrants are forced by their situation to live with? How much longer can we tolerate the paradox of a society which spends so much time, energy, and money reaching for the moon and beyond while it refuses to guarantee the minimum necessities for a decent life to a substantial group of its citizens?

We can no longer claim ignorance of the urgent problems faced by migrant workers, and it is inexcusable that we have not acted to alleviate the miserable conditions in which some of our fellow citizens live. The Senate Subcommittee on Migratory Labor, established ten years ago, has gathered a wealth of information on the desperate situation and has proposed legislation which would begin to deal with the migrant problem.

But legislation is not the whole solution; it is only the first step. Protective legislation is worthless without effective means of enforcing it. Furthermore, there must be public awareness and recognition that migrants should be guaranteed the right to a decent living, that migrants, too, should be entitled to better wages, housing, health care, and education, and—most important—an effective voice in controlling their own lives. Efforts by scholars such as Dr. Friedland and Mrs. Nelkin are playing an increasingly important role in educating legislators and the general public about the pressing needs of the most neglected and unprotected segment of our society.

It is the absence of power to press for their own needs and aspirations that consigns farmworkers to the bottom rung of the ladder. They often remain today in virtual peonage and invisible to the masses of our population; their needs remain unheeded; their problems remain unsolved. Farmworkers have seen this and are pulling themselves together in a movement to garner a measure of power, as evidenced by farm labor organizing in California. Therein may lie the hope of lasting change. To understand more fully where that movement is going, and why it is going in that direction, it is essential that we examine in some detail the farmworkers' experience of powerlessness and hopelessness. In this regard, Dr. Friedland and Mrs. Nelkin have made an important contribution to the literature, for by analyzing the conditions of the farmworkers' life, perhaps all of us will gain insight into possible ways to improve their lot.

SENATOR WALTER F. MONDALE

Acknowledgments

Social research is characteristically an activity that involves the energies of many people. That is especially true of this volume, which is based upon the field work of many students. We find ourselves indebted to a great many individuals and agencies and can only mention a small number of those who have contributed to our work.

First, we wish to acknowledge the enthusiastic participation of the student contributors whose research has provided the essence of this volume. There were, in addition, many individuals who assisted in the complex arrangements for placing students in camps, who provided valuable information and advice, who assisted in the instructional activities that accompanied the research, and who facilitated the research process. Among those whose contribution was considerable we include Henry Anderson, Gene Bedford, Daniel Daly, Charles Green, Brian How, William Howell, John Kirby, Richard Klatt, George Lamont, Frank Losurdo, Richard Norton, and Joseph Salvato. We owe a special debt to the migrant team of the American Friends Service Committee, to its director, Bill Channel, and to his staff, Jim Pollard and Sam Jackson. Dr. John Radebaugh, of the University of Rochester Medical School, was a constant help. Professor Eric Krystall, then of Tuskegee Institute, provided invaluable assistance in the recruitment of Tuskegee students for the project.

The research was done when the authors were both at the New York State School of Industrial and Labor Relations at Cornell University. David G. Moore, then dean of the school, encouraged the project and provided continuing support, moral and otherwise. We are greatly indebted to the organizations that provided financial support to sustain the project, the Manpower Administration of the U.S. Department of Labor, the New York State Agricultural Experiment Station at Cornell University, and the College of Agriculture at Cornell. The Ford Foundation also provided support for the substantive study and encouraged the integration of research and teaching, thereby facilitating a key aspect of the entire project.

During the final stages of the preparation of the manuscript, William Friedland was on the faculty of the University of California at Santa Cruz and Dorothy Nelkin was at the Centre Internationale Universitaire in Paris and with the Program on Science, Technology and Society at Cornell University. Each of these institutions cooperated in making time and facilities available and we wish to express our gratitude.

Student Contributors

The students listed below participated in a migrant labor research project from 1966 through 1968. Five of the students (indicated by T) were from Tuskegee Institute; the remainder were from Cornell University. Specific contributions from the students' field diaries are identified in the text by their authors' initials.

Jane Avery
Janet Perkins Carter (T)
Les Durant
Howard Gladston
David Gruenberg
Harry Hutchinson (T)
Arthur Kimmel
Sandra Grotberg Kistler
Craig Leslie
Iles Minoff
Lee Packer (T)
Jessalyn Pendarvis (T)
George Price

David Rindos
Michael Rotkin
John Rounds
Leonard Rubin
Lucy Whyte Russo
Nedra Sanfilipo
Marie-Celeste Scully
Roger Stetter
Judith Stewart
Edd Taub
Lillian Trager
Graham Wiggins (T)

WILLIAM H. FRIEDLAND
DOROTHY NELKIN

Contents

Foreword by Senator Walter F. Mondale   vii

Acknowledgments   xi

Introduction   1

Themes, 1
Migrants in Florida, 3
The Camps in the North, 7
Methods of Study, 15

Part One   THE SETTING   17

   1. Going North on the Season   19

Recruitment, 20
The Trip North, 22

   2. Migrant Labor Camps   35

Housing, 37
Privacy, 43
Food and Eating Arrangements, 45
People in Isolation, 48

   3. The Crew Leader and His Control   51

Crew Leader Portraits, 52
Means of Control, 61
Crew Leader Mobility: A Case Study, 66

   4. Work   70

Grower/Crew Leader Relations, 71
Piecework Crops, 76
Hourly Work, 90

Part Two   CHAOS AS ORDER   97

  5. Personal Behavior   99

      Sex and Deviance, 99
      Personal Dress, 102
      Hygiene, 104
      Health, 109
      Religion and the Supernatural, 111

  6. Interpersonal Relations   121

      Marriages, Muck Marriages, and Mother, 122
      Communication, 129
      Reciprocity and Exchange, 134
      Tension and Mistrust, 138
      Violence, 143

  7. Leisure Time   149

      Stories and Jokes, 150
      The Social Functions of Humor, 155
      Games, 159
      The Piccolo, 164
      Wining Up, 167

  8. It Cut My Spirit and I Can't Pick a Thing   173

      The Image of Work, 174
      Attitudes toward Supervision, 177
      The "Spirit" of Work, 179
      Productivity, 182
      Wages, 186

Part Three   PERSISTENCE OR CHANGE   193

  9. The Migrant and the Outside World   195

      Black Folks, White Folks, 195
      Poor Folks, Rich Folks, 205
      Prisons and Police, 207
      Our Town, 210
      National Crises, 211
      The World of Television, 219

10. The Search for Solutions 221

Dropping Out, 222
Preorganizational Gropings, 227
Unionization, 235
A Successful Organization, 237

11. The Children 243

Kids, 244
Adolescents, 247
Child-Rearing Practices, 249
Education, 252

Appendix OUTSIDERS IN THE SYSTEM 257

The External Network, 258
Government Services, 267
Social Work Services, 271
The Church and Its Volunteers, 275

Bibliography 281

MIGRANT

Agricultural Workers in America's Northeast

INTRODUCTION

Themes

This book is about migrant farmworkers. Many crops, especially fresh fruits and vegetables, are still harvested by hand by people who "work the seasons," moving with the ripening crops to provide labor where it is needed. Thousands of these migrants live close to Florida's Gold Coast just inland from Miami, Fort Lauderdale, and Palm Beach. For the casual northern tourist traveling south, migrant farmworkers are as unobtrusive as they are in the north where, during the summer, they cluster in large numbers in eastern Suffolk County outside of New York City, as well as on the margins of Rochester, Syracuse, and other western New York cities, or in southern New Jersey.

This study explores the migrant labor system as it operates in the northeastern United States. The study is concerned with how the system affects its participants, the migrant workers themselves. Detailed information on the economics of migrant labor, and on its history and demography, can be found elsewhere.[1] Here we are concerned with life in migrant labor crews: the details of daily routine and the problems and the adjustments made by the people to the circumstances in which they live.

Three themes pervade this book. The first is the disorganized and unpredictable character of migrant life. Intrinsic to the migrant labor system is its irregularity. A labor crew is formed for a period of three to five months, and there is little continuity in many groups from year to year. A migrant may find himself in a camp that is in good or in poor condition; it may be

---

[1] A brief bibliography appears at the end of the book.

1

overcrowded or spacious; he may have a single room or live in a "bullpen"; his neighbors or roommates may be affable or disagreeable. Often he has little idea of where he is located geographically and, in any case, seldom has means to move elsewhere. He is paid for most activities on a piecework basis so that if it rains, he has no earnings. He is totally dependent on the efficiency of the grower for whom he works, on the whim of his crew leader, and on the quality of the crop. He has practically no way of controlling his environment with respect to either his home or his work. It is within these erratic conditions that the migrant must create a viable mode of existence.

The second theme is concerned with the migrant's adaptation in day-to-day life to the disorganized character of his existence. The ways migrants relate to one another, their understandings and expectations, reflect the conditions in which they find themselves. The behavior of individuals is bounded by expectations that develop through past experience. There are certain attitudes and behaviors that we have come to expect as "normal" in American society; namely, those fostered by an environment characterized by regularity and a well-defined system of rewards. These circumstances encourage orientation toward planning, productivity, and an expectation of control. Within organized frameworks, ambiguity is managed by attempts to control the environment, to identify problems, and to reaffirm order. In contrast, the adaptive response to the disorganized circumstances of migrant life is apathy and escapism. This response does not necessarily indicate that migrants have different values than the rest of society; nor does it imply that their behavior is pathological or deviant. Rather, such behavior is consonant with the needs and definitions imposed by their social context. Although some patterns of behavior in migrant labor camps appear disorganized, they serve in fact to make life viable under conditions of uncertainty, ambiguity, and dependence.

A third theme is the extent to which the migrant social system traps its participants. Adaptive behavior is self-perpetuating. Social patterns that make life viable in one set of circumstances may differ from those necessary to succeed in others. They tend to become fixed, impeding adaptation to new conditions. The tendency for the system to perpetuate itself is revealed in the relationship between the migrant and the larger society and in the socialization of children. In practical terms, this tendency implies that there are obstacles to social change within the system that are not easily removed merely by providing "opportunities." But it is not only the internal features of a system that perpetuate it; we will illustrate how the network of organizations that constitute the system around migrant labor also impedes significant change.

The migrant labor system in the northeastern United States, the area of concern in this book, is part of a larger system. There are three patterns of seasonal agricultural migration in the United States. On the West Coast, migration takes place over relatively short distances, largely within the state of California. The midcontinent stream, originating in Texas, distributes itself broadly in a variety of crops. One group goes north into Michigan and Wisconsin, working mainly in soft fruits. A small number, largely skilled workers, operates harvesting machinery in the wheat states. The East Coast stream originates in Florida and moves up the Atlantic seaboard to the Eastern shore, to New York State, New Jersey, and New England, working in vegetables and fruits.

The three streams vary ethnically: the western and midcontinent streams are predominantly Mexican American; the eastern stream is primarily Negro. But many other ethnic groups work in California and thousands of Puerto Ricans work in the northeast each summer.

It is difficult to establish how many migrant workers there are in the United States: census enumerations provide estimates varying from 400,000 to 2,000,000. The discrepancies arise largely from technical difficulties in the enumeration of a mobile people. The eastern stream is estimated at about 50,000 people. With the decline of the plantation economy, Negroes from agricultural communities in the south moved to a variety of areas, including the rich agricultural lands of Florida. There they now work in citrus or vegetables throughout the winter. During the summer, the available agricultural work is limited. Because few can subsist for four to five months on the meagre income earned during the winter growing season, this group is the main source of the labor that moves north to harvest the crops in the northeastern United States.

Migrants in Florida

The life of migrants in Florida has an important bearing on the character and expectations of crews as they move north. A brief review suggests the diversity of arrangements available to agricultural workers in Florida, yet the dependence characteristic of each option. Unlike the more affluent migrants who inhabit the Gold Coast hotels on Florida's coastline, most black farmworkers who come to New York state make their winter homes on the "Range Line," which borders U.S. 441 a few miles west of the Florida coastal cities, or they cluster in and around the towns of Belle Glade and Pahokee on the southern shore of Lake Okeechobee.

The town of Belle Glade is the home of about 20,000 people, about half of whom are black. Except for teachers, shopkeepers, and others in service occupations, the entire black population consists of migrant agricultural workers.

MIGRANT HOUSING IN FLORIDA

Migrant housing on the Range Line consists of rented rooms or small apartments in stucco motel-type buildings or in slum buildings over stores. Although there are some families living in the towns, those with children prefer to live out of town if possible. Single men can be observed eating out of cans in grocery stores to avoid cooking. Families, often without kitchens, cook on burners in their rooms. There are no communal cooking arrangements as in the camps in the north. A small two-room apartment rents for $18.00 per week. Because rooms are scarce, many people hold their apartments when they go north; to do so, they must pay full rent during their absence.

The most important housing for most Florida migrants consists of large camps called "centers" or "projects" on the fringes of the towns. The Okeechobee camp, for example, is owned by the Belle Glade Housing Authority, a private organization of local property owners. The camp is located one mile out of town and, having no public transportation, is isolated; at the entrance, a sign reads: "No Trespassing, Visitors Register." Because the camp is reputed to be the best housing in the area and a better place to raise a family than the town, there is always demand when vacancies occur. The main part of the camp consists of several hundred identical, small gray wood dwellings renting from $10.00 to $14.00 a week. In one section, set apart from the main area—and conspicuous in that the yards are planted with bushes and flowers—are the residences of local ministers, teachers, and year-round agricultural workers. During the summer most residents go north; to hold their houses for the next season many pay half rent during their absence. The camp is self-sufficient, containing a school, an assembly building, a nursery, and a hot dog concession. A white manager and a black assistant manager maintain the grounds, collect rent, and decide what activities may take place within the camp. For example, a request to show the film *Harvest of Shame* on the premises was denied.

Three similar projects, despite being condemned for several years, house hundreds of migrants in the Pahokee area. There are plans to replace them with new camps, but in the meantime the migrants still live in wooden shacks, most of which have no running water or heat.

Physically, the Pompano Beach camp, housing 2000 people, resembles the Okeechobee camp. This is, however, a "grower camp" in that individual growers rent sections to house those who work on their farms. Residents pay no rent but must, in exchange, work for only the one grower or they will be evicted. This assures the grower of his labor force. Other grower camps are smaller and located on individual farms. In this sense, the pattern resembles the system in the north, with a high degree of paternalistic dependence on the grower and the arrangements he provides. Residents of these camps may not work for any other grower without permission and must accept the conditions of work and the limitations on their nonwork activities. There are cases where growers have evicted people who joined an adult education program, which was felt to distract them from work. Families and single men often live in grower camps when they come to Florida with no money. Because other living arrangements require advance rent, people are often forced into this system.

Similar dependency prevails in "crew camps" except that crew leaders rather than growers run them. The crew leader contracts his crew to different growers of his choosing. This again is similar to arrangements in the north, and many crew leaders retain at least a core of a crew year-round.

In addition, there are, along the Range Line, many clusters of barracks and motel-type structures. Some are decrepit wooden buildings; others are of stucco or concrete-block construction. Each cluster is focused around a commissary, a liquor store, a "juke,"[2] and a gas station. Commissaries sell food of poor quality at high prices. Chicken, ribs, pig tails and necks, pork chops, and cold cuts cost about 10 cents a pound more than equivalent meat in small groceries in town. Camp commissaries, however, provide credit for those who shop regularly. People living in these rural barracks go north during the summer, and do not hold their rooms. In the fall, the rooms are rented on a first-come, first-served basis.

WORK ORGANIZATION

The organization of the work process in Florida differs from the pattern in the north. For those in towns such as Belle Glade, the day begins at the "loading ramp," a large square in the middle of town. Each morning at 5:00 A.M., the loading ramp is crowded with buses, trucks, contractors, and people shopping for a day's work. The contractors make arrangements with

---

[2] Juke (pronounced "jook"): a separate room or building (sometimes open to the elements) where prepared food and drinks are sold and where there may be dancing to the music of a "piccolo" (jukebox).

the growers to hire and transport workers to the fields where, on larger farms, the grower (or his hired help) assume supervisory roles. Some contractors work for a single grower for the entire season; others seek contracts by the job, by the week, or even by the day. Contractors go to the ramp to recruit daily. This is called the "day haul" system and it is the predominant pattern. Although people make motions of shopping around between contractors, they tend to choose their contractor on his reputation, rather than for the particular deal he offers. "He promises a good deal," they say of one contractor, "but he never comes through with it." Thus, a grapevine operates as an essential part of recruitment. Some contractors recruit from the fringe camps such as Okeechobee, and throughout the Range Line there are small loading ramps in rural centers so that even those in the rural motel units work on a day haul basis if they are not tied to a particular crew or grower.

Buses leave between 5:00 and 6:00 A.M. and often do not return until 7:00 or 8:00 in the evening. Long rides to work, delays, and labor wastage are daily problems for migrants in Florida as well as in the north. There is also considerable irregularity in work, although weather patterns and the large scale of the farming operations make the season more predictable. Despite the claims of farmers that there is always much work and insufficient labor, most people are able to find work only three or four days each week.

There are distinctions between "contractors" and "crew leaders" in Florida and the north. Contractors have more limited roles than do crew leaders, contracting with growers to recruit and haul labor. Crew leaders not only contract with growers, but also maintain their crews as social units in nonwork contexts. There is overlap between these two types and, indeed, our terminology—based on social realities—is not identical to that used by administrative organizations. Of relevance here is the fact that most Florida contractors merely recruit workers in the south, but when these same contractors move north with crews, they become crew leaders, undertaking management of their crews in all respects for the entire season.

Farming on the Range Line is devoted mostly to vegetables; citrus is grown elsewhere. In vegetables, there is variety in wage payment systems. In some cases, the farmer pays the contractor a lump sum for the entire day's work or for a given job. The contractor, in turn, distributes wages to his crew according to the agreement made in the morning, keeping the remainder. In other situations, the grower pays each worker by the hour, and the contractor receives a fixed percentage. In still another arrangement, the contractor receives a fixed amount for the day, and each worker is paid as he turns in a full hamper of produce. The picker himself has little economic leverage unless there is a serious labor shortage, since the large growers can manipulate market prices if productivity is low and tend to agree among themselves as to wage levels to avoid competition for labor. There is no state agricultural minimum wage law so that the levels are based on federal wage legislation, which, at the time of our study, required a minimum wage of $1.00 an hour. This figure has since risen to $1.30 an hour, the maximum to which it will rise under current federal legislation. According to an informant, wages in a day haul are higher than those in the grower camps and compensate for the "free" rent in these camps.

As the summer sets in and Florida's harvest peters out, most agricultural workers leave for the north. Some try to remain in the south year-round, eking out a subsistence from odd jobs. There is little work, however, and few have sufficient savings to permit them to remain. Although this is the pattern year after year, few people make the decision to go north until the last minute. During the winter they are reluctant to admit that they might again have to move.

As the workers move north, the patterns of living and work organization change substantially, except for year-round crews. The migrants are solicited by crew leaders and form into new crews for the trip north. Friends often try to join the same crew but there is no systematic perpetuation of the Florida groups in the north. Many of those who work with relative independence in the south under the day haul system become crew members for purposes of migration. Some families, owning their own cars, make private arrangements with northern growers and avoid the crew leader system. Depending upon the size of the crew needed and his capacity to keep a stable core of workers, a crew leader may fill out his crew through last-minute recruitment.

The Camps in the North

This book has developed from the study of fourteen camps that were almost entirely ethnically homogeneous, composed of Florida Negroes. The camps displayed many common features as well as significant variations. Here, six of the fourteen camps in which detailed study took place are described to provide a picture of the migrant labor system.

The systemic aspects of migrant labor should be kept in mind by the reader. Migrant labor is not a "normal" occupation in which work is distinct from such social factors as housing and kinship. Social and work satisfactions are closely related in crews that live and work together with only limited outside contact.

HOUSE CAMP (MR)[3]

The smallest camp studied consisted of a single tenant house owned by a small grower who had no involvement with the camp or the work organization. The grower maintained contact with the crew through a year-round hired man, who arranged the work but had little direct contact with crew members.

The camp was an ancient frame house in a marshy area on an isolated dirt road a mile from a hamlet. Nearby lived a community of "stagrants," migrants who had dropped out of the stream to remain north year-round. The house was in poor condition, with broken plasterboard partitions, a leaking roof, and two outhouses (one of which burned early in the season). The crew consisted of twenty-eight people, including the crew leader, his wife, and ten children. This large family lived in a separate house nearby. Aside from the crew leader's family and one other, the remaining people were single. Although most crew members had been north on the season before, no member of the crew had known the others for more than a few months. The crew leader required medical care early in the season and delegated total responsibility to his driver. The driver and his "muck wife"[4] cooked for the crew, charging them $12.50 each per week.

The farm on which the crew worked was only a short walk from the camp. The main crop was cherries, and only one person in the crew had ever picked this crop before. Supervision by the driver was lax, and when the original crew leader reappeared on the scene and began to tighten control of the crew, the change was resented. The crew ultimately split; the crew leader, his family, and two others departed, leaving the driver with the rest of the crew.

Productivity was extremely low in this crew; the tendency of many people here, as in other crews, was to claim that the next crop, apples, was the one in which they would make "big money." Inefficiency in the management of work was marked. There were long waits each day to get cherries checked in and tickets punched, and a poor system of labor allocation required the

---

[3] Initials indicate the name of the participant-observer who lived in the camp and provide a means to associate events and statements appearing later in the text with a particular camp. To identify the observer, see the list of contributors on p. xvi.

[4] Muck wife: migrant terminology for a free marital liaison, usually arranged for the season.

faster pickers to wait for the slower ones. The availability of work was intermittent, and behavior within the camp was affected by the large amount of spare time.

Spare time was taken up largely by drinking and card playing, but there was relatively little gambling. There were many fights on weekends, instigated largely by one person, an old man close to eighty. There were no "winos"[5] in the camp and heavy drinking was usually limited to the weekend. Partial or nonattendance at work on Mondays was usual. Much of the sociability occurred in the house, but occasionally groups of men would go to a juke in the neighboring stagrant community.

MODERN CAMP (LD)

This camp is located on a relatively large and modern farm owned and operated by a grower concerned about keeping abreast of recent scientific developments in agriculture and in farm management.

The housing in Modern Camp was widely dispersed: indeed, it cannot be described as a single physical facility. The migrants were scattered over a considerable distance in trailers, tenant houses, and shacks. It was possible to walk from place to place, but this took about five or ten minutes and therefore affected social patterns considerably. The dispersal of the housing and the nonexistence of a juke were viewed by the grower as a solution to the problem of "trouble"—drinking, violence, and gambling.

The housing units were in fair condition. Because each housed no more than fourteen people, the grower was relieved from some regulations of the housing code. Three dollars weekly rent was charged per person. Each family or individual made his own cooking arrangements, each unit having cooking facilities. Shopping was facilitated by the unusually high number of cars in the camp.

Housing, as well as other aspects of labor policy, represented the carefully thought-out philosophy of the grower with respect to the recruitment, direction, and management of labor. He viewed the crew leader system as exploitative and avoided it. Workers were recruited entirely through informal contacts maintained in a single rural county in Alabama.[6] Because they found work satisfactory, earnings relatively high, and housing and other conditions reasonable, a basic core of workers returned to the camp year after year, bringing with them enough new workers to keep the labor force in balance. By establishing a reputation in a single small southern

---

[5] Winos: those who remain drunk to the point of incapacity most of the week.

[6] This case is an exception to the statement on p. 7 about Florida-based migrants.

community, the grower was able to recruit without using a crew leader, relying instead on an informal social network.

The crew was remarkable if only for its unusual kinship relations. Of approximately sixty people in the camp, thirty-six were members of three extended family groups. Most of the others also had some kin relation in the camp, and, indeed, there were only eight unattached people.

Another aspect of labor policy was the careful way in which the grower planned work for the migrants. There was a gap between the two major harvests of cherries and apples. As a matter of policy, the grower was energetic in his belief that regular work had to be provided for this period, and he planted vegetable crops for this purpose.

Supervision was lax during the time of observation, which coincided with the slack period. Both the grower and the migrants agreed, however, that there was a tightening up during the busiest part of the season. The grower personally assumed responsibility for supervision, but the normative controls existing by virtue of kinship substituted to a considerable degree for external supervision. The work groups regulated themselves with minimal direction. The result was comparatively high productivity, particularly among older workers with family responsibilities. The grower handled wage payments directly. Since neither wine nor food was sold, there were few deductions, no credit manipulations, and most migrants were able to save.

Sociability was based largely on proximity of living units and marital status. There was a relatively high level of trust and practically no violence or destruction of physical facilities.

Motel camp (LR)

This camp was owned by a grower working a specialized crop. The crew was also specialized, preferring this crop to others. However, the season for this crop was short and, in fact, the crew was occupied with secondary crops for much of the season. The grower was disinterested in the management and direction of the crew, and this was reflected in the physical condition of the camp, the organization of the crew, and the work.

The crew, a prototype of the migrant labor system, was directed by a large entrepreneur owning a substantial amount of equipment. Of the seventy-five people, about two-thirds had worked for the crew leader during previous seasons. About 20 percent of the crew consisted of small family groupings, and there were some couples who arranged muck marriages for the season. Most of the crew members were single males, younger than twenty-two or older than thirty-five.

Physically speaking, the camp was in poor condition and in violation of the New York State Sanitary Code on a number of counts, most conspicuously with respect to its wood-frame, nonfireproof construction. The bulk of the workers, about sixty in number, were housed in a large wooden motel-type unit; families were housed in wooden shacks. The seventy-five people in the camp shared a single juke, where the crew leader provided prepared meals at high prices and sold alcohol at double the retail price.

The juke was the center of social activity for most of the younger people staying in the camp because of the "piccolo" which blared its music at full volume day and night. Older men gathered at a side entrance to the building—during their many off-work hours—where they drank, told stories and jokes, and argued. Generally, people clustered according to age groups with the exception of the families.

The camp was located 5 miles from the nearest town and in most cases far from work sites. The crew leader's personal control over transportation, the provision of work, and the wage payments, as well as over the provision of food, enabled him to maintain a situation of social dependency and tight control.

The grower's lack of interest in the management of labor was conspicuous at work. Supervision was erratic but, for the most part, lax. There was no indication that the crew leader encouraged people to work provided they earned enough to pay their bills to him. When work was available, only a small fraction of the crew worked; but there were many days when there was no work for anyone. Piecework earnings were extremely low. During the period in which we studied the crew, there were few who saved money.

There was a great deal of gambling in the camp, which often developed into physical violence, especially among the younger men. Drinking was a major pastime and at least half the crew, men and women alike, were drunk each weekend; productivity declined noticeably on Mondays. There were also more winos in this crew than in any other which we studied.

BEAN CAMP (IM)

Situated in a remote location one mile from the nearest telephone, Bean Camp housed a bean-picking crew of sixty. The crew worked primarily for one grower. The extent of his participation in the camp consisted of a morning visit to make arrangements with the crew leader about work for the day.

The camp itself contained three motel-type structures of cinder block and wood. At one end of the camp was the juke, a roofed wooden platform without walls. There were also a combination washhouse and public kitchen and two latrines. The showers had occasional hot water but collected the odor of urine from the nearby latrines. A major drainage problem existed and, on rainy days, a marsh separated the latrines from the camp so that they were inaccessible.

The crew leader, a man of sixty, had been bringing crews north for twenty-five years; but this was his first time in this camp. His wife, a vigorous and imposing woman, played the major role in running the crew in the camp and at work. It was she who woke the crew each morning, assigned people to their rows, and provided general supervision. The crew leader seldom went to the fields and, at best, supervision was irregular. The crew operated, then, with little control either at work or in the camp.

Food was not provided by the crew leader; each family or individual cooked in his room or shared the overcrowded facilities of the cookhouse. Each evening after work the bus stopped at the grocery store on the way back to camp. The storekeeper had an arrangement with the crew leader that permitted people to pay for their purchases with bean tickets.

The crew members ranged in age from two to seventy-six. There were twelve couples married or living together, two single women with children, eighteen single men, and sixteen children (under fifteen). Most families had been north with the crew leader before.

Families, including the children, worked together, with the head of each family acting as supervisor. Loading and other jobs were performed by the son and grandson of the crew leader's wife. Productivity varied a great deal. There were many good pickers in the crew, but older people and young children fared less well. Moreover, the bean crop was extremely poor during much of the season. The crew leader's wife converted the bean tickets into cash. There were no deductions for Social Security, and because there was no credit system, debts did not accumulate.

Social activities focused on the piccolo, which blared most of the night. There was a great deal of drinking, particularly on weekends, but few people were winos. Although there were many daily arguments to pass the time, few resulted in fights; violence and property damage were minimal.

Main camp (GP)

Owned by a cooperative farmers' association, Main Camp could house up to 750 people. During the period studied, the camp contained seven crews, which constituted the labor pool for farmers scattered over a radius of 50 miles. The camp occupied 15 acres with ten cinder-block, motel-type housing units, a camp store, an office and barber shop, a shower building, a recreation center, and, during the season, a fully equipped medical trailer within which a clinic operated several days a week. The road through the camp was unpaved and there were few grassy areas; thus the camp was either muddy or dusty at most times. Otherwise, because of the size of this camp and its conspicuousness, the management had to conform to housing regulations. Also due to its size, it was the focus of a great deal of social service activity.

The areas encompassed by each crew were referred to as separate "camps," each of which was associated with the name of its crew leader. Each had its own juke, used primarily by the members of a single crew although serving occasionally as centers for general sociability between the members of several crews. Although a camp manager was employed by the coop, intervention and control by the coop was minimal in the camp and at work. The crew leaders had exclusive responsibility for maintaining control, feeding the crew, and organizing work. The character of each crew was influenced by the multicrew structure of the camp and the style of the individual crew leader.

The main crew studied consisted of sixty people, mostly families and older people, many of whom had been with the same crew leader for years. In addition to these regulars there were a number of workers new to the crew. Extending favors by way of credit arrangements for food, loans, and rides into town, the crew leader maintained relations with the crew through a system of social dependency.

The primary crop was beans. The crew traveled considerable distances to work each day, and, working on many different farms, confronted widely varying conditions. For the most part, these conditions were characterized by poor planning and considerable labor wastage. Limited supervision was provided by several field walkers appointed by the crew leader. The crew leader himself appeared in the fields only occasionally. Pay was in the form of tickets, which were exchanged each evening for cash. Debts were deducted regularly from earnings and became a means of exploitation and control. Productivity within this crew varied. Many of the older people were winos whose earnings were less than $3.00 a day. The best picker in the crew earned an average of $9.60 before deductions on a good day at the peak of the season. The common range of earnings was between $4.50 and $7.00.

Drinking was heavy during the week as well as on weekends, for money was generally available because of the daily payoff. Gambling for relatively high stakes was common, encouraged by the large number of weekend visitors, some of whom were ex-migrants and professional gamblers. Violence usually occurred between members of different crews.

Camp faith (CL)

Camp Faith was owned by a farmer who had contracted with the same crew for many seasons. The grower himself allocated all responsibility to the crew leader, who, after many years, was familiar with the farm's operation. The camp contained two wooden motel-type units with forty-two small rooms, several one-room shacks, a store, a juke, quarters for the crew leader and his family, and a cookhouse/washhouse combination. Located on a major U.S. highway, the camp had limited land area and its buildings were close together. The camp was approved to house 87 people; but during the peak season, it housed 130, with an average of 3 persons per room. The overcrowded and primitive facilities and nonexistent maintenance resulted in a substandard housing situation. Washhouse sinks emptied onto the ground, which drained poorly; and outhouses, unmaintained, were seldom used. Bed pans and garbage were dumped either in the grass or over a fence; the fly population thrived.

The camp was located 25 miles from the nearest town, but food could be purchased at a concession in the camp. On Saturdays the bus took people to a nearby hamlet, charging each person $1.00 for the ride.

Most of the migrants in this camp were experienced agricultural workers from Florida, except for eight "jitterbugs," young boys from twelve to seventeen, disdained by the others as noisy and disruptive. Otherwise the crew was divided on a religious basis. The crew leader, a large, persuasive man, was an elder of a pentecostal church, which shall be referred to as "The Church of A to Z." The core of his crew, about thirty-five people, were members of his church. The religious people formed a cohesive group, held together by their beliefs, sustained by regular evening services, and by kinship ties. Contact within this group was maintained year-round. Another conspicuous group in the camp was the ten winos. The various groups lived in different sections of the camp. The religious group cooked and ate separately, using their own stoves and often sharing food and cooking facilities. The rest of the camp used the communal cookhouse. Leisure activities were also separate; the religious group participated regularly in the services from which others were excluded. Thus the striking feature of this camp was its polarization, which extended to the work situation.

To the extent that a hierarchy existed at work, the religious people were favored. The crew leader, his son-in-law, and several appointed field walkers supervised the picking. Jobs such as loading, driving, and weighing were assigned within the religious group. There was considerable in-group pressure, which minimized the need for supervision. The families, working together, were relatively productive, considering the possibilities. These were often limited, for the crop was poor and there were periods with no work available. During part of the summer a group of men left the camp and their families for two weeks to pick corn in another part of the state. Welfare food had to be brought in for the others. Nevertheless, when work was available, productivity was relatively high.

The beliefs of the religious people prohibited drinking and gambling. Among others, except for the winos in the camp, drinking was moderate. Unlike other camps, the juke was not a busy social center. Violence was avoided.

These six cases illustrate the diversity in the migrant labor system; but they also suggest similarities in life-style that reflect the position of the migrant in American society and the pattern of camp life. Migrant labor is a "sanctuary" for those outside the mainstream of America's social system, as shall be shown in Part III. Unable to find other employment for many reasons, many southern Negroes become migrants as a last resort. They find themselves involved in a self-perpetuating system that is difficult to escape. The dynamics of the migrant labor system constitute the substance of this volume.

Methods of Study

The research from which this book developed has provided unique possibilities to view the migrant labor system from an internal perspective. During the summers of 1966–1968, sixteen students from Cornell University and Tuskegee Institute became migrants. Each lived individually in a labor camp and worked in the fields with a crew. For a season, each shared the same experiences, confronted the same problems, tolerated the same conditions, and faced the same frustrations of life that the migrants do in a labor camp. Most students entered the camps, not as students, but as "drifters," broke and in need of work. They placed themselves in situations where they could not fall back on the companionship and support of colleagues. They immersed themselves totally in the system and its daily routine. In almost all cases, the students found easy acceptance despite the fact that twelve of the sixteen were white. There was somewhat greater skepticism among the crew leaders, and indifference or hostility among growers. In two cases, growers cooperated willingly with the study and another cooperated only after considerable negotiation.

The students entered the camps to gain firsthand insight into the life of migrant workers. They remained in their camps for five to nine weeks, long enough to know most co-workers and to experience not only the obvious consequences of the system but to understand the subtle ways in which people in this setting adjust their life-style and personal relationships to conditions they cannot control. They were there long enough to perceive social forms underlying an outwardly chaotic and disrupted way of life.

The method of participant-observation, employed as the basic field research technique, has yielded rich material on the day-to-day life of migrants. Observations were carried on as a systematic program. Students left the camps about every third evening to tape-record field diaries. These diaries were loosely structured to permit as wide a range of data as possible, but certain categories were probed and systematic outlines were followed. Diaries were recorded with the assistance of a liaison person, who served to maintain balance in the observations, to probe specific areas, and to prevent the researcher from lapsing into generalizations due to personal familiarity with the milieu.

Prior to their stay in the camps, students also conducted informal interviews with people in migrant communities who were involved with some aspect of the system. These included police, labor department employees, inspectors, social workers, physicians, teachers, and clergy, as well as growers.

This book is constructed of excerpts from the field diaries. In addition, some material is included from papers written by the students analyzing their experiences. All have been edited, and analytic and explanatory sections are interspersed in italics to provide continuity. The selections include verbatim records of conversations and stories and documentation of special events as well as routine activities. Through these selections, it is hoped that the way of life in a migrant labor camp will be revealed to the reader.

The book is organized in three parts developing the themes suggested earlier. Part I will describe the conditions of migrant labor: recruitment and the trip north, the physical setting, the crew leader system, and the organization of work. Part II relates to the organization of life in these circumstances: the personal habits of individuals, interpersonal relations, leisure-time activities, and work-related attitudes and behavior. Part III develops material on the potential for social change: migrants' perceptions of the outside world, their own efforts to create change, and their children.

An Appendix reviews some of the outside agencies that form a peripheral part of the migrant labor system.

Part One

THE SETTING

The physical and social circumstances of migrant labor are described in this book as they are perceived by the participants in the migrant labor system. Like the perceptions of any human group, they have their subjective aspects and are crucial in influencing behavior. If, for example, migrants believe and act on the basis that they have been recruited to come north by false promises, the extent to which their beliefs are based on fact is not relevant. And, in an examination of the dynamics of daily life in the camps, actual physical conditions proved less important than details that irritate migrants on a minute-to-minute basis.

Here we provide the setting for four aspects of the migrants' lives: recruitment and the trip north, the camp, the crew leader, and the work. This setting has a characteristic disorder, anomalous in the highly structured and organized context of American society. Ambiguity, uncertainty, and disorganization—themes that appear throughout this book—are rooted in the fortuitous conditions that are the setting of the migrant labor system.

1

Going North on the Season

Migrants are recruited formally by the Farm Labor Service of the United States Employment Service, an agency of the United States Department of Labor. At the local level, growers make their needs known to local agents. These needs are communicated to state employment service representatives, who do the actual recruiting in Florida. In some cases, the grower specifies a crew with whom he has had previous contact; in others, he indicates only manpower needs. "Contracts" are negotiated in the spring with crew leaders, specifying wages, housing arrangements, crew size and composition, and dates for the season. Here formal administrative functions terminate. During this process, which establishes the conditions under which he will work, the migrant has been completely uninvolved.

The migrant is recruited in several ways. In some cases, people drive north in their own cars, picking up information through word of mouth. More commonly, migrants are recruited by a crew leader who either lives in their own town or who passes through en route north. Practically no migrants use such formal government agencies as the Farm Labor Service to find work: recruitment is highly casual and fortuitous. A friend may know that a crew leader will be coming through and that he promises high wages. The possibility of a free trip presents itself. Many decisions to come "on the season" are made at the last minute, sometimes the day of departure. During the winter, few people plan to go north, but as citrus and vegetables end in May in Florida and employment opportunities cease, crew leaders make their contacts. Most crew leaders spend their winters as day haul contractors, recruiting workers on a daily basis from central locations in *rural communities. As the season ends, they recruit people in their local communities for the season in the north, filling out their crews with strangers picked up elsewhere.*

Recruitment

Why do people come north on the season? There are some who see the trip as a way to expand their horizons. Some are sucked into the system for the first time, believing the extravagant promises made by the crew leader. Others are restless and prefer the loose schedules of migrant work to the routine of more regular employment. Many are unable to hold other types of jobs. Some are physically handicapped, others are alcoholics or have jail records. Most have no alternative. They must subsist during the summer when there is no work in Florida. Most claim that their decision to come on the season was made spontaneously because the opportunity presented itself at a convenient moment. Although migrants do not analyze their motives, they occasionally talk about why they came north and how they were recruited.

Lonnie was born and raised, the oldest of four children, in Alabama, where his father worked as a farm laborer. He went to a county training school. At the age of seventeen he began to feel restricted. "The only thing a white man wanted a Negro to do in this county was to grow up knowing as little as possible about anything." He finished the tenth grade and decided to leave school. Feeling frustrated and discouraged, he needed to get out of the county. He heard about Pole, a migrant labor crew leader in Selma, Alabama, who was recruiting a crew to go north. He would be coming through the county on the way to Florida to do the early summer harvest of the citrus crop. Lonnie had no money and regarded the chance to travel with the crew as an opportunity. Encouraged by several people who told him that he could make some money, he joined the crew and went with them to Florida. There he began to have regrets; but because he had no money to pay his return fare, his decision could not be reversed.

The crew remained in Florida for several weeks and then headed to a labor camp in New York State. Lonnie stayed at the camp for two weeks. He claims he left because the crew leader beat the members of the crew. Two other disaffected migrants left with him when offered a job by our present crew leader, who recruits his entire crew by collecting them from camps where they are dissatisfied. (GW)

*　　　　　*　　　　　*

Major found out about the trip north when he saw a big poster in a restaurant in his hometown. He and his sister decided to come up, so they just got on the bus. There are buses leaving from his area all the time and if anyone wants to come, he can. It was better than staying down home because the season is usually slack during the summer and supposedly you can make better money in the north. This, however, has been a bad year.

Moe also talked about how he came to the camp. He saw notices posted in front of the employment office at home about jobs available for people who are willing to travel north. To get one of these jobs all you have to do is to give the people your name. Most people, he claims, give false names. You get a date and on that date buses will be out in front of the building. You can go with any crew you want to. Sometimes people just flag the buses down on the road or, if you know someone who is going, you can just go along and get on the bus without signing. No one says anything. If the bus isn't full, the drivers will go around to the bars to recruit people. (GP)

*　　　　*　　　　*

Pops is drunk most of the time but when sober he is very articulate. This morning he talked about various jobs he has held, and why he is here. He said that some people come north on the season thinking there will be good money. Others come up because, "It's just a thing they want to do. They just want to get away from home." He knew things weren't so good here and that he would have done just as well or better staying home. But he had lost several good jobs in the south because of his heavy drinking. He just couldn't go back to the ordinary life, working as a steady man. The only thing left for him was to work in a camp. (GW)

*　　　　*　　　　*

Hart is originally from Baton Rouge, Louisiana, and has been moving between Chicago, Michigan, and New York State doing odd jobs. He said that if his parents knew what he was doing now they would really be angry. They believe he is in Rochester working in a factory and doing pretty well. He says that farm labor is the best he can do. He had a good job once but his record as a juvenile delinquent and a later criminal record kept him from holding decent jobs. This is why he became a migrant. "People here don't ask questions and they really don't care what your past is all about or anything." (GW)

*　　　　*　　　　*

The women were talking about how they weren't going to come back next year. They came up this year on the promise that they would make money. Emma told how she heard a radio advertisement in Belle Glade about coming north with Frank. The broadcast promised a real good time, lots of money, lots of fun. She really thought she would be doing well to come. (LR)

*   *   *

Ben, age thirty-five and with a tenth-grade education, has worked the seasons for three summers, but this is his first summer with this crew. He was originally from North Carolina, but had grown up in Bridgeport, Connecticut. He then moved to Boston, Buffalo, and finally to Florida, where, until three years ago, he was making $2.50 an hour as a construction worker. However, he was restless and wanted a change. Some girl told him about a crew and he got in touch with the crew leader just as he was leaving for the north. He joined them and took off. (DG)

*   *   *

A wino who had left the camp met me in town and asked if there was any work in my camp yet. I told him there wasn't and that people were leaving. He was trying to get back to Florida. When he was picked up by the crew leader at the beginning of the summer, he had been drunk. He was offered a couple of bottles of wine and told that if he came up here he could make all kinds of money. If he had realized there was so little work, he never would have left. Not having worked for about three weeks, and now badly in debt, he had no money to get home. (CL)

*   *   *

A group of Florida boys complained about how they had been recruited. A man came by and told them he was bringing people up to work in a small town just outside New York City. He told them the wages on the job were very good. There was a labor shortage in New York and the crop was ready, but there weren't enough people to pick it. Wages were going up for they needed men badly. When they heard they were going to be near New York City, they hopped on the bus and then found they were stuck way out in the woods, several hundred miles from the city. (GP)

The Trip North

The bus trip north shares many of the fortuitous aspects of recruitment. The trip is made in one stretch with no overnight breaks; however, with frequent stops for food and inevitable bus breakdowns, it takes three to four days. During the trip, relationships develop among members of the crew and social patterns for the summer begin to be established. The style of leadership, often unfamiliar to many people in the group, becomes apparent as the crew leader handles crises during these initial days of the season. People arrive in the camp, then, with some expectations concerning each other, developed after days of close contact under tiresome circumstances. Strains begin to develop during the trip, but at the same time internal cohesion is stimulated by the blatant distaste often expressed by many garage attendants, store-keepers, and police encountered en route.

Attitudes that will assume later significance take shape and are reinforced during the bus trip. Mechanical breakdowns and other disagreeable incidents, considered routine and unavoidable, foster attitudes of resignation and apathy. These attitudes are also manifest in the lack of planning and in the minimal discussion concerning expectations for the summer.

I walked into a black neighborhood in Pompano Beach about 3:00 P.M. on Wednesday and asked around if there were any crews going north. I found that Hook was leaving that day and was now driving around town picking up his crew. I found Hook's truck outside a small restaurant and I asked him if he could use some more people. He regarded me briefly and asking no questions, said, "Okay, get on the bus." I waited for him to volunteer information about what we would be doing; when he didn't I asked him what we would be picking. He said we would be chopping cabbage and picking tomatoes.

The bus was a blue 1956 International Harvester in pretty good shape. On the front it said, "Catch me and you won't go wrong." There were eleven people on the bus: eight older men sitting in the back, and several younger people, in their twenties, in the front. Everyone, except me, was Negro. I walked back three seats and collapsed in an empty seat, with my head against the window. The men in the back of the bus were each sitting alone. In the front, however, the younger men were sitting together.

After about a minute a man across from me asked if I was going north. I nodded and someone from the back of the bus added, "It looks like he has had a rough day." I said, "Yeah," and he offered me a cigarette. No one asked further questions about my background or what I was doing there. In the first five minutes a young man sitting next to me introduced himself as Grease. I told him my first name and we shook hands. He introduced me to Jitterbug, a younger boy of eighteen, who said, "How are you doin', man?" A girl came over and introduced herself by her first name. I asked her what was happening and she said, "Nothing, we're fixing to go north." There was not much talk. The young guys in front were trying to get some wine before they started. One of them leaned out and asked a girl in the street to lend him some money to get a bottle of wine, but she told him to go to hell. The older people in the back said absolutely nothing while waiting.

Finally, John, the bus driver, appeared and we left to pick up some others. The bus driver knew where to go. We drove first to Flat Top's apartment about five blocks away. When we got there, we found that Flat Top had started his car engine and then locked the outer door of the car, leaving the key inside in the ignition. The car was still running and he had broken a back window trying to get in. When we arrived, he had not succeeded in turning the engine off so he just left the car running as we left, expecting that it would run out of gas eventually.

We spent about an hour and a half picking up people and waiting for them to get organized. One of the guys brought a bottle of wine on the bus and asked Sugar if she wanted a drink. She said she would drink only if her boyfriend, Ed, would join her. He agreed, so she passed him the bottle, but he refused to drink. Annoyed, she threatened to pour the wine over him. The other people were worried about wasting the wine and convinced Ed that he had better drink some. Kidding of this sort, concerning drinking, occupied time while waiting to leave. There were few comments about crops, or about the season in the north.

The older men in the back remained sedentary. All of them seemed to be awake but they were not talking. Grease became a little friendlier, and, moving to the seat in front of me, he talked about the crew. Most people had known Hook for a number of years and several were related to him. The crew, then, was not composed of strangers; its members were all recruited from the same town in the south. While I was in the cafe, for example, I heard Hook say to Jitterbug, "Hell, you know you better go with me because you are going to have to." Jitterbug did not reply but got on the bus. People have to go north and they know when Hook is leaving. There is no need for much salesmanship on his part. Half the people in the crew had been north with him before to the same camp where we were planning to go this year. The others had been north with other crew leaders. Everyone on the bus with the exception of Jitterbug, the youngest member of the crew, had been on the seasons previously. There was some variation, however, in their backgrounds. All had picked crops before but not continuously. Grease had driven a truck; Ed had spent some time during the past year working in Georgia as a driver hauling logs for a pulp company. Others had done yard work and various service jobs. Everyone in the crew was originally from elsewhere in the south, but considered himself a resident of Pompano Beach, having lived there for at least two years.

As we rode around Pompano Beach, people joked about getting off the bus. "Hell, I'm going to get my suitcase and get off." "Sit down, you know you ain't going nowhere." It was considered funny to joke about making your mind up and then changing it at the last minute and getting off the bus. People would stand up and then sit back down again and say, "Well, I guess I'm going to go after all." But no one actually got off.

Most people were aware that they were going to Virginia to pick cabbage, but during the first few hours no one appeared to be concerned about what they were picking or the camp that would be their home for at least four months.

At 5:30 P.M. we left Pompano Beach in a caravan of four vehicles. The bus held twenty-one people, four of whom were women. John was driving. There were also Hook's 1967 Dodge sedan, driven by his girl friend; a new Ford pickup truck, driven by Hook: and the large truck, driven by Flat Top. In all, there were twenty-five people in the four vehicles. The bus driver, John, is Hook's nephew and has been driving the bus north for him for four years. Before that time he was a picker in the crew. John and Flat Top each earn $40.00 for driving north.

We were on the road five minutes when a woman who had been arguing with a man in the back of the bus pulled out a knife and put it on his throat. It was not clear whether she was kidding or not, but at that time, the bus driver's girlfriend said that she had to go to the toilet. We happened to be in front of a service exit on the turnpike, and the bus driver swerved to make it on time. The knife was put away. Bobby and three women went to the toilet. No one else moved. The bus driver was told abruptly by an unpleasant gas station attendant that he had better move his bus fast; that he was breaking the law because he had stopped in front of a gas pump.

When we got back on the road, we drove for about a mile and saw Hook and his pickup truck on the side of the road. We stopped the bus behind him and Hook was very angry. He told John never to stop again without telling what he was doing. He had just gotten some trouble from a cop for waiting on the side of the road. For the rest of the trip we traveled almost always within sight of the other vehicles.

Talk during the first three hours of the trip was mostly wisecracks about wine, but one interesting conversation occurred concerning Ed's relationship with his girlfriend, Sugar. Ed was angry because Sugar was talking to other men in the crew. He moved back two seats and she followed him. The other guys moved back with the two of them and Sugar put her hands behind her back on another man's knee. She was teasing several people at the same time. Everyone realized this and Ed was getting a lot of kidding. Finally at about 7:30, he moved to the back of the bus, away from the young people, and went to sleep. Sugar followed him and the interest in that momentary distraction waned. Meanwhile, there were three women sitting together on the left drinking wine. When they first sat down on the bus, there were comments like, "Twenty damn men on the bus and the women go and sit together." At one point, one of Hook's nephews decided that he was going to break it up, and he grabbed one of the women and moved her to another seat and sat down next to her.

At 8:30 we were still in Florida, south of Ft. Pierce, on U.S. 1. We stopped at a little food store on the side of the road, run by white people. I was given very hard stares but they did not say anything. People bought bread, prepackaged hot dogs, baloney, Spam, luncheon meat, and cokes. A few bought beer. Each person paid for the things himself, having started the trip with about $5.00 apiece. There was some sharing of food: one person bought a whole loaf of bread and someone else bought hot dogs. Hot dogs and lunch meat were eaten cold. The older men just ate bread. Hook and Flat Top apparently had food with them, because they did not go inside. This stop lasted about fifteen minutes. There was no toilet, but a number of men went into the bushes.

When we got back on the bus, the same seating arrangements were resumed. Some of the older men started talking, mostly about the food and their hopes to get wherever they were going in a hurry. Several of them fell asleep in a sitting position with their heads leaning against the window. During the entire trip, the eight men sitting in the back of the bus never lay down in their seats or slumped down completely, although there was room to do so. The young people in the front, however, stretched out, putting their feet across someone's lap on the other side or dangling them on the floor.

We stopped again at 11:30 P.M. for gas in a large truck-stop gas station, still in Florida. Almost everyone went to the toilet, and several of the younger people went to a cafe next door for coffee. At this stop I had the first in a series of difficulties with white outsiders. During the entire trip I had no trouble with the people in the crew, but at almost every stop I was harassed by white people. Here, I was called a "nigger lover" by the gas station attendant. No one in the crew overheard and, since we left immediately, there was no discussion.

There was no singing at all on the bus except by Hook's nephew, who sang: "You wanna get poor, then get you a car and get rid of the bitch. Do it today, don't wait 'til tomorrow." He had a few similar songs and he hummed a little bit, but no one joined him. He was also the only storyteller on the bus. He told some very long, drawn-out jokes, sometimes taking fifteen or twenty minutes. They seemed to be extemporaneous, since he would come to a point, pause for a while, and then make up another detail.

The stories, about people going to the hospital for swallowing dogs and eating dog food, and women trying to poison their husbands, were repetitious. They included long details that had nothing at all to do with the main point of the story. Most people did not seem very interested, and the punch lines always fell dead by the time he got to the end.

Soon, one of the three women, who had been drinking heavily, fell asleep and three of the younger men spent a lot of time feeling her breasts and playing with her. She was oblivious to the whole affair. They did it all very quietly without much excitement and kidded each other about "feeling her up." Jitterbug laughed and said it was the first breast he had ever felt, "Didn't she have nice knockers—just out of sight."

About midnight everyone was falling asleep. There was only the one driver for each vehicle so they were expected to go through without sleeping. There was one stop, about four in the morning, for gas, and two or three people got up to use the rest rooms. At 5:30 A.M. Thursday, we entered Georgia. Most of the people were up by this time. During the night two of the women had left the bus and were riding next to Hook in the pickup truck. Sugar had left Ed alone in the back seat and was riding with Flat Top and his wife in the furniture truck. Ed then moved to sit next to his brother in the front. At eight in the morning we stopped at a large gas station. I thought the men's room would be inside the garage so I went in. I was told, "It's around the back, nigger lover," by four rednecks, big, husky-looking white boys with crew cuts. There was just one toilet that we all shared. The women waited in the same line as the men, although there was a separate ladies' room. The bathroom we were using was not labeled "colored" but people knew what was expected, not because they had stopped here before, but just because this was where you went to the bathroom at this kind of truck stop. After only four of us had used the bathroom, one of the white boys came back and said he was sorry, he was closing up. There were still fifteen people waiting to go and there was some grumbling. Grease said he would like to "have a chance to beat that motherfucker's ass." Most people, however, took the situation in stride. Only the younger men said anything, and aside from Grease's comment, complaints were veiled. They generalized the problem, saying how bad the trip north was, rather than focusing on this particular incident.

We drove on for ten minutes and the bus engine started knocking. We pulled over immediately, Hook stopping behind us. Fortunately, about 50 yards down the road there was a garage, owned by a Negro garageman. He and one helper were working on four large transport trucks. The bus was pushed to the back of the garage and the garageman started working on it immediately, ignoring the trucks he had been servicing. He found that there was no oil, absolutely none at all. The bus driver was supposed to be responsible for keeping oil in the bus. He had checked it during most of the stops, but the bus had been losing oil rapidly and he had not checked it at the last stop at 8:30. Hook was angry, but only said one thing to John, "You know you've got to keep oil in there. Now look what you've done." He mentioned to Grease, his nephew, that he was going to wait until we got to the camp before he said anything further because John had to drive the rest of the way anyway.

While waiting for the bus to be fixed, we sat around in the back of the garage on the frame of an old truck. Some of us sat in the bus. There was very little complaining or comment about the breakdown. I was much more upset about it than anyone else. Everyone took it as a matter of course. Grease said, "You have to expect the bus to break down during a trip." It wasn't even worth discussing.

Ed had a little portable tape recorder, and to pass the time, we were talking about each other on a tape. For example, a guy with a hanging lower lip was described as "looking like a mule with a tire in his lip." Then they insulted Hook, talking about his weight; that he couldn't sit down in a chair without crushing it. I was labeled on the tape as "bread man" because I ate two slices of bread with nothing between them the night before, so for the rest of the trip I had this nickname. They described my physical features, "There's this guy over there that's got curly hair, got blue jeans on and he is wearing a blue shirt. He's O.K., but . . . we'd better not say too much more about him." At that time the guy talking was nudged by two others as if he had better watch what he said about me. He looked confused and then turned the recorder off without completing the description. I asked for the microphone and gave a withering description of him, going on at great lengths about the size of his feet. Then he took the microphone back and described me as a "son of a bitch who doesn't have a damn cent to his name." Relations were more relaxed after this. There was a long description of someone called Geech who bends over when he walks. He can't straighten his back up. A stutterer was also called Geech, so apparently the term is used in this crew for persons with physical disabilities.

Next door was a white-owned gas station. We used the rest room in the gas station and bought candy in a little store inside. When we needed more substantial food, we went to another store about a quarter of a mile down the road from the garage. The people in the store ignored me at first, perhaps not noticing that I was with the crew. Later they began to give me hostile and contemptuous stares. Grease noticed this and went to great lengths to explain to me why they were staring. He was very anxious to make it clear that there was nothing wrong with me and that I should not worry.

"They're staring at you." "Yeah, I know." "That's because you're white and we're black." I replied, "I know. That's why they do that and it really pisses me off." And Grease responded, "They wouldn't stare at you like that if you weren't with us." He went on for five minutes, essentially apologizing and taking the blame for these incidents.

During the day the young people stayed together, playing the tape recorder and occasionally walking to the store. The older members of the crew also stuck together, but they talked very little, only commenting occasionally about the weather or about getting something to eat. Hook had a Swinger camera and took some pictures of people. Some of the young guys went into the woods with some dice. They were playing for small stakes, nickels, dimes, and pennies. There were some people who remained sitting on the bus the entire time, getting off only to use the toilet or to go to the store.

For many hours there was no speculation at all as to how long the repairs would take, or what was wrong with the bus. People were completely disinterested. After a while I learned that the bus had trouble with its crankshaft. The damage was serious, and they were stripping the engine down to the block and doing a complete overhaul. They had to send to Savannah for a part. At two in the afternoon we were told that we might get on the road late that evening; then at 7:00 P.M. the garageman, who had been working on the engine all day, left to go to church. At eight o'clock Grease got a TV set from the truck. He set it up in the back of the bus and ran an extension cord to a plug in the garage. The only station we could get was National Educational TV, so we watched an exploration of music theory program. Two or three people seemed to be watching the program. I tried to probe if they were really watching it, commenting how much sweat a conductor worked up waving his arms around in the air. People said, "Yeah," and let it drop. There was no discussion. They watched the show to its end, however, and then turned the TV off when they saw that the next program was a news analysis.

We were told that the garageman would return at 11:30 P.M. with a part from Savannah, which was to be sent to his home, and that we might get out at two or three in the morning. He did come back but the part had never been delivered to his home and it was clear that we would be there at least until the next morning. Then a man drove up, and was talked into taking some of the people to the nearest town to get some wine. They returned later with a two-gallon jug and we went to the back of the truck and started drinking. There was not quite enough for anyone to get seriously drunk. During this time there was a fight between Ed and Grease. Ed had been taunting Grease, saying that he wasn't worth shit; Grease claimed that Ed owed him 80 cents, but this was denied. "All right, then don't pay me that money but don't be messing with me again." As the dialogue started to get nasty, Ed said, "All right, I'll pay you back the 80 cents as soon I get it." But Grease refused to accept the conciliatory gesture, "You can keep your damn money. I'm not interested in money any more. Just don't mess with me. I don't want you fuckin' with me for nothing." The exchange went on but neither one wanted to start an actual fight. Eventually Grease complained to the crew leader and the argument petered out. Later in the evening Grease and Sugar, who had been ignoring Ed, went off into the woods. Later, when she started playing up to Ed again, Grease declared that she was just another whore anyway and that he didn't give a damn. Meanwhile, Jitterbug was getting very excited over a woman who was old enough to be his mother. There was a lot of joking among the other people about this. "You're just a boy. You don't know what to do anyway."

At about two or three in the morning people started drifting back into the bus and fell asleep. It was chilly, and mosquitoes were very heavy. I tried to fall asleep, but kept getting kicked by Jitterbug, who was across from me. Finally I got out of the bus and found a junk car nearby and went to sleep in that. I woke up at seven o'clock. People were standing around a little wood fire that had been built several yards from the garage. A group of us went to the store to buy hot dogs for breakfast. The garageman showed up about 9:15 with the part and resumed work on the bus. Then we all waited again, out in back of the garage, and on the bus, walking back and forth.

There was one incident involving Jitterbug, the eighteen-year-old who had not been north before, and the crew leader. Hook walked up to Jitterbug and said, "You think you can beat me. You think you can do something to me. We're going to have it out right now and get this thing over with instead of messing around for the whole season. Come on out here and let's have it out." Jitterbug said, "Okay, all right, why don't you back up a little bit so I can stand up." Hook backed up some and said, "Is that far enough?" "A little further, a little further." He backed up far enough, and Jitterbug jumped up and ran away. Hook laughed.

People were still not interested in the bus repairs, but about noon on Friday they started to grumble. We were told that we would leave soon. At 2:30 the engine was finally put back together and John was asked to drive a few miles. The bus seemed all right but then a broken radiator hose was discovered, which took another hour to fix. While waiting, the men played a "give and take" game that continued on the bus later in the trip. A cigarette is offered, accepted, and then is pulled back. The giver then takes it out again and says, "Oh, I was only kidding"; when it is accepted, he again withdraws it. This game is played with cigarettes and matches, or, more abstractly, with friendship. For example, Grease would try to make up with Ed about Sugar saying, "Let's be friends. No sense in us messing around over a whore." He'd offer his hand, Ed would reach out and Grease would withdraw it. In another version, the game was played with changing seats on the bus.

About four o'clock we finally got on the bus. Although there had been little complaining while waiting, there was indication of relief at this time: "About time we got going. Waited long enough. About time we were moving." But these comments were brief; people forgot completely, it seemed, although we had stopped for almost two days. It seemed unimportant and not unusual to them. As we rode through various parts of Georgia, several people would call out, "That's my home, I've got relatives there." They would play a game where they would pick out the worst-looking shack and say, "That must be where you were born"; or, "Hey, that's where I was born—in that place." "I didn't seen nothin' except bushes. You were born in the bushes?"

At about 10:30 on Friday night in South Carolina we were pulled over by a state policeman, who said, "You driving this bus, boy?" to the driver. John got off the bus and came back with a warning ticket that one of his headlights was out. He was about to drive away when the officer knocked on the door and got on the bus. He walked all the way down the aisle of the bus and back again and stopped by me. He stared at me for a long time and asked, "Are you riding this bus north?" I said, "Yep." He said, "I mean are you riding up with all these people?" "Yes sir." He looked real hard at me for a few minutes and then said, "Damn," and got off. After he left, people were surprisingly quiet, but Grease said to me, "Sometimes the Man will really piss you off." A few others said, "Yeah, the son of a bitch." That was it. No one seemed surprised or excited by the incident.

As we drove off after getting the ticket, people kidded John about his speeding. He insisted that he was stopped only because of his headlight and we looked for a place to get it replaced. As we made a left turn across the traffic to a garage, another cop pulled up. I scrunched down on the floor of the bus this time and pretended to sleep, hoping to avoid trouble. John explained that he already had a ticket for his light and was stopping to get it fixed and the cop left. At this stop, I was again called "nigger lover" by someone behind the counter.

The next stop was at an all-night gas station. We went to the bathroom and bought cokes. It was very cold and there were only about five or six blankets shared among the younger people. The older men continued to sit up all night in the middle of their seats, staring straight ahead, occasionally dozing off. There was almost no conversation. Everyone was groggy.

I woke up at 5:00 A.M. Saturday in Virginia. At midday, about 25 miles south of the new Bay Bridge Tunnel, the truck broke down. We left the truck behind, and Hook and Flat Top and his wife stayed with it. The car and the bus continued to the camp, driving through the tunnel and bridge complex. "Hey, look at this, man, we're going through the tunnel." There was a lot of kidding about how great tunnels were and how high the bridge was. At about three in the afternoon on Saturday we arrived at the camp. We had been together for 72 hours without any break.

The camp had 136 separate little cabins, some of which were attached as doubles and occasionally as triples. Another crew was there before us, and two hours after we arrived a third crew came in. Six crews were expected altogether. People walked around saying that it was a pretty nice camp. It was clean; the buildings, made of wood on raised cinder block, were in good repair. There were sixteen outhouses, eight for men and eight for women, distributed throughout the area. They were clean, although they smelled bad and were full of flies. There was a food store in the camp, open on weekends. Bread was sold at 32 cents, hamburger meat, which looked bad, was priced at 45 cents a pound. They were also selling sandwiches at 45 cents, cokes for 25 cents, and cigarettes at 49 cents. There was no alcohol. Two pinball machines and a jukebox stood against one of the walls of the store.

Hook arrived and told us to pair off and see the Man for room assignments. The pairing, which had nothing to do with the previous seating on the bus, depended on whoever was standing together at the moment. The only people who indicated that they had preferences concerning roommates for the next four months were the four young guys, who decided that they would get together in one place.

The rates for the cabins ranged from $2.00–3.00 a week if we shared a room, and $5.00 for a single person in a larger cabin. There was a rate schedule on the wall of the office, but the rates were never announced and few people noticed the posted schedule. The white man in the office took our names with difficulty. He had trouble understanding us, and most names had to be spelled six or seven times. He needed nothing but names and ages, and then he assigned us our cabins.

Grease and I were located in cabin 62, next to the "bullpen," as the four guys called their place. Most of the people had little furniture or clothing. They had a washtub, perhaps, and some work clothes, which they hung on the wall, and some blankets and sheets. Hook, however, had a refrigerator, a huge double bed (with box spring, slats, and headboard), ironing board, TV, radio, and a chest of drawers. He completely furnished his place, which was larger than the other cabins. Hook had the room next to his fixed up as a kitchen with a big stove, and a gasman came later with some propane tanks. Flat Top and John and their wives also had stoves that were already in the camp. Several other people brought small kerosene gas burners with them.

At about 4:30, Hook called everybody together to ask about cooking arrangements. The choice was to cook alone or eat with him, and he said it was completely up to us. Most of the people said that they would cook for themselves, at which point Hook said, "Well, if you haven't got any money now, I would rather you eat with us just for a week and then do what you want to after that. I would rather do that than lend you the money to buy food yourself. It would be cheaper for me. It's up to you. It doesn't matter to me, any way you want to do it." After this urging, the crew decided that they would eat with him after all. No one knew how much it would cost to eat with him. Hook's girlfriend, who was to do the cooking, had never done this sort of thing before and she said she didn't know how much it would cost.

Previously, there had been little discussion about picking or wage rates, but now that we were in the camp, there was concern about the crop and the wages. We found out we would start the season with cabbage but were not told the wage. Sugar said that the minimum wage in Virginia was $1.50 an hour. Someone else said it was 85 cents. No one was sure of what was really going to happen. Several people in the crew were nervous because they had not cut cabbage at all before. We later found out that the crew cut cabbage in eight-man teams. At the end of the day, the amount that the eight men have picked is divided between them. Hook does the supervising himself. He has no permanent supervisors in the crew, so that those who drove north have no special status once they arrive. John is a picker, Hook's other nephew is a loader. Women place the cabbages in the boxes, so the work is divided more by sex than by status.

Later, on Saturday, Hook called the crew together again and asked if we could use three dollars to get started. Everyone said yes, and thus, from the start, everyone owed him at least this amount.

Grease decided the very first day that he had to leave the camp and said he had some plans to stay with a girl he knew from Ohio. He told Hook he was leaving, and asked him if he would give him some money for his pots and pans and TV set. Hook gave him $10.00 for the lot, including the TV, which Grease said had cost him $180.00 just before he left Pompano. He had already paid $75.00 down, but the $10.00 was all that he needed to leave; so he took it and left the first day.

At dinner time we wandered into the kitchen. Hook's girlfriend prepared the "plates" one at a time and handed them out. Some people took their plates back to their rooms, some sat around, and others stood up and ate. Hook got himself a special can to sit on because the bench would not hold him. We ate on paper plates with yellow plastic forks. The chicken was the greasiest I had ever eaten. It was sitting in a quarter of an inch of fat but it tasted good. We talked mostly about the food and flattered the cook. One man, however, who was already drunk, told her she was a terrible cook, that the food was poison, and there was not enough of it. Most people didn't talk at all. They just ate in a hurry. There was still no mention of a price for the meal.

Later, after dinner, people were busy fixing up their cabins. The older people never left the camp, but the others went back and forth to town, shopping for small items, such as electric plugs and light bulbs.

The next day, Sunday, was quiet. Many people slept for the whole day. Others fixed up their cabins and stood around waiting for meals or trying to get enough money together to buy a bottle. One group began to play a game with belts and electric cords. Jitterbug sided with the women, who had formed a team against the men, and they were each trying to hit each other with a belt or a cord. They were swinging the cords for about an hour, raising amazing welts on each other. It was a way to pass the time, since there was nothing at all to do in the camp and it was boring. The women finally quit and left the camp, actually locking Jitterbug in their room to protect him; however, about five minutes after the women left, the guys ripped the lock off the door, broke the door down, and dragged Jitterbug outside. They held him down and beat him with an electric cord for siding with the women. They did it all in a kidding manner but they made it hurt. The guys had been beaten worse than the women and they took it out on Jitterbug, each one taking turns getting even. A couple of people from another crew came over and tried to egg them on.

Sunday night, people went to bed around midnight, because they expected to go to work the next day. However, at 7:00 A.M. on Monday we were told that we wouldn't be going out after all. The camp was flooded with four inches of water from a storm during the night, and apparently the fields were also submerged and could not be worked. I said I was going out to do the laundry and left the camp. (MR)

2

Migrant Labor Camps

Migrants are housed in barracks, tenant houses, cabins, shacks, or trailers, generally grouped in camps during their three- to five-month stay in the north. Camps are privately owned by individual farmers or farmer cooperatives and vary considerably in size and character. Some small camps have facilities for only a few people, others house hundreds. Most camps contain small sleeping rooms, plus a "juke," the center for sociability, eating, drinking, and gambling for the entire crew. The condition of the camps, although ostensibly regulated, varies. Even in the best camps, however, there is little maintenance during the season; with many people sharing limited facilities, dirt and run-down conditions are ubiquitous.

Poor physical conditions and the need to share inadequate facilities are sources of constant irritation; but other more subtle aspects of the physical setting, such as lack of privacy and the impersonality of the housing, are equally significant in shaping the character of camp life. Each unit is undifferentiated from the others: each room is merely a place to sleep—with no associations, no history, no mark of identification or personalization.

Eating habits vary. Families tend to cook for themselves, in most cases sharing cooking facilities. In larger crews, or crews with many single men, it is common for the crew leader's wife to prepare food, charging by the plate or by the week. The individual migrant has little choice as to which system he will use. His alternatives are limited by the decision of the crew leader, the availability of cooking facilities,

Inadequate housing. These units are probably not in violation of the housing code.   Photo by Bill Siebert/Glad Day Press.

and access to town. If food is provided by the crew leader, the content of the meals, their price, and their regularity cannot be controlled, and food is potentially a mechanism of social control for the crew leader. In the camps studied, weekly board charges ranged from $10.00–15.00. The cost of individual plates averaged $1.00. Wine and beer were sold in the camps for double the price normally charged in bars.

The pressures of group living are aggravated by another physical fact of the environment, the isolation of the migrant labor camps. Camps are usually located far from town, and problems of transportation are serious. Where the crew leader has transported people north on a bus, there are few cars available and those who own cars charge for rides. If people are able to get to town, there are social barriers limiting the use of facilities. Migrants do not feel welcome in local bars and stores and their experiences often reinforce their inital concerns. Moreover, they are often unfamiliar with the northern environment both geographically and culturally. Unsure of where to go or how to act, they are easy prey to vague fears and anxieties. As a consequence, during nonworking hours many people remain in the camp, where boredom is a constant problem. These, then, are some of the physical facts of camp life that help to create the migrant's conception of himself and that set the background for his activities and relationships.

Housing

The first selections describe physical conditions in the camps. They focus on those conditions that preoccupy the migrants; these are the irritating aspects—the flies, the outhouses, and the lack of privacy.

My camp is a two-story wood-frame house on a dirt road a mile from the nearest phone and grocery store. The house is heated by a Franklin wood stove and has no window on the first floor. The rooms are created by pasteboard partitions; although most rooms can be entered over the top of the partitions, the doors have a place to fasten a lock. The floor of the second level is made of logs covered with planking. The first floor can be seen through holes in the planking. The windows in the second level are covered with screens but cannot be closed. A set of rickety stairs with one broken step connects the first and second floors, and a fire escape stands outside one of the screened windows. Although it is impossible to locate any holes in the roof, the building leaks enough on the east side to make sleeping there impossible when it rains.

In the kitchen there are two wood stoves and a small propane gas range. One of the wood stoves heats a five-gallon tank, and cold water from the well is piped into the kitchen sink. A shower has been created in the backyard by nailing a hose to the wall. There is only one outhouse, the second having burned down early in the summer.

When I first arrived at the camp early in the season before it was crowded, there were not many flies. But when people increased, so did the flies. Now, when you sit down, your body literally becomes covered by them. There are several things that account for the flies. Once the crew arrived, the men's latrine steadily filled until there was no possibility of using it. Recently someone wedged the door shut and placed a rock in front of it. We now have to go to the toilet in the woods, but some people just go against the wall. We have some new garbage cans, but they are always overflowing. People still throw their garbage on top of the cans, trying not to litter the ground. I don't know what provision has been made for them to be emptied. The flies breed in the yard. The water from the sink goes out in a pipe that runs over the back steps close to the door. The pipe is broken and waste water pours over the step so that the yard is flooded with about an inch of water.

We are not charged for these living quarters, and wood for cooking and heating is supplied gratis by the farmer. (MR)

*   *   *

The buildings in my camp are made of wood and cinder block. The main building is old and falling apart; the screen door leading into it is ripped to shreds, giving free access to the flies. Each room contains a stove, a bed, and sometimes several shelves. Right in the middle of the hallway are a jukebox, a crap table, and two sofas. Besides this main building, there are several family houses.

There are two kitchens, each with a refrigerator and stove, but there is no inside plumbing; no sinks to wash hands, brush teeth, or wash dishes. There is a pump outside with a little faucet, which is temporarily broken. For drinking water one must walk up the dirt road for a few hundred yards to the farm. There we use the water from an outside tap that has a hose attached to it. There is a small building with two showers, neither of which work. The shower is a pipe that comes straight up and then curves down with no head on the end of it. One must wet part of one's body at a time, because there is just a trickle of cold water. There are also two dilapidated outhouses. The first has a little hole in the door with a screen over it and no other ventilation. The other has a full window with no screen, but it doesn't smell as bad, for there is more air. In any case, only one person uses the outhouse; everyone else uses a pan or the bushes. (ET)

*　　　　*　　　　*

During the night there were some interesting visitors in the room: two rats that scampered across the floor and numerous bedbugs. The other three men in the room all had sprays to kill the insects, but didn't use them. These bedbugs were large, and when you killed them they were full of blood. The

Stagrant housing.   Photo by Bill Siebert/Glad Day Press.

bugs that I had in my bed in another room in the camp were small, black, and about the size of a crystal of sand. This room also had a number of ticks running up and down the walls. The four of us slept poorly because of the bugs, which bite all exposed areas. Vance says that my bed is bad because Clyde slept there before and he was dirty. In the morning we all woke up at 4:30 and found blood spots all over the sheets from killing the bugs during the night. (AK)

* * *

Joe instructed me on the proper use of flypaper. We unwound the roll and hung the paper in the middle of the room, directly in front of the door. The flypaper was up for twenty minutes and I counted twenty flies on it. During the afternoon the fatality rate was incredibly high. Roy saw the flypaper and came in to borrow some. He claimed that his room was so full of flies that he could barely sleep because they landed on his head and arms all night. There are messy splotches all over the walls and ceiling where people have killed them. However, there was little discussion concerning the problem until Joe brought the flypaper into the camp. The possibility of easing the problem has stimulated people to talk about their miserable experiences. (CL)

* * *

Inadequate housing. These units are probably not in violation of the housing code.   Photo by Bill Siebert/Glad Day Press.

When I first arrived, the camp was in fairly good condition, but over the summer there has been a lot of damage. Most of it is accidental. There are, for example, large holes in the yard from horseshoes. And there are a number of broken screens and windows that have been hit by balls since the kids have no alternative but to play ball right near the barracks. Some of the destruction has been for constructive purposes. Nate tore a shelf out of his room and used the wood for a much-needed shelf for the washing area. There has been relatively little deliberate damage and most accidental destruction could have been prevented with better construction. The screens, for example, are not stapled and come out with very little pressure. The major source of destruction, however, is the fact that there are so many people occupying a very limited space. (CL)

*   *   *

I got some toilet paper from my room and set off for the nearest outhouse, which was seldom used. I soon realized why. The screen on the door was torn and there were flies swarming inside of it. The seats were dirty and the place smelled. So I walked over to the other outhouse. The floor of this room was all wet, either from urine or clorox. Very frequently diarrhea can be found on the back side of the toilet seat. It is most likely from the children, who have trouble using the outhouse seat, which is built up at a rather high level. (DR)

*   *   *

There were two other men in the outhouse and the place smelled like an ammonia factory. The men were complaining about the terrible smell, how dirty it was, and how a camp this large with this many people should have some kind of flush toilets or at least a better system than this. A third man came in and all four of us were talking about how terrible it was. It seems that everyone gripes about the toilet all the time, but just among themselves. They don't take their complaints to the camp management. (GP)

*   *   *

Around dinner time, people come into the kitchen to get buckets of water for drinking, bathing, and cooking. The water runs very slowly. I would estimate it takes about three minutes to fill up a quart container. I remember Johnny saying to Mr. Ed when he came in, "I can piss faster than that water. Do you want a cup of that to drink?" However, the water problem was somewhat remedied by Geech. There is a filter from the pump that gets plugged by sediment that comes in through the pump water. So Geech

Good housing.   Photo by Bill Siebert/Glad Day Press.

took the filter apart and cleaned it out. The water pressure increased slightly. He remarked that a bigger filter was needed because this one just didn't handle the number of people who used the water.

The waterlines run first to the kitchens, then to the showers along the same pipeline. If someone turns on a faucet in the first kitchen, the water pressure falls in the second kitchen. During peak-use periods there is no water at all in the second kitchen or in the shower. The kitchens are the only place in the camp where there is hot water, and it runs for an hour in the morning and an hour in the evening. (DR)

Privacy

The close quarters, the shared rooms with thin walls, and the common cooking and eating arrangements preclude privacy. There are few places where one can be alone and away from group pressure, where one can avoid contacts that may, for some reason, be disagreeable. There is little respite from the social life of the camp and this, in itself, generates considerable tension.

Tom had lived in a bullpen last year, but only for three nights, then he moved out. He now lives in a single room, separated from the bullpen by

Fires often begin in camps because of overloading of inadequate electrical facilities. Photo by Thomas J. Pollicano.

the juke. He hated the bullpen because there was noise all the time. What bothered him most was that he couldn't leave anything hanging around. He was afraid even to go to the bathroom, suspecting that people would go into his room and steal things while he was gone. He is much more at ease in his own room. (DG)

* * *

There are six men in my room; three of them sleep in the same bed. Bull sleeps by himself in the other half of the room. He has the entire front half of the room all to himself, despite the fact that the rest of us are crowded. Everyone avoids him. Bull is an ex-con who spent six years in jail for killing a man. Three of the guys keep lead pipes under the beds to have them ready if he causes trouble. (GP)

* * *

Our corridor is at the end of the barracks, right next to the juke. It is six feet wide and contains a stove and refrigerator for common use. No one keeps anything in the refrigerator because food is stolen, but everyone uses the stove.

On each side of the corridor there are three rooms, one of which is the juke. Large pictures of the Temptations and smaller pictures of Martin Luther King and Robert Kennedy decorate the walls of the juke, which is furnished with an icebox for beer and soft drinks, a couple of tables, and a pool table which costs 25 cents for a rack of balls. A jukebox features soul music: Motown, Smoky Robinson and the Miracles, B. B. King, and Otis Redding. The juke looks like it is always ready for a party, with crepe paper hanging from the walls and ceiling. The music is very loud and carries to all the rooms in our corridor.

This morning I got up around 7:00 and met Bertha in the juke. She explained to me that she had been grouchy the day before because she was very tired and couldn't get any sleep. She sleeps in a corner of the juke that is covered off with hanging blankets. She is unable to sleep when other people are up late playing cards. (DG)

* * *

I went out for the day Sunday and, on arriving back at the camp in the evening, I met Paul walking through the yard. He asked me if I had a good time and I said, "Yes." He asked me who had dropped me off out on the road. I told him I had just caught a ride from town with a stranger; and he said, "That's good. Don't ever let any girl know that you live in a place like this, if you got a good girl somewhere." (GW)

Lack of privacy.   Photo by Thomas J. Pollicano.

Food and Eating Arrangements

Eating arrangements in migrant labor camps illustrate the extent of the migrants' dependence upon the crew leader. The migrant, in most situations, must accept the irregularity of meals, their price, and their quality. Dissatisfaction is prevalent but complaints are subdued. With no possibility of controlling the arrangements or of seeking alternatives, active protest can only result in frustration and humiliation.

The people in my camp preferred certain types of food and contrasted their taste with that of white people. The crew leader's wife told a story about a white boy who worked with her in Florida. "He liked colored people's cooking so much, he liked it better than white folk's cooking." She asked me if I liked chitterlings. I said I ate everything and she noted, "That's the way it should be. There are lots of white folks who don't eat chitterlings." It was commonly believed that white people do not like fried chicken and that they serve their chicken pink in the middle, instead of well done. Identification with "black food" is also suggested in the popularity of a song on the jukebox called "Soul Food, That's What I Like," a catalog of traditional southern foods. Migrants are familiar with foods such as 'coon, 'gator, 'possum, and armadillo: 'coon is popular, but armadillo is "starvation food." There are several foods thought of as luxurious. The crew leader's children, who occasionally ate ice cream and watermelon, which are relatively expensive in the north, were regarded with envy.

Some people brag about their odd tastes, such as the man who claimed to have eaten dog and cat meat, worms, bumblebees, and caterpillars. More often, however, those with deviant tastes are a source of humor. Bean told a story about a guy down south who was real drunk and took a can of dog food off the shelf in a grocery store, thinking it was a can of meat. He gave it to the storeowner and asked him to open it for him right there. The man looked around and didn't see a dog but he took the top off anyway. "That nigger was so drunk he just ate the whole thing right there and said how good it was and walked out." People who can cook well are admired. "You haven't tasted anything until you've tried Ernestine's cooking." Conversely, those who can't cook are criticized. Flo offered me a cheeseburger sandwich, deep fried in lard, which turned out to be of cardboard consistency. She was quick to remark that there was something wrong with the meat when she bought it. She had spent $6.00 for a 10-pound box of hamburger, but now she thinks they must have sold her horsemeat.

Whatever the food, it is often shared. Shorty offered me a plate of food the first day I arrived in camp and many times since. One day, Fats, on discovering that I hadn't eaten breakfast, offered me some food saying, "This is a tramp camp but that doesn't mean that anybody is going to go hungry. We all eat. We'll share whatever we have." (DR)

* * *

Jessamay put my name on the list of people who will pay $15.00 a week for food. All of the single people were told they must either join the meal plan or get out of the camp. Jessamay does the cooking and there is plenty of food. It is very greasy, however, and I find myself, along with everyone else, consuming a lot of bread to push it down. For breakfast Tuesday we had French toast and a hot dog. There was no coffee for the second time this week and everyone grumbled; but most people had never eaten French toast before and enjoyed it. At every breakfast there is something missing. One day it is coffee, another day bread, another day butter.

For dinner we had rice, baked beans, corn bread, and some kind of fatty cut from a pig, all soaked in gravy. For lunch, as usual, we had a peanut-butter sandwich, a lunch-meat sandwich, and two cookies. Sometimes, when there is not a full day's work, we get only two meals a day. In any case, there is no fixed lunch period. Today, people ate one sandwich in the morning around 10:30 and another around 1:00, both out in the field. We eat our meals in five or ten minutes. Since there is room for only seven or eight people at the table, everyone else eats breakfast and dinner standing around the stove. (MR)

*   *   *

The crew leader's wife, who cooks for the crew, doesn't have a particular time to serve, and we eat whenever she calls us. She gives us about an hour to get there after she calls the first time. If we don't eat then, we miss the meal, although it is paid for by the week. This morning we had to travel to work, so we got up at 5:30 A.M. No one complained too much about the early hour except those who were working on the afternoon shift at the canning plant. They also had to get up at 5:30 to eat breakfast. They had paid for it anyhow and didn't want to go without it. (GW)

*   *   *

A common expression in the kitchen is "whatcha got there smelling so good." This is said as a friendly comment regardless of how the food smells. The burners in the kitchen are crowded and there is a good deal of "burner stealing." One person might have a pot on a burner and take it off for just a minute. In that minute, someone who had been waiting would put his pot on the free burner. The person originally using the stove would ask

Dining facilities are often unappetizing.   Photo by Bill Siebert/Glad Day Press.

who took his burner, but no one would answer. I heard people complaining the other day how people just can't be civilized when it comes to cooking. (IM)

*   *   *

Generally irritated one day, people focused their complaints on the food, which was actually the least of our problems. They complained about the price, "$10.00 a week for two damn meals a day," and they griped about the amount and the quality of the food. "All we had for dinner was bread and grits. I never get enough to eat." Generally meals weren't too bad, although there were more grits or rice than anything else. But people were feeling dissatisfied and said they would never again eat on the meal plan; that it was ridiculous to pay $10.00 for this food. Nevertheless, the next day, when Jessamay fixed a chicken dinner with rice, yams and peas, Kool-aid, and bread, a good meal by any standards, people drifted in slowly and reluctantly to the kitchen. She asked, "Are you getting on the meal plan this week?" Most people said, "Yes." She confronted them with the trouble they had given her earlier, and they all denied they were the ones making trouble. They never thought anything was wrong with the meal plan. There were, however, a few holdouts. Coonie and Spaceman refused to eat that night, though over the weekend they found themselves without money and were brought back to the plan. Sitting at the table eating dinner, Pete was trying, like everyone else, to rationalize the fact that he was again on the meal plan. He had been quite emphatic in saying that he would never eat any of Jessamay's cooking again. He said, "Well, understanding is all we need," the idea being that he had misunderstood the food system. He had thought originally that $10.00 was for three meals a day rather than two. Now that he understood, there was no problem. The people needed food and had no other way to get it. (MR)

People in Isolation

Migrants are isolated in two senses. First, camps are physically isolated from population centers. But even more significant is the social isolation that is a product of their fears of the local community. These fears are often founded on an accurate assessment of local attitudes. In the insulated and unsophisticated milieu of small rural townships, there are many who do not bother to mask their feelings that migrants should remain invisible in their camps. At the same time, conditions in the camps and the nature of the work make it difficult for migrants to meet middle-class standards of presentability. Their appearance, shop-

ping in town after a day's work in the fields, serves to reinforce community stereotypes and perpetuates their isolation. Their response is to remain in tight groups when in town and to avoid contact insofar as possible. The consequent boredom, a significant aspect of the conditions of migrant labor, is a striking feature of camp life.

Sam commented how he envies me for getting out of the camp occasionally; how he sits in his room afraid to go to the juke because of all the fighting that goes on there. Miss Bea complained that everyone was always dying to get out of camp but they never can. At some camps there were cars and at others there were stores nearby. Here we were 4 miles from any store. I decided to walk into town one day to see how long, in fact, it would take. It took me 45 minutes; it is not an easy walk and this dissuades many people from leaving the camp. The only regular opportunity to go to town is on Saturday, when the crew leader provides a bus so that people can buy food for the week. Since most people have no refrigerator, however, they can only buy meat for one day. This affects their diet, limiting it to canned foods. Actually it discourages most people from cooking for themselves and increases their dependence on the crew leader. (LR)

*   *   *

The camp is 4 miles from town, and once a week the crew leader drives us in on the back of his truck to buy groceries. The time we are allowed to stay in town is limited. The truck makes two trips, and each group stays in town about an hour. I went in with a couple of people who were afraid to go into the stores. There was no Negro bar; no separate barber shop or pool room; no Negro hangout. They found this shocking and just stayed on the streets. Finally, I convinced Larry that he could go into a clothing store and buy a pair of pants he needed. Four of us walked in, but the clerk in the store gave us a very dirty look. We bought the pants fast and when we left, Larry said, "See, I told you we weren't supposed to go in there." In another store, later that day, I got the best service I ever received in my life. There were three elderly women waiting at the cash register but the saleslady left them and ran over to me. I was in the hardware section of the store looking for a lock, a light bulb, and a little rope. She gathered up these items and brought them to the cash register, where the three women stepped back five or six healthy steps to give me room. The saleslady rang up the total and asked me if that was all.

A similar awkward experience occurred in a hotel bar. All the migrants were congregated around a small bar in one room, although they were buying their drinks in the next room. I went to the larger bar and noticed there were all white men there. I stood for a minute to size up the situation and a man turned around and said, "The toilet is in there." I wasn't looking for it but went in anyhow for a few minutes when I finally realized that the bar was segregated. The migrants were going in to the large bar only to buy their drinks and brought them directly back to the other room. (GP)

*   *   *

In town, the migrants hang out together in a parking lot near a store that caters to migrant trade. This store provides credit and stocks such southern foods as ham hocks, tripe, frozen collard greens, and black-eyed peas. The townspeople walk the other way when they see us coming. We always look dirty and grubby, for the pump is broken and we can't get a shower. People look at us as if we were really strange and young kids poke fun or conspicuously step to the other side of the sidewalk. Nate asked one day, while we were chatting in the parking lot, "What's the matter with the people in this town? This is the unhappiest town I ever saw. Nobody smiles, nobody laughs. They just can't be happy here." (ET)

*   *   *

There is a cab that comes out to the camp regularly, and one day I took it to town. The cabdriver's wife was driving the cab and she had her daughter with her. There was also a large pile of clothes and boxes in the front seat, so it was very crowded. She said she had to pick up another person first on the way downtown. When the other lady, who was also white, got in, they conspicuously piled all the clothes on their laps, and the three of them plus the clothes shared the front seat. I mentioned the incident later in the camp and people said that "it's that way up here." (GW)

*   *   *

Yesterday, at around one o'clock in the afternoon, a thunderstorm broke and we couldn't work. We sat around the yard all afternoon doing nothing, just talking and sitting. We talked of what we might do. Somebody suggested that we could go to the drive-in in the evening. But we didn't have any way to get there. There was a car at the camp that we could occasionally borrow. But this time the man who owned the car didn't want to go to the drive-in himself nor would he let us borrow his car. Lamb even offered him $10.00 to use the car, but he refused. The only thing we talked about that day was getting away. Paul suggested that at J.B.'s place we might have something to do because there are a few women around and a pool hall in the juke and that is better than sitting around doing nothing. Some of the fellows who had been to Rochester said that in the city you always have someplace to go and something to do. But there we were, sitting around the place with nothing to do and it was very lonesome and very, very quiet. So after a few games of checkers in the juke, we decided we wouldn't be going anywhere that night and there was nothing better to do than to sleep. (GW)

*   *   *

While walking into town with a group of young men the other day, we passed an antique yoke on someone's front lawn. Several people had never seen one before. Larry asked, "I wonder what they use that for?" "Man, that's a nigger beater." "What do ya mean by that?" "Don't you know? They do it once every three years. They come into the camp and bring everyone down here and put the two biggest and strongest guys through the loop with one ass facing north and the other facing south. All the other migrants sit in a circle and watch. And they come out with boards with nails in them and beat the guys. That's how they keep people in check up here." "Then they might get us when we're coming through here." "You don't know what these people might do. Let's get back to camp." Larry's timidity was a source of great humor at the time, but the group turned around and returned to the camp. (GP)

3

The Crew Leader and His Control

A crew leader has many tasks. He is an owner and an entrepreneur: he owns equipment, usually in the form of old school buses and trucks; and he must risk his capital in contracts with employers and in recruiting workers. The crew leader establishes contracts with northern employers and assembles the crew. He must schedule the movements of his crew and arrange for their transportation to the north. Upon arrival in the north, the crew leader becomes a camp manager, responsible for the direction and control of the crew in the camp. He is provider of food, tobacco, alcohol, and a variety of auxiliary services, including transportation. He brings his crew to the work site, where he acts as supervisor, allocating tasks, directing work in the field, maintaining inspection procedures, and often managing all aspects of the operation until the produce is delivered to the packing house. A crew leader is also a banker to his crew, lending them money directly or allocating credit for food, alcohol, and services. He considers himself, and is considered to be, responsible for the behavior of the crew in the camp and in other contexts, at work and in the local community.

What is striking about crew leaders is the variety of tasks that must be assumed by a single individual. This must be understood in terms of the leader's ability to articulate between black crew members and the white world. Crew members view the white world as unpredictable and dangerous; they prefer to have as little contact with it as possible. Similarly, white growers usually want to have as little to do with the migrants as possible, for they feel that migrants are unpredictable and dangerous. Both groups look to the crew leader as a liaison. His ability

51

to deal with white people and to have worked out some understanding of the predictable aspects of the white world gives him enormous power over his crew.

The crew leader's many functions provide him with mechanisms to maintain control. Most important is the credit system. Most migrants, by the time they begin working, are heavily in debt to the crew leader. Once they start earning, debts are deducted regularly from their pay. Continued dependence on the crew leader's provision of food, whiskey, and loans often compounds the debt. Responsible for the sustaining of individuals who have limited alternatives, the crew leader has few constraints on what he charges for his services. Moreover, all expenses (with the exception of alcohol) are usually charged, and the migrant invariably keeps no records of transactions. When the crew leader deducts debts, he rarely itemizes them: credit books, if kept, indicate a reliance on memory, for entries show large unitemized totals, although transactions tend to be small and numerous. The arbitrary aspects of the credit system permit the possibility of extraordinary leverage if the crew leader wishes to exercise it. In part, this leverage becomes operable because of the isolation of the camps and the crew leader's control of transportation. Alternatives to the system are only possible where there is access to town; since transportation is contingent on the crew leader's favor, his ownership of the bus becomes another means of control.

The crew leader's varied responsibilities provide him with several sources of income. Formally, he draws his income from the override on the crops harvested. For example, in beans most crew leaders receive a 30-cent override on each bushel; out of this they operate trucks and buses and pay lower-ranking supervisors. In addition, they obtain income through the sale of food, wine, and auxiliary services, which may be more lucrative than the override. The crew leader's stake in the productivity of his crew, therefore, is often minimal beyond the point where crew members earn enough to pay off their debts to him.

Crew Leader Portraits

A crew leader's style in carrying out his many tasks and maintaining control is highly personal. Some exercise considerable force in managing a crew, manipulating the credit system, threatening expulsion, refusing to pay wages or to provide loans. Others are paternalistic, controlling through a system of social obligations and by fostering dependency. Still others manipulate their crews through the ingenious use of social techniques, such as humor and teasing. Styles of crew leaders vary, not with the demands of the task at hand, but with the personality and temperament of the individual.

Frank has been a crew leader for twenty-four years. He is about 6′4″ and weighs between 250 and 300 pounds. He has three trucks, three buses, and two cars, a fleet that indicates his success. Most of the time he is distant and aloof from the people in the crew outside of his own family. People may drink, gamble, and fight all they want, and he will never interfere. Frank, as he said himself one day, is not going to change people. In the fields, however, he has mastered the art of manipulation. He does exactly the right thing at the right time to keep his crew happy and working. He operates on the assumption that his people cannot move to a different job. They depend on him for money, rides to work, a place to stay, and the ride back to Florida. Therefore, he functions just enough to keep them minimally content and to provide them with enough work so they can eat and drink. Frank once said that he didn't like the idea of shooting in the camp because he didn't want children to get hurt. He said nothing about adults.

Until we started picking cherries, Frank rarely came to the field to supervise. He contracted out the crew for a fixed rate. But in cherries his income is based on a percentage of the crop picked. The more we pick, the more he earns. During the cherry season, he has been going around talking to people while they work, and occasionally he picks a few cherries and throws them into their buckets. When he helps them pick cherries, people feel that he is really caring for them. He handles the crew beautifully in the grove, telling stories and keeping people laughing and encouraged.

He is a master storyteller. In the orchard he was telling a story about a man who picked 125 buckets a day. He holds his audience well, but he doesn't perform often. He tells stories only when necessary, and then manages to create just the right mood. For example, when ten of us decided to quit work at 5:15, Frank was annoyed. He had planned to fill up the last truck and wanted us to go back to work for another hour; but we were tired and irritable and wanted to leave. Frank got on the truck with us and told some old stories about polecats. Within five minutes everyone was laughing and went back to work.

But Frank has other means of control. If you have been working, he will give you credit for food. If you haven't been working, he will not give you credit and few people have cash to buy food. People occasionally express awareness of Frank's control over them. One day he was complaining to Sonny about the registration fees for trucks in New York. Frank said there

The crew leader keeps track of production in the field.
Photo by Paul S. Buck.

was no longer a six-month registration, that he had to license for a whole year. Red, who was picking nearby, interrupted, "What are you complaining about? You've got it!" Frank asked, "Whatdaya mean, I've got it?" "You know you've got it, you're loaded. You make a fortune off poor people." "How do you know? I've got a big family to take care of." And Red replied, "For what you make a week, you could take care of ten big families. We're poor and we've got nothing. You're rich and you've got everything." Frank sort of snickered. Just then Joe came up and told him that the people who were grading were moving very slowly and when they were told to speed up they had said, "We're working by the hour, we don't have to worry about that." Frank's response was, "We'll see how they like it working for 75 cents an hour," and Red noted, "See what I mean?" (LR)

*   *   *

Pole had by far the largest of the seven crews in my camp: about 100 people. It was composed largely of young men between eighteen and twenty-five, the majority of whom were with him for the first time. There were a few families in the crew, but most of these did not include children. Pole's assistants were his son, Reece, and two other workers who drove the buses. All responsibility at work, such as field walking, weighing, driving, and checking, fell on these three men. The others all worked as regular pickers. Decisions for the crew were made by Pole alone. Even his son knew little about what was going on. When asked whether the crew would be going to work the next day, Reece replied, "You know I don't know. Why don't you go and ask my daddy." Reece simply carried out orders and did not share in making the decisions. Pole kept himself aloof from his workers. He was seldom to be seen except in the mornings and on payday. He was also very strict. Everybody went out to the fields, whether they worked or not. This rule was enforced by his son, who checked all of the rooms each morning before the buses departed. The only workers left behind were those who hid.

Physical force, or the threat of it, was used to keep disobedient workers in line. A threat was usually sufficient, because most of Pole's workers feared him. Where he could not use physical force, he relied on the force of camp authority. One such case involved three girls who refused to work one day. Pole promptly asked the camp authorities to remove the girls from the camp. Pole's credit system was the tightest in the camp. Workers were allowed no credit unless they had worked that day in the fields. He paid off his crew members weekly in private, and stories were told of his extracting debts by violence. Favors often made available by other crew leaders in the camp, such as transportation and loans, were not provided.

Jones' crew operated differently; it was smaller and more stable. Most of his workers had been with him for some time and, in fact, most were related to him. There were several elderly people and many women and children. Decision making was shared with several sons, who also acted as his assistants, supervising in the fields, driving, and grading. They made many decisions independently without consulting their father. When a group of social workers wanted to borrow a bus to take the children swimming, Jones' son was able to say on the spot that his crew could provide a bus, while Reece had to ask his father.

Jones himself had closer contact with his crew than Pole. He was available to them at any time because he was in the field with his crew during working hours and sat in the juke after work. No physical force or threat of force was used to control workers because it was not needed. Control came from a sense of mutual commitment between the crew leader and his kin. They basically trusted one another, and there was little question of exploitation or desertion.

The credit system in the Jones crew was informal. If there was no one behind the counter, workers would take what they wanted and write it down or wait until Mrs. Jones came back to tell her what they had taken. This degree of trust, not evident in any of the other crews in the camp, was due to the family ties among the members of the crew.

Emmet's crew differed from both of the above. Crew members varied widely in age, and there were many women and families; but, unlike Jones, he had few kin in the crew. Emmet had a number of people who assisted him, but he shifted responsibilities within his group frequently. Although a man might be a driver one week, he was only a checker or picker the following week. The favors were, therefore, spread thin. Decisions about the crew were made by consensus. Once, when the crew had to be split, he first discussed the move with his assistants. Then the workers were told about the situation, and several volunteered to go to the new field. This worked well, because those who were doing poorly in the first field were the ones who left. Emmet was always around the crew, but usually silent. He never used physical force to punish or control a worker; but social pressure was exerted, usually in a humorous way. When a worker was sleeping under a bus instead of working, Emmet removed his belt, swung it around his head, and playfully chased the lazy worker back into the field.

Emmet's credit system was not as rigid as Pole's nor as relaxed as Jones'. A worker would usually get credit for food, no matter how much money he owed. Not only was credit relatively easy to obtain, but Emmet also did many favors for crew members, providing transportation or loans when necessary. Essentially, Emmet relied on social pressure and a sense of social obligation in controlling his crew. (GP)

*   *   *

Tom, the crew leader, lives with his wife and four children in a cinder-block house in the camp. Last winter he remained north, trimming trees and doing odd jobs on the farm. During the summer, he continues as a general handyman while supervising the crew. Occasionally he picks in the fields himself, but for the most part he grades the cherries as we bring them in. He pays us as we bring the buckets to him rather than at end of the day or the week. In paying us, he calculates what he owes us in his head and never writes anything down. He is seldom questioned, for he maintains a distance between himself and the crew and it is difficult to approach him. The work crew is much larger than the group that lives in the camp, since Tom also serves as a contractor for day haul labor, that is, he hires people to come in and pick for the day. He supervises all of us with a style that combines nagging and sweet talk. He has difficulty, however, in controlling the crew and keeping them working steadily. He feels that the method of wage payment in which he cannot hold pay for the day or the week does not allow him much leverage. The best he can do is to say, "Okay, bring in some more cherries and I'll give you more money." He has no way of threatening to withhold funds or loans to keep people working an extra few days or hours. The crew members have little respect for him. "Tom ain't shit. You shouldn't take anything from him because he's nothing. He just thinks he's a lot." "Tom wants to be a big wheel but he's not even a hub-cap yet." (ET)

*   *   *

Preacher, the crew leader, was talking about how he and Ed, his brother, used to hoe up the field themselves in half the time it was taking the whole crew. He also talked about how he used to run his crew with physical force. Preacher no longer uses violence since he has been "saved" by God. Although he will jokingly threaten people, most of the time he is pater-nalistic. The other day Kelly asked him for $5.00 to send to his kid in a hospital in Florida. Preacher said that he would give him $5.00 under the condition that Kelly go to Western Union and wire the money and show him a receipt.

Today we were supposed to start weeding at 7:00 A.M. because Preacher decided it would be best if the crew works five hours in the morning, from 7:00 to 12:00, and then from 1:00 until 4:00. In this way we would get in eight hours and miss the hottest part of the late afternoon. The crew thought this was a good idea; however, a number of people were late boarding the bus, so we did not actually get out to the field until 7:15. Preacher was annoyed and made a big point of saying that we had started at 7:15 and now we had to work until 4:15 to get in our eight hours. He was very firm about this, as if he was paying us out of his own pocket. Once we reached the field, we were each given a hoe and assigned a double row. While we were working, Preacher wandered around telling stories about himself and Ed and the way they used to fight in their younger days.

Preacher is a master in handling people. He refers to us as his children, and rather than yell at us for doing something wrong or working slowly, he merely gives us firm but fatherly reprimands such as, "Come on children, tighten up there children." He occasionally works with us while hoeing; he is much faster than anyone else in his crew. This stimulates people to hurry to keep up with him. (AK)

*　　　　　*　　　　　*

Clyde, our crew leader, can be described as a Puritan. I commented one day, "How many potatoes is this guy going to plow up for us to pick today, anyway?" He replied, "What do you think we came here for? We came here to work. Work, boy, get to work! You shouldn't care if the man plows up for the next three days. It's more work for you to do. You should be glad that he's plowing." He is always asking the young boys, "How do you expect to be a fine young man unless you learn to work? You've got to learn to work so when you get old you can look back and say to your children, 'Well, when I was young, I did it. I did my part.' I want you to work now because I've worked, and I know what it is, and I know it's good for you. You should always be honest with people, you should never tell a lie, you should never cheat a man, you should always deal fair with him so that when you die the man can say, 'Well, Clyde never did anything wrong.' " Clyde says it's the crooks, the liars, the cheats that "shake on their deathbed. If you live an honest life, when you are on your deathbed, you can die in peace because you know you've done no wrong."

Clyde came to this country from the West Indies in 1947. He first worked in a migrant labor camp in Texas. He met his wife in Georgia, and they moved to Florida, where they worked in a peach grove. Eventually he bought a couple of trucks, became a crew leader, and started coming north on the season. In the south he doesn't have a crew and makes his living by picking peaches. He claims he can make $40.00 a day doing that and would rather pick than hassle with a crew in Florida.

Last year he had a completely different crew. No one here this season had ever been north with him before. He recruited this crew partly in Florida and the rest joined him in South Carolina, where he worked for a while before coming to New York. People just walked in and joined the crew while they worked there.

Clyde is always warning us to stay away from other camps because, he claims, he doesn't want us to get into trouble. He doesn't insist, he just advises us not to go. He generally controls his crew skillfully, but gently. The camp is so isolated that the location itself naturally tends to make people dependent upon him. It is difficult to leave the camp and there is little to do but to work hard. Clyde will loan money to anyone in his crew, whenever needed, and a few people are permitted to use his truck. When someone needs to go to town, he will usually find a driver. Even if a food bill goes unpaid for a long time, you can always eat; but he will not advance money for wine. He will never withhold a meal as a means of control. Rather, Clyde tries to convince us that we should work harder for our own benefit, "You'll sleep tighter, you'll sleep sounder if you work hard." One of his techniques of ensuring productivity is to get a good core of workers in the first place and then others tend to follow. "Boy, all the people, they just work so hard. I can't goof off here; man, if I don't want everybody on my back, I got to work hard."

I am a slow worker, but am not treated differently in terms of favors. Clyde, however, is constantly teasing me and talking about how much I eat and how little I work. He waits until everyone is in the kitchen, and when his wife is about to give me a plate, he says, "Don't give that boy a plate, he didn't want to do anything today. He didn't do anything. Boy, he eats so much. You're never going to be anything. How do you expect to be a man if you don't learn to work?" He was joking, but at the same time he was trying to control me by criticizing me in front of other people in the crew. People respect Clyde, but they still resent their dependence on him. "He must be crazy. He wants everyone to work themselves to death around here. I'm not here to make his family rich. I'm here to work for me and me alone." People also complain that he makes much more money than they make and does less work, riding around on the truck or walking around the field while others are down on their hands and knees. (GP)

*   *   *

I was sitting outside the bullpen when Reverend, the crew leader, started speaking over the PA system. He has a loudspeaker hooked up to his house that he occasionally uses to address the crew. It had been raining for about ten minutes, and Reverend said in forced humor, "Even if it snows tonight and even if it snows tomorrow, we'll be picking tomatoes." He announced that if people preferred, he would send one bus to a cucumber field and one bus to tomatoes. He advised everyone to keep himself in shape, meaning not to drink too much. Reverend feels, in fact, that people should not drink at all and makes continual references to the Bible on the evils of alcohol. However, he also makes money selling wine in the camp at a 100 percent markup. In the package store in town the winos can buy a pint for 52 cents. The crew leader sells it at $1.00. I once asked Clinton if he thought it was right that Reverend should charge such a high price. Clinton said, "Well, if I went to the store to get it, I would have to spend a dollar to drive there and back." "Well, should he make that much profit?" Clinton just shrugged his shoulders and said, "Well, you know." Reverend is generally an ineffective supervisor. One day he threatened to turn off the refrigerator if we didn't work. This was ineffective because the refrigerator hadn't been working for about three weeks. But then he threatened to nail up the bullpen. There was a lot of talk about his threats, but the general feeling was the Reverend could neither make us leave nor make us work. The bullpen belonged to the grower, and it was up to him who would live there. Reverend could not kick us out of the crew because he had promised to take us back to Florida.

Roosevelt, the driver, claims that Reverend is losing his people because he doesn't do anything to win their favor, and doesn't even get up early and go out to the fields with them in the morning. Yesterday he first showed up at 12:30, when we were eating sandwiches. Later, a white man who had supervised us in the morning came out again and started prodding us to work, but Reverend did nothing to encourage anyone. He just sat in the shade of the tree and talked to Honey about all the new machines—blueberry-picking machines, bean-picking machines, cucumber-picking machines —that were coming. Honey said that if there were more machines there would be a lot more crime and violence and that jails would be filled. She suggested praying as a way to stop the machines. "If everyone got down on their knees and prayed to the Lord to keep the machines from coming, they wouldn't come." Both Reverend and Honey agreed that wine was partly responsible for the machines, because the pickers wouldn't work.

This morning Reverend came to the field with us. When we first got there, the grower was handing out tickets and giving us instructions about which tomatoes to pick. During the first hour or two we picked green tomatoes and later changed to the red, ripe ones. The grower stressed that he wanted only the really red tomatoes and Reverend echoed him, "Yes, we want only the red ripes. No vines, no pink ones." However, later in the day when the grower had left, Reverend came along, picking behind me. He picked a few tomatoes for my basket. They were hardly blood red, as the grower wanted them, but quite orange. Reverend does not really do any picking himself. He just walks around and jokes with the crew. He seldom urges us to pick, and is not listened to when he does. He suggested that Punk help finish up Clinton's row because Clinton was going very slowly. Punk just shook his head and ignored the suggestion. Around 3:00 one day, Reverend told us just to finish the rows that were already started and not start new rows. However, he did not stay out in the fields to enforce his rules. He sat in the back of the truck and when he saw a person starting a new row, said, "Oh, you just can't tell these folks anything." (DG)

Means of Control

Because of the variety of roles they perform, crew leaders have many techniques of control at their disposal. There are several ways in which transportation becomes a means of control over a crew. The use of force is illustrated by the extreme case of "Blind Man," who enjoyed a somewhat legendary reputation. Also described are techniques of control that employ humor and teasing (cajoling people into cooperation), and that create social pressures within the crew.

"WHEELS"

"Wheels" are a crucial means of control in labor camps, where lack of physical mobility isolates the migrant and forces his dependence on the crew leader. Camps are located in remote rural sections, far from public transportation. Most migrants do not own automobiles and rely on the crew leader to get north in the spring, to get to work each day once they are in the camp, and to get food and other necessities. Because automobiles are crucial but scarce, they become a source of prestige and a means by which a crew leader can distribute favors among his crew and exercise control over them.

The crew leader, because he owns the bus, decides who will make the bus trip north with him. Once at the camp, the bus is used to transport workers to and from work sites, often miles away. By controlling movement to and from work the crew leader can determine what type of work will be done by whom and for how long. If he decides to reach the work site at 6:00 A.M., rather than at 7:00 A.M., that is the way it is, regardless of the desires of crew members. Similarly, if alternatives are available, control of transportation gives the crew leader the possibility of deciding the work site on the basis of his own interests. His override rather than the worker's wage can determine the field to be picked. If work is limited and there is not enough to go around, then someone must decide if the crew is to share the poverty or if some are allowed to earn while others do without. Clyde often used this power. When the work called for only part of the crew, he decided who was to ride in the truck to the work site, justifying the decision by saying, "This man has more responsibility."

Once in the field, the worker must remain there until the crew leader decides it is time to go. In one case, two boys decided to stop working early and to wait in the bus. Two hours later the crew leader made the boys get off the bus and walk home. The crew leader also controls his crew's access to nearby urban areas. When Clyde drove his crew to town, he put a time limit on their stay. Those who were not back on the truck would have to walk the 4 miles back to camp. Pole never took his crew to town, for it contained mostly young men who might stay and refuse to return to camp. He attempted to control dropping-out by discouraging contact with urban areas.

Since migrants cannot easily shop without transportation, the crew leader decides what products are brought into the camp and thus controls the eating and drinking habits of his crew. If a man is hungry or thirsty, he must pay the price the crew leader asks.

The automobile can be used as a source of favors, to build social dependence and a sense of obligation. Clyde loaned the truck to Carl, who said, "I'll take good care of it because maybe I'll want to use it again sometime." Clyde had a small crew. He could not afford dissatisfaction, and carefully used his truck and car to develop loyalty. (GP)

*   *   *

We had been picking corn for several weeks about 200 miles from the camp where we had been working most of the summer. Many of the men had their families back there and wanted to return. The crew leader refused to drive us, but we finally talked Bear into giving us a ride for $5.00 apiece. He was leaving, in any case, that night. One problem developed. Earlier in the week, the crew leader had offered to take our clothes to town to have them laundered. Four of us had a large pile of clothes in town, although the crew leader had promised to have it back before the weekend so that we could leave. Now that we were planning to leave, we found out that the crew leader had neglected to go to town to pick up the laundry. It was now too late since the laundry had closed, and Joe was unwilling to leave without his clothing. It seemed that this was a means of keeping people in the camp another week. (CL)

*   *   *

We sat on the bus until 4:15, when J.B., the crew leader, came and said, "We still have another field to pick." There were cries on the bus of "Hell, no, we ain't going to pick anymore today, we've picked enough." But J.B. drove around to the other side of the field, parked the bus, and said, "Come on, pick one hamper here. We can go home then." There was no motion in the bus. Everyone sat still. J.B. insisted, "You get back to work. White men get tired, niggers don't get tired." He walked off the bus, and his family and girlfriend followed. Two or three minutes later, another family group got off and started picking. People watched them quietly. There wasn't much talk on the bus. Occasionally someone would ask for a cigarette or would crack, "Hell, I don't feel like picking no more." We sat on the bus until 5:00, when Freddy arrived at the work site in J.B.'s station wagon. Whiskers and Bean walked over to the car, hoping to get a ride back to camp, but they returned after a brief conversation, saying, "I don't give a fuck if J.B. is going to be that way. I don't give a fuck." J.B. had told the driver not to give any rides. (DR)

Withholding food

When we got back from work, I sat down in front of the kitchen. Shorty was there, saying, "I don't understand how J.B. keeps anybody in this camp. I just don't understand it. They won't give me anything to eat because I just picked one bushel. I can't have any dinner." J.B. said, "If you only picked one bushel, you can't have anything on the book." (DR)

* * *

Johnny had gotten a job directly with the grower, driving a tractor. His wife was working in the grower's house as a maid. They were paid directly by the grower instead of through the crew leader. Previously both of them had been pickers in the crew and they were still living in the camp. One day, Johnny asked me to get some food from the kitchen for him. "I'll make it good with you. The crew leader won't let me have anything on the book because he says that I am working for the grower now and not for him." The crew leader often manipulated the food system in order to control the crew. By limiting the amount of food available for breakfast, he forced people to get up and out to work early, since there was no food left for those who were late. Besides making credit unavailable for those who did not work, in one case he cut off all credit for the entire camp for two days. This followed an incident of violence and was an unambiguous warning to the crew to "shape up." (DR)

Force

There are some crew leaders who seem to be legendary: "Snow, he's a mean man. Snow is real bad." Then Bear said, "What about Pole? Nobody messes with him. He comes down the line, he tells you to do something, and you get down that line in three or four minutes because his feet are as big as half the line." He treats his people so bad that "I don't think they even let him into Maryland or New York State. I don't think they let old Pole out of Florida anymore. Old Pole, he's a bad-assed man." Another infamous crew boss they call Blind Man; but he apparently isn't blind. Bear said, "Yah, I was out there one time with Roy. Blind Man grabbed his cane and hooked it around Roy's neck, asking what he was doing there. He pulled Roy up to him with the cane and then let him go. That man's not blind." James told about the time he and his brother went down to his camp. Blind Man pointed toward his no trespassing sign about 50 yards away and asked, "Can't you read?"

On Sunday a new man came into the camp to work for us. He came from the Blind Man's camp and told us some details to support the rumors. Blind Man is a crew leader from Florida who owns a migrant camp and cherry grove in New York. He runs his crew with "pimps and henchmen." These are people who get paid a regular wage and keep control by force over the people in the crew. This year there are thirty-five people in his camp, fifteen of whom are supposedly "pimps or henchmen." The others are all new workers, up with him for their first season. Blind Man robs them as much as he can, because he knows they will never come back another year. Picking cherries for Blind Man, a worker received 3 cents for a ten-quart bucket. When Blind Man contracts his men out to pick for someone else, they receive 6 cents a pound. Out of that Blind Man keeps 3 cents and gives the people only 3 cents. They were pulling weeds one day. The total wage per man per hour was $1.75. Blind Man received 10 cents a man from the grower and was supposed to distribute the hourly wage among his workers. What the workers actually saw of that $1.75 was 87 cents. Blind Man kept 75 cents and deducted 13 cents for Social Security.

People are afraid to warn others about Blind Man, for it is rumored that one man who told "had his head layed open with a pipe." Blind Man, they say, has spent a total of $42,000 keeping his friends out of prison. Most people in Blind Man's crew are picked up en route to the north. He has an air-conditioned bus made to order, with staggered seats so people can stretch out. Blind Man fools his people. They see a nice bus and they are told there is a new camp in New York State. They are tempted to come with him and are sorry later. (ET)

HUMOR AND TEASING

Big Time tells stories whenever there is time to kill. In the morning when the dew is still on the ground, or if it's raining and we can't go to work, we sit around and Big Time talks. He tells about when he was in the army, about truck-driving experiences, and about his childhood. The stories are always told in a very personal form. Even stories that do not relate to him at all are reconstructed to fit into something that happened in his life. "I know you aren't going to believe this really happened, but this is true. It did. It happened to me." He tells the same stories over and over in a monologue style, as if they have been worked over for years. The first time, at least, the stories—a mixture of adventure and humor—are usually interesting. Many are tales of superhuman feats. For example, two people were trying unsuccessfully to hold a wagon up so the wheel could be fixed. A third guy came along and said, "Come on, raise that wagon higher, get that thing higher up." The two people strained but were unable to move it, whereupon the third guy knocked both of them down on the ground, sat on them, picked up the wagon with one hand, and shoved the wheel on with the other. This story has been told at least five times now. It has its own location in a series of stories, and each one seems to recall the next. As Big Time tells his stories, he laughs to himself for as long as two or three minutes at a time. He has a very funny and contagious laugh and everyone laughs with him.

The stories that he tells keep people's minds off their problems. Groups that are sitting around grumbling are distracted from their concerns when Big Time arrives. (MR)

*   *   *

We arrived at the field at 6:45 A.M. During the day, we put up 1,300 bags of corn. There was a great deal of singing while bagging the corn, but it was very hot in the field and the work was tiring. Near the end of the day, at 6:00 P.M., two men started to complain that they were tired and threatened to quit. Such a situation, if allowed to happen, could stop the crew, all of whom were equally tired. The crew leader was on the mule train[1] at the time. He came down and helped the two men pull their rows for a while. They continued to complain that they had to work long hours and were getting little money. The crew leader successfully put down the insurrection. He began to insult the two men. He accused them of being winos, unable to hold onto any of their money. He ridiculed them with a stream of insults for about five minutes. At first the situation seemed tense, then gradually the men responded with humor. They started rapping the crew leader and joking about the fact that he did nothing but "sit on his big ass on the mule train" while they worked. The tension of the situation dissipated and people continued to work.

A crew leader from another crew working in the same field was mocking

---

[1] Mule train: a mechanically powered machine onto which pickers throw crops. Packers on the machine pack the crops into boxes or crates.

his people while they were picking. He made comparisons between his crew and ours, which he refers to as "those Belle Glade people." From time to time he brought his people over to "watch the hands of those Belle Glade people. Watch how they work." He frequently singled out Big Betty as being the one to follow. "You'd better come over here. You watch how this woman works. See how those hands do it? You watch her hands." Betty meanwhile just continued with her picking. After watching her for a while, the crew leader pointed out an old wino in his own crew who was picking one or two beans at a time, "Now, just look at *those* hands." (CL)

Crew Leader Mobility: A Case Study

A shift of leadership occurred within one crew during the middle of the season. In the process of change, differences in crew leader style and the use of effective techniques of control were revealed. The superficial attachments that generally characterize the relationships between a crew leader and his crew come to light in this observation of the chance circumstances that led to the transition.

St. Louis, the crew leader, had in the past contracted as many as five crews to go north on the season. This season he hired Big Time, whom he met briefly in Florida, to drive his bus. Big Time had done some day hauling in Florida and talked fourteen people into going north on the bus. St. Louis and his family followed a few days later in his car.

St. Louis had obtained the contract with the grower, but delegated recruitment to Big Time. St. Louis provided transportation, capital for gas, and loans for food and liquor; but Big Time drove the crew north. After some moving around, due to confusion in the terms of the contract, the crew moved into Benny's camp, Benny being the supervisor of the farm. During this initial period of confusion, the crew lived off St. Louis' money (though *they* were under the impression that the money was Big Time's).

Benny's camp consists of two buildings about one-quarter of a mile apart on a back road. The crew, including Big Time, lived in one building, while St. Louis and his family moved into the other house. Thus the crew was much closer physically to Big Time than to St. Louis.

The third day in the camp, St. Louis was taken to the hospital for minor surgery. He was in the hospital for more than a week, and during this time Big Time continued to assume leadership, making loans where necessary (using St. Louis' capital), and supervising at work. His supervisory style was light and intermittent and, although he was the only person supervising the crew directly, he always asked Benny in the morning exactly what was to be done.

Food was provided at $12.50 a week for two meals a day by Big Time's "muck wife," and again, capital for food purchased was provided by St. Louis. The last and perhaps most important function of the crew leader (in the eyes of the crew) was also assumed by Big Time, as he paid the crew at the end of this initial week. Thus, early in the season, Big Time's position vis-à-vis the crew was already changing. Although he was initially hired as a driver, after this first week the crew members spoke of the debts they owed him. It was Big Time who was often referred to as the crew leader, though at the end of the first week, when the pay was disappointingly low, hostility was expressed against Big Time: "Well, he's just a bus driver; wait 'til St. Louis gets out of the hospital, he'll fix us all up."

Meanwhile, during the week that St. Louis was in the hospital, Big Time made another move toward crew leader status. He established contact with the grower, and was put directly on his payroll to drive cherries to the process plant. He not only gained an "in" with the farmer but a source of income independent of the crew leader. On several occasions Big Time turned aside Benny's offers to bring the market receipts for the day's cherries to the grower, obviously intent on presenting the "good news" of the day's profits himself. Also during this time, Big Time spent a great deal of time with Benny, asking advice on picking techniques. On several occasions, Big Time was overheard talking to his "muck wife" about his hopes to get a small crew some day.

For several days after St. Louis came out of the hospital he was in poor physical condition, but eventually he began to get about and made an obvious attempt to assert his position as crew leader. This was manifest in the new tone of supervision in the field, which was much firmer and more regular than it had been previously under Big Time. In this way, St. Louis managed to alienate both the crew members, who felt he was crowding them, and Benny, who was no longer consulted about field procedure. In fact, as Benny was later to mention, St. Louis was picking rows of trees perpendicular to the way that they had been picked for "more than seven years now." Crew members complained that St. Louis showed favoritism toward his own children and gave them better rows of trees. Sensing that Big Time had influence over the crew, St. Louis was hesitant to countermand his orders, tending rather to compromise with them. Work continued with an ambiguity in leadership through the second and part of the third week.

Halfway through the third week the stress became evident as Big Time acted out his aggression toward St. Louis through verbal assaults, to the entertainment of the crew. As the week progressed, he began to direct more and more of his aggression toward St. Louis, although at first not by name and always behind his back. Big Time's verbal skill became a significant factor later in the week. Benny spoke of St. Louis getting "too big for his britches" and mentioned that he had taken the profit from the piccolo (jukebox) in "Big Time's building." Benny then defined his relationship with the grower. "I am his right hand, not his right-hand man, but his right hand. What I tell him he hears, see!" He then returned to criticizing St. Louis. The scene proceeded like a bridge game, with each player bidding to his partner's unseen hand; Benny took the lead. "I knew St. Louis when he started in the contracting business, I knew him when he came to Waitville, walking." He offered the information that St. Louis had on several occasions threatened to leave. "If he threatens it one more time, I'm going to let him go. I know you'll stick with your job, Big Time, won't you? And this crew will stay with you?" Big Time responded quickly to this bid. "Yeh, this crew is not goin' away. This is my crew, they stay with me." With this final show of support, Benny closed the bidding with "Yeh, if that son of a bitch tries anything again, I'm just going to give him his walking papers and he can go." During this conversation Big Time had been asking the members of the crew standing around for support, "Don't I treat you boys right?"

By the fourth week the rivalry between Big Time and St. Louis was open, each "putting down" the other, by name, behind his back. St. Louis' approach was usually a rational one. He pointed out his financial advantage: "Why do you want to stick with Big Time when you know he hasn't got a bicycle to carry you to town?" Big Time's approach was humorous: "St. Louis is so fat he's got to ground them trees, he can't climb them." During this time Benny had seen the grower, who was only interested in one thing, a crew to pick his apples. He had talked him into letting St. Louis go but keeping Big Time and the crew.

St. Louis finally announced that the crew would have to leave in two days. The crew members agreed, but then told Big Time they would stick with him. There was, at this time, ambiguity as to which way the crew members would finally go. Big Time reinforced his position by buying beer and lending money more freely than usual. For the next two days, St. Louis drove people to work in his bus, and on both occasions gave a short speech to convince people to go with him. The people nodded, but on the third day, when he finally left, only two men went with him, one whom he had promised to take to the doctor for an ulcer and one who, the night before, had a fight with Benny about his daughter. The rest of the crew remained with Big Time.

Meanwhile there was considerable financial manipulation; Big Time borrowed enough from the grower to pay off his debt to St. Louis. The crew members were forced to give up almost a whole paycheck to pay off a store bill borrowed on St. Louis' "good name." Big Time also made contact with a few growers to fill in work until apple time. Since the bus belonged to St. Louis, the crew had to depend on the growers to pick them up at the camp. This immediately became a cause of discontent, but Big Time was able to borrow enough from the grower (who badly needed the crew as the peak season approached) to buy a station wagon.

Thus at last Big Time had all that he needed to be a crew leader in his own right: a crew, transportation, a place for his crew to live, and, most importantly, a source of whatever capital he needed for his operation.

The most crucial aspects of this transition were the chance events of those first two weeks of the season. During that period Big Time filled the role of crew leader in the eyes of the crew members; and in migrant farm labor, where the work period itself is so short, those first few weeks are more important than they might be in other situations. To a certain extent Big Time's personal style helped his position. The crew was more receptive to his humorous banter than to St. Louis' more rational assessment of the material picture. The broader social needs of the crew were better served by Big Time and, in this case, were more salient than the material benefits offered by St. Louis.

Also illustrated here is the casual nature of the migrant system. A mass of unrelated, chance circumstances contributed to the transition: Benny's insecurity, the wide spatial separation between St. Louis' house and the crew's quarters, his hospitalization, and his need to reassert himself on his return. In particular, underlying the casual nature of the transition is the lack of attention that the grower paid to his labor problems. (MR)

4

Work

The migrant labor crew, formed by definition for the purpose of work, must be considered with respect to the character and organization of this work. There are many crops that still require hand harvesting, and many farms, particularly in the eastern United States, where hand labor is still more economical than mechanization. The crews studied harvested cherries, lettuce, snap beans, peas, tomatoes, corn, strawberries, potatoes, and onions. In addition to picking crops, migrants did odd jobs such as weeding, haying, laying irrigation pipes, and packing produce. Most crews did not specialize in a special crop; although preferences were voiced, crews took whatever work was available.

The technology of harvesting most crops is not complex. With the exception of those who pick corn, which involves a larger number of procedures, most migrant workers are pickers. The skills required to pick crops are simple, but they are, nevertheless, considerable—a fact that became painfully clear to student participants in the crews. The difference between an experienced picker and a novice is striking, in both speed and stamina. Migrants also perform related tasks, such as loading trucks, weighing produce, supervising, and driving. In smaller crews the crew leader performs many of these tasks personally, but even in large crews relatively few people are required for intermediate jobs. Except for driving, most tasks require no special skills, and are interchanged or handled by one or two persons. Pickers may also act occasionally as loaders and weighers. Given this fluid situation, no permanent intermediate stratum develops between the picker and the crew leader. Both the requirements of work and the policies of crew leaders discourage stratification.

70

The conditions of work vary. On many farms, harvesting proceeds with relative efficiency. Generally these are farms on which the grower, or a permanent supervisory staff, is involved in managing the labor force. More commonly, however, the grower abdicates responsibility for this aspect of farm management and delegates responsibility for the harvest to the crew leader. This abdication usually results in poor management or no management at all, a fact that is reflected in the daily experience of the migrants. The workday is poorly planned, and multiple delays preclude high productivity. Labor wastage hurts the farmer, who must get his crop harvested within a given time; more directly, it hurts the migrant, who is not paid when he is not actually working. There is no system of protection as in many other industries that are dependent on the weather. The cost of all delays, natural or otherwise, is assumed by the migrant. There is little uniformity in the system of wage payment, a fact that compounds the uncertainty that stems from weather and labor wastage. Harvesting wages are usually paid on a piecework basis, but the same crops, picked in the same area, sometimes yield different piecework rates. Minimum wage regulations, based on hourly earnings, are difficult to enforce in a piecework system where hours are erratic and may be falsely adjusted to conform to regulations. Various systems for payment of piecework are employed. Often tickets with a fixed value are provided for each unit of production. These are exchanged for cash in the evening or at the end of the week; and, in some cases, are used directly as currency in gambling or for local purchases. A punch-card system is also common. In some cases, crew leaders keep only mental records, and no tangible evidence is provided of the number of units picked.

The conditions of work are characteristically uncertain and unpredictable. The availability of work is dependent on the weather, the quality of the crop, and the whims of the grower and the crew leader. The migrant himself is often poorly informed, seldom knowing where he will be working, for how long, or the wages he will be paid. There is no established routine that enables the individual to plan his day or his savings. He has few alternatives but to accept conditions as they are or not to work at all.

Grower/Crew Leader Relations

The existing conditions of migrant labor are rooted to a large extent in the management of labor: in the crucial relationship between the grower as employer, and the crew leader, who, as we have seen, serves in many capacities as the middleman between the grower and his labor force. To explore this relationship, growers, crew leaders, and migrants were interviewed in a survey of twelve farms selected as representative of the variety of situations in which migrant labor crews are employed. This section summarizes the relationships found to exist.

Relationships between growers and crew leaders are not well specified; the rights, duties, and powers of each develop according to the beliefs a particular grower may have on how to manage a crew, the personalities of the individuals involved, and the demands of the situation. Various kinds of relations have developed with implications for the migrants.

From the perspective of the crew, the most important characteristic of a grower is his ability to provide regular work. Many of the factors relating to this ability are outside the grower's control; others are based on general economic considerations. His predicted need for labor may change due to weather conditions, his own crop conditions and those in competing areas, or the state of the market when his crop is ready for harvest. The timing and type of the harvest in relation to whether the crop is picked for processing or fresh market are also important factors in the availability of regular work for the migrant labor crew.

Economic considerations such as these shape the character of the season for the crew; but far more important for the migrant are the arrangements that develop between the grower and crew leader for the management of labor. These arrangements have more than mere economic importance for the migrant. In addition to his need for work, all other needs—food, shelter, rest, recreation, order—must somehow be met within the migrant labor system. With only minimal ability to secure these things for himself, the potential for control rests with the crew leader and the grower. Conflict frequently develops because growers fail to recognize that their responsibilities include the migrant's noneconomic situation and that non-work activities feed back on work performance. Most growers also fail to recognize that they are employers of labor as well as producers of crops. With one notable exception, no grower in this study showed evidence of having shaped his work organization and supervisory practices so that the worker would be channeled to efficiently bring about the ends for which he was employed.

There are several aspects of work process that must be defined and allocated by each grower and crew leader. In defining responsibilities, four predominant patterns were found. These vary as to the extent to which the grower abdicates responsibility for various aspects of the work process to the crew leader. Those growers with the closest involvement in the work process tried to exercise some control over work and minimize exploitation by seeing to it that the crew leader's interests were inseparable from their own and the crew's. The crew leader's main function in this kind of arrangement was to provide the grower with a specified number of workers; beyond this he was essentially an employee of the grower. His earnings were a combination of wages earned from his own picking and a commission based on his workers' productivity. Although the commission provided incentive to get as much work out of the crew as possible, he was also intimately aware of the crew's problems because he worked in the fields with them under the same conditions. Thus, the possibility existed for upward communication of problems to the grower before they got out of hand. Supervisory responsibilities were usually shared between the crew leader and a full-time foreman employed by the grower. In practice the foreman supervised, but directed any problems concerning crew members to the crew leader. The structure of the work, the allocation of work roles and work sites, and the supervision were loose, with many individuals stating that they worked completely on their own, despite the obvious presence of a foreman in the fields. On farms where this relationship prevailed, there was nothing in the technology itself that dictated such arrangements.

A different pattern of relationship developed in several cases where a more complex organization was required to pick celery. Working on a mule train (celery harvester) requires close coordination of many workers and maintenance of a steady work pace; one person slower than the others can bring the entire operation to a standstill. Supervision is therefore crucial. One grower took advantage of this interdependence to create a self-supervisory situation. Instead of paying workers by the hour, he developed a complicated piece rate for each of five jobs on the mule train. When someone jeopardized the wages of others, he was controlled by the work group. In contrast, another grower created a situation that resulted in chaotic and inefficient work. This crew was exploited by several methods, including manipulation of credit at the only local store (owned by the grower's brother), nightly harassment by a local state trooper who was also a brother, reduction of the hourly rate promised prior to the season, illegal holdback of part of the wage as an end-of-season "bonus," and a charge of $2.00 for transportation to a nearby town. Workers believed that the grower consistently underrecorded the number of hours they worked, and morale was very low.

The crew leader in this situation was powerless. Although he had recruited the people, he had no bus; the crew had traveled by public transportation, with the grower paying the return fare. Therefore the crew leader could not threaten to pull his crew off the job if the grower did not meet his demands. Furthermore, his mode of pay cut him off from effective control. Part of his earnings was a commission based on the number of workers recruited, rather than on the crew's productivity. The rest was a weekly salary for supervising and training people to work on the mule train. Although completely dependent on the grower, he had little opportunity to talk with him. He noted bitterly that the previous year he had only one meeting with the grower during the season to discuss the progress of work. This year, by mid-August, he had none. Crew members felt it was his job to bring their complaints to the grower, but the crew leader said his appeals were ignored. His crew, however, noted that his salary was "$150.00 a week, rain or shine."

Another grower, with a similar mule train operation, paid the crew leader a fixed wage and a commission—not on output, but on the number of people he recruited. An ineffective recruiter, he hired winos or anyone who wandered in. Still unable to get a full crew, the grower arranged for a group of Puerto Ricans to supplement the crew. Integrating the complex and interdependent tasks on the mule train was, in this case, nearly impossible. The crew leader's ineffectiveness extended to supervision, and since his pay was not dependent upon the crew's productivity, he relaxed and collected his salary, much to the grower's frustration.

A third type of relationship between growers and crew leaders developed as a response to changing requirements for hand labor. The crew leaders in these crews are really entrepreneurs, taking maximum advantage of shifts in technology as they occur. The crew leader owns and operates the labor camp in which his workers are housed and makes use of local labor as well. Crews are large with high turnover, although some members live in the camp year-round, doing whatever winter work is available. One large grower reported that mechanization had reduced his migrant labor needs to six men for weeding during the growing season and about one hundred men for a few days at harvest time. By being prepared to meet the short-term specific needs of many such growers in a wide geographical area, this type of crew leader can keep his workers busy, and the grower can have labor available when he needs it without high overhead costs. The contractor's normal commission in these cases is 15 percent of the wages paid. He also earns additional income doing hauling jobs with his own equipment, and through other normal channels such as the sale of food, liquor, and women to the crew. This type of crew promises to become more common in the future.

Finally, there is the situation where the grower transfers all responsibility for the provision and supervision of labor to the crew leader, who must decide upon the most appropriate work organization, fill the required jobs, and provide whatever equipment is needed. The crew leader's earnings may be based on a prearranged share of the yield (in one case, one-half of the crop) or on a specified amount per unit yield. Beyond the initial arrangements, the grower has no interest and disclaims all knowledge of what goes on. Some growers in this category claimed not to know what the workers were paid; this was the crew leader's affair.

Growers' attitudes toward the crew in these cases were highly stereotyped. They rarely went into the fields and almost never went into the camp. They avoided all contact with workers, whom they regarded as highly unpredictable. "The less you say to them yourself, the better." When one grower was asked what he would do if he saw a worker deliberately damaging plants or throwing trash in the hamper, he replied that he would not say a word; if the crew leader didn't do anything on his own, the condition would merely remain. "I don't really know what's going on and even if I did, there's nothing I could do about it. I just have to take whatever the crew leader's handing out."

Of the farms surveyed, there was one unique situation in which many of the problems described above were eliminated. This grower provides an interesting contrast to other situations because of his awareness of management practices and the close relationship between economic and noneconomic factors in developing an efficient work force. This grower's entire crop consists of apples for fresh market. Apples that are bruised at any stage of the harvest must be thrown away. Under these conditions labor is an important cost, and he rationally sets about to see that his labor worked under the best conditions possible. This grower retains complete control of the work organization by reinforcing and channeling the authority that the crew leader already has over his crew.

The crew leader and an assistant direct all operations in the orchards; one of them is present all the time. Four orchard bosses, year-round employees of the grower, each supervise fifteen men. These six people are also responsible for on-the-job training of workers, which consists primarily of showing them how to pick apples without bruising them. The grower is also present in the orchards during much of the harvest, encouraging the workers, but if he observes any problems, he always goes to the crew leader.

The work itself is organized to accomplish two ends: (1) completion of the harvest with minimum wastage of time and effort and minimum damage to the crop; and (2) the elimination of any beliefs on the part of workers that favoritism has been shown in the allocation of work sites or that they are being cheated out of their earnings. The crew of sixty workers is divided into thirty pairs, each assigned a picking number that it keeps throughout the season. Tickets numbered with the picking numbers are drawn from a hat, and people are then assigned to a row in a block of trees in the order that they are drawn. Each pair is responsible for cleaning every tree on the row, regardless of yield. No time is wasted waiting for crates or carrying loaded boxes to a truck after they are filled. Before the season begins, the grower and orchard bosses estimate the number of boxes that can be gotten from each tree. Boxes and ladders are placed where they will be needed before the crew arrives. During the harvest, a separate loading crew collects the loaded boxes from each tree.

Each couple keeps a written record of the number of boxes picked from each tree. They also put a ticket with their number on each filled box, thus providing the grower with a record of the yield of each tree in his orchard, and the worker with a record of his own earnings. The loading crew collects boxes and tickets and checks to see that the correct number of boxes has been counted for each tree. If they find an error, they must tell the worker to recheck the count. A third check is made when the tickets from the loaded truck are given to the grower. If the worker has any complaint about his pay, there are three sources that can be checked.

In an industrial setting, this kind of rational organization is typical and the effort to describe it a belabored irrelevancy. However, in the seasonal agricultural labor context, this case is unique. The more common situation suggests that although technology, natural conditions, and market conditions affect the relationship between grower and crew, there are large areas in which this relationship can be improved. What is surprising is the unwillingness of growers to structure work organization to their economic advantage. Instead, the "power vacuum" is filled by the crew leader with unanticipated and unwelcome consequences for both grower and crew. (JS)

Piecework Crops

The technology of picking, and the consequent organization of work, varies with each crop as well as with supervisory practices. Work experiences are described below, either because they are routine or because they shed light on the migrants' perceptions of such ubiquitous problems as the inefficient waste of labor and the poor planning characteristic of seasonal farmwork.

CHERRIES

Monday we got up at 6:30. At 7:00 we were sitting on the front porch when Benny, the foreman, drove up on his tractor and asked if we wanted to ride to the fields with him. We climbed on the tractor and drove about half a mile. In the field an old man, his wife, and three boys were picking cherries. Benny gave me a bucket and a piece of string, which I used to tie the bucket around my body. I asked him what I was supposed to do and he said, "Just pick some cherries." When I got up on the ladder, I asked the old man whether I should pick all the cherries or just the red ones of a certain size. He said, "Just pick 'em all, pick 'em all." So I filled a bucket and passed it in and they stamped my ticket for 60 cents.

While picking cherries that day and later in the season, I learned several things about cherry picking. When you finish your tree you must take the next available one in the row, even if it is very scrawny. Occasionally one row will have some very bad trees and when this happens, people will hide in the grove, waiting for someone else to get stuck with the bad trees. At first, I complained about the scrawny trees, and the field walker gave me a lecture about how every man had to take whatever came to him. Someone had to do these trees, after all. He talked to me as if taking these trees was the Christian thing for me to do. In finishing a tree, you are not supposed to leave any cherries on it at all. The checker says the farmer gets on her if he sees any cherries, even little white ones that look like they're not any good, left on the trees.

There are three grades of cherries, and we were picking the best grade. When we filled a bucket, we brought it to the checker, a woman who punched tickets and dumped the bucket into a large box. She then spread the cherries out and pulled off any remaining stems, complaining from time to time that too many people leave stems. She also complains that the grower wants the little white cherries picked, but at the same time, he wants to maintain the grade. She feels she is getting it from both ends. "Well, if I pick all the white cherries I am going to bring the grade down and the man is going to tell me I'm picking the wrong cherries; but if I don't pick the white cherries he's going to tell me that I left them on the tree, so there is nothing I can do about it." She seems to try to split the difference, sometimes telling us to pick the whites, sometimes telling us to skip them.

On Tuesday, some of us started working early in the morning, about 6:30, while others kept wandering into the fields until 8:00 or 8:30, having waited for the grass to dry. The grass in the field is about a foot high and when you work before it dries, your feet and legs are wet for most of the day. It was hot and people complained that we had no water. They yelled across the field to the man, "Hey, bring us some water, bring us some water now. I can't get up in this tree without some water." About half an hour after this shouting started, the man who drives the forklift brought out a large tin can of water. The water was pretty dirty because the can had sticks in it when the water was poured in. It was, however, drinkable. Later he brought some ice from the cherry tank and threw it in. The ice was also dirty but it cooled the water. The water can is usually left in the shade but it is tepid anyway. No one seems to mind the dirt in the water. They brush it out of the way with the back of a cup and scoop the water up quickly. Jessamay makes some attempt to clean the dirt out, but others just drink the pieces of sticks and leaves without worrying.

Around noon, lunch was eaten in about five minutes. By this time, the good trees were finished. A bad tree is one that has small cherries that take a long time to pick, or one where the ladder has to be moved often because the limbs are far apart, or where it is hard to get a ladder to stay in the tree at all without breaking limbs. A further problem is that some trees are covered with poison ivy vines, in which case people will usually not pick them. People often work with partners. Sometimes a man will see a friend working on a good tree when most of the other trees are bad. He will ask to "help hit this tree," until someone else gets the bad ones. Occasionally someone who is stuck with a poor tree will ask a friend to help him in order to finish it off fast.

One day, we were taken to a cherry grove far away from the camp. A man took us over to it in a pickup truck. We rode in the back and sat on crates. The truck itself had been used to carry boxes of cherries and had not been cleaned out. There were gnats, mosquitoes, and flies. Big Time and Jessamay, his wife, sat in the front of the truck with the man. No one asked Big Time where we were going to be working. When we first arrived at the field, there were no buckets or ladders. Another crew was there already, using the equipment, and we waited while someone went to get more for our group. The cherries seemed to be very good and the trees had few bare spots. However, they were quite tall and it was a very windy day. People commented how scary it was up in the trees, and we decided to start picking our first bucket on the ground while waiting for the ladders and more buckets to show up. In about forty-five minutes they arrived. By 2:00 most people were tired and fed up with the big trees. "Man, I can't pick any more cherries, I ain't gonna pick any more cherries." They complained how much they hated cherry picking and started slowing down. Several people were beating the trees with sticks, trying to knock cherries down rather than pick them. This was done quite violently, as if they hated the trees and were trying to kill them. While ostensibly this was done in order to avoid climbing the ladder in the wind, it turned out to be more an act of frustration. However, in some cases beating trees, a common practice, has an economic motive. If the tree is bad and the person feels that he is being slowed down by having to pick it, he will often knock the cherries down just so he can move on to a better tree where he will be able to make money much faster.

Finally, Big Time decided we should leave this section of the orchard and pick the last two untouched rows of trees. These were small and fairly good. He tried to explain to the farmer, "Since the people are tired, we are going to get to work on those small trees and we'll get these later. I've got to pace them a bit. Everyone has to have a little rest and get their wind on the littler trees. We'll get these other ones later." The farmer was reluctant but finally acquiesced and let us move. People were so tired, however, that they were unable to finish even the small trees. "Those big trees beat me down, they just beat me down." (MR)

*   *   *

Wednesday morning the camp was buzzing. At about 5:30 Frank, the crew leader, walked down the hall, blowing a whistle to get people up. When they realized there was work, they moved fast, because work had been scarce. Everyone was very excited about going to pick cherries and there was a lot of noise and good spirits. When it was time to leave in the buses, everyone in the camp was out on time. We got on the road around 6:45. Frank drove down a truck full of pails and ladders. We were given two large pails and a smaller one and told that the going price was 55 cents a pail. We signed up with a lady and she gave us a number. Joe, the foreman, assigned trees. We worked in teams: husbands and wives worked together, as did friends. We were to pick with the smaller bucket, and when it was full we dumped that into the larger one. When the larger bucket was full, it was brought to a bin where three members of the crew were dumping all the buckets. There the lady who had given me the number was checking the number of pails. They were quite strict, and the first time I brought up two pails she told me that I would have to go back and fill them up some more.

The trees were about 7 to 8 feet tall, and if you were lucky you could get one bucket off of each. People were talking about "topping," that is, getting the cherries off the top of the tree, and "grounding" or getting the lower parts, either by using a small stepladder or standing on the ground. Each person or couple takes a tree and must clean it completely before moving to another one. Joe, the foreman, checks each tree before assigning another. You can hear people calling him to check their trees throughout the grove.

The first day we started picking at 7:00 and by 8:30 there was a downpour. We ran through the grove to the bus. Most people had only gotten two or three buckets, but we had to stop. Spirits were still high, however, since at last we had gotten out to work.

The following day we went out at 6:00. When we reached the grove, Joe showed us the trees we should pick. They were loaded with cherries and the atmosphere in the grove was cheery. Several people had brought radios and many were singing and whistling. We started grounding since the ladders had not arrived, and when the trailer finally came, there was a mad rush. There were not enough ladders, and those of us without them had to stop picking and wait for the trailer to return. It finally came, and when I finished my tree, Joe told me to get the next one while Miss Bea, my partner, waited to check all the buckets. The next tree was a sickly one, but Joe said it must be picked. When Miss Bea returned, however, she refused to touch it and said we should merely shake the branches to get the cherries off and to make it look like the tree had been picked.

While we were working on this tree, a plane came by and sprayed the grove. Everyone climbed down and went under the trees to avoid being sprayed. Meanwhile the plane circled over the grove. People crouched, since the plane sweeps down very close to the tops of the trees. They complained that the man shouldn't spray while there were people in the grove. Someone shouted something about this to the crew leader but he didn't respond.

At noon, another predicament occurred. There were many filled buckets, but one loading truck had left and the other had not arrived. There was nowhere to empty our buckets and we had to stop picking when they filled up. Most people brought their buckets to the area where they usually empty them and sat around waiting for the truck. Others just dumped their buckets out, left, and walked back to camp. Miss Bea asked if I would wait and check her five buckets for her. I agreed, so she left them with me and walked back.

Each person takes two big buckets and one small picking bucket home every evening and keeps them in his room. People complain about this because rooms are small and they have scarcely enough space for their own things; but there is a shortage of buckets and if you leave them, you may not have them the next day. (LR)

*　　　　*　　　　*

The cherry season was almost over. Sara, Miss Bea, and Emma, working on adjacent trees, were complaining how rotten the cherries were. They swore they weren't going to come back next year. They said they came here on a promise that they could make money, but this was impossible. Finally six of us began to use a new method of picking. We slapped the cherries down with sticks. Each of us took a stick and violently attacked each tree. We really didn't care about the number of buckets, we just wanted to get the trees finished. We moved to the final two trees, where Red and I were assigned the job of topping while the girls grounded. We picked for a few minutes and soon got the sticks again and slapped the cherries. Finally, I told the checker that I was through and asked what to do with the buckets. "Do anything you want with them." I noticed people throwing their

Picking beans.   Photo by Paul S. Buck.

buckets up in the air. Buckets were flying all over. People were happy, the end of cherry season was here. The crew leader told us to slap a few more cherries off the last tree. He wanted to see the trees clean. I walked back to the camp with Miss Bea. She said that this season had been just a complete flop. They had made no money either in strawberries or cherries. (LR)

BEANS

As people got off the bus at the bean field, they remarked, "You won't need more than one basket here because there ain't many beans on these vines." The rows, indeed, were sparse. The beans were growing on bushes about a foot high. They were spaced far enough apart so that one bush barely touched the next one. About eight or ten beans grew on each bush. You grab them with one or both hands and pull them off and throw them in a basket. I picked a good hundred feet before I filled my first hamper. I then walked to the bus where Freddy, Butterman, and the truck driver were sitting. They griped about the poor picking, that the beans weren't much better than the peas and "we weren't going to get anything done this way." After listening for ten minutes, I walked back into the fields and sat down near Florida Joe. He had arrived late and had not finished his first basket. He was also complaining. This was his first time north and he had not been told it was piecework. He would never come again. He felt the crew leader, who gets 30 cents a bushel while we get 70 cents, was getting too much money. "In Florida, people would refuse to pick this poor a field."

The next day, we were again brought to poor fields. There were huge holes in the rows where there were no bean plants but only weeds. The plants were very small, and the beans were shriveled and difficult to pick. The field was a sorry sight. As we got off the bus, which was parked at the edge of the field, J.B. said we should go out and pick only one hamper. The day was hot and it took about two hours to fill a hamper. I settled down near the truck with Freddy and Florida Joe. There was no fresh water, so we drank some warm water left over from the day before, drinking it directly out of the milk can. The water was warm and there were rust specks in it. At 11:30, twenty people were on the bus; the others had walked back to camp. We then drove to another bean field, one that had been picked before. It was in bad shape, but J.B. said to try to get another basket. At this point, Geech and four others walked away, refusing to pick. Those of us remaining went out and started working. We were in the field only fifteen minutes when it started to rain, so we combined our pickings to fill a single hamper and left. (DR)

             *   *   *

Spaceman, the field walker, woke us up at 6:00 to get the bus early; but we sat there for an hour before we went anywhere. At 6:50 A.M., when forty people had arrived, he finally decided to leave; but then the women had to wait until the nursery opened so they could leave their children, and this caused further delay. Finally on the road, we drove for about 20 miles and then stopped because the driver was unable to find the field. The crew leader was supposed to have been leading us but his car was nowhere to be seen. Eventually, he showed up and led us to the field. Two other crews were already there, and we all rushed to grab available rows. I worked with Major, who gave me some tips on how to become a faster bean picker. He said my rhythm was all wrong. He told me to get behind someone who was really fast and then try to keep up as he goes down the row, not worrying about the beans I missed. "Just pick the ones you can pick while keeping up and you'll learn to pick up more beans as you go along." That was how his mother taught him and his sister to pick beans. I picked three hampers and brought them in for tickets. Spaceman said to wait on the bus since we were moving to another field. Most of us had finished and were on the bus, but there were still twelve people in the field, and we all had to wait for them. Those on the bus complained, "Why don't those fools come on; they hold up everyone else." It took the last man another forty-five minutes to finish, and this meant time wasted for more than twenty-five of us, for the entire crew must wait until the last man finishes picking the hamper he is working on.

The time wasted in the field is striking. For example, Wednesday morning thirty of us arrived at work, but the weighing truck—where we put the beans after we pick them—had not come and there were only ten hampers available. Those who were already picking had two apiece and some of these were already full, so we had to wait for about forty minutes. Some people started to pick, putting the beans on the ground, while the rest of us just sat. On Thursday there were other problems. There was a confusion about the lineup, and arguments resulted in a loss of twenty minutes. But most of the wastage comes from the poor condition of many of the bean fields. One day we went into a field that had almost no beans in it. Here, people set very low goals. Tussy, who was the best picker in the crew, said that he would try to get only three bushels. Others set goals of only one bushel. As we worked down the field, people commented, "There's no beans here. Look how far I've come with no beans." "I'm getting one bushel and then I'm quitting." We picked for two hours. As soon as people got their tickets for the first bushel they sat down. Sleepy, who was the field walker that day, asked what was the matter. "Now come on out here in the field and let's get those beans out. Tighten up and we can finish this field and get out of here by 1:00 and go on to another field." Tussy replied, "Another field, my ass, you know there is no other field." Tina said, "I'm not working out there. You have to go a mile to get one bean. Why did you bring us out here anyway?" Sleepy backed off. "I only do what I am told. You have to see the crew leader about that. He's the man you want to see." Field walkers support themselves by passing responsibility to the crew leader, saying, "I only do what I am told." The women refused to go back to work, and ten of them sat on the bus, where they continued to gripe about conditions, second pickings, and the lack of beans. They claimed they were not going to work any more unless there were good beans. They would just sit all day.

There is a marked contrast on days when fields are good. Tussy says, "I think I might knock out eighteen or twenty today." Others aim for twelve or fourteen. Those who set the highest goals work at a faster pace, but everyone in the crew picks faster when the beans are full, and there is often competition.

Tussy is a fantastic picker with incredibly fast hands. When he arrives at a field, he starts picking immediately and is soon way ahead of everyone else. He will set a goal for himself and then, after he makes it, move around the field helping others finish their bushels if they are short. He is a wino and there are many days when he can't work. He helps those from whom he is likely to want to borrow money when he is down and out. There are many people obliged to him.

One day a bean-picking machine was used in a field adjacent to the one in which we were working. This had a tremendous effect on the workers. At first, everyone was trying to beat the machine, setting goals that were simply fantastic. "That's what's going to be picking all the beans next year." "That's what is picking the best beans. Look, they're giving the best rows to the machine." "Let's pick these beans over quickly so we can get over there before the machine picks them all." We worked fast for about an hour, until it became clear that it is impossible to beat the machine. Then there was a slowdown. One man who had said he was going to get thirty bushels now said, "Well, I might settle for twenty today," and there were several people who quit working altogether. Later, they began to criticize the machine, saying it left most of the beans in the field. "It may go down a row quicker but it can't get as many bushels per row as we can."

It is commonly believed that the scales for weighing the beans are fixed, but sometimes complaints about the scales are merely a focus for a more fundamental problem. For example, one day these suspicions started a discussion that revealed that no one really knew what we were earning. The field walker had said, "You can make a lot of money today, if you work hard," but he never told us the rate per bushel. When someone asked him, he said 60 cents, but ten minutes later he told someone else 50 cents. A few people asked about the discrepancy and he replied, "Now don't give me any lip." There was a great deal of quiet complaining about the ambiguity, but no one said anything further to the field walker, who complained that he himself was not going to make any money either. He said that he would be lucky to receive $5.00, while we could make more since we had the opportunity to pick. "I can't pick and be a boss too because the crew leader won't let me." Another day, when asked the wage rate, the field walker said we would be paid "the regular price," but when asked what that was, he replied, "Don't bother me. Can't you see I'm busy?" Rumors began to circulate. One woman said she had seen a sign saying 75 cents a bushel but a man said that was ridiculous. "75 cents means that we are only going to get 50 cents because the crew leader takes something out of each bushel that we pick." Another woman said she thought it was 60 cents because she heard the crew leaders were getting 80 cents. We did eventually get 60 cents, but people worried about the rate throughout the entire day. (GP)

*   *   *

We got up at 5:30 A.M. and reached the field at 7:30. This was the same field we had picked the day before and the beans were poor. People were very slow in getting off the bus. First, they just sat there without moving, and when they did get off, they straggled toward the field slowly. No one joked or showed any enthusiasm. When we actually got into the rows and realized how bad things really were, everyone started grumbling. "I want to be taken home. I'm not going to waste my time here." Several people came over and tried to cope with the complaints. One of the field walkers said in an aggressive voice, "You're not going home until you pick a bushel." Another field walker who works for the grower came by and said, "Well, I've never come to a field and not picked something. I always pick at least a bushel and figure once I get here I might as well do something." This did not ease the dissatisfaction, and one man got up and said, "What we need is a revolution"; but then he added, "Well, I guess I'll pick my bushel today." We began picking, and complaints changed to platitudes about how there were some good and some bad days. "When I was doing tomatoes, sometimes it rained and the truck would get mired in. But we also have some good days." James replied, "A lot of people think they're going to make it when tomatoes come in but you never can tell—it may be a bad year— you never can tell." (DG)

TOMATOES

Monday morning Preacher pounded on the window at 6:15 and we climbed onto the bus. The atmosphere was more relaxed than when we were cutting onions. As each person got on the bus he said "good morning" and was answered with a cheery reply. Ben did a parody of what he had said many times before during the onion season. "Well, I ain't gonna make it in tomatoes, but just you wait until them potatoes start. That's where I'm gonna make my money, in potatoes." Later it was modified: he was going to make it in apples; and then finally he said that he was not going to make it in tomatoes but "you just wait till them onions come up again."

Everyone seemed happy to start the tomato season. When we got to the fields, we were lined up in rows. Preacher and Ed, the crew leaders, assigned each person the number of rows requested. Single people took two rows, and those who worked in pairs took three or four. We were instructed that there were three kinds of tomatoes in the field: the red ripe, the pinks, and the sunscalded. We were to pick the red ripe and the sunscalded but were to leave the pinks. The sunscalded tomatoes have a big wide splotch on them; the red ripes are just very red, soft, and ripe. Everyone takes baskets and puts them out at intervals along his row. As you fill one basket you move on to the next one. Unlike onions you do not handle tomatoes twice. You put them directly into a basket as you pick them. There was a great deal of conversation in the field. Johnny began telling the same jokes Ben had told on the bus. Ed overheard this and made up a joke of his own, "Some of you guys come to me and say, 'Boss, you can't expect me to work on Monday, but you just wait until Tuesday.' Comes Tuesday and you say, 'Boss, I can't do shit on Tuesday, but you just wait until Thursday.' And it comes around to Saturday and you say, 'Boss, I just can't do shit on Saturday.' It comes Sunday night and you say, 'I'm just going to pick me a hundred, you just wait.'"

Twice during the day Preacher and Ed came around to see if we were picking pink tomatoes. They didn't check in the basket, but just looked at the top and warned us not to pick the pink ones. By twelve I had twenty-seven baskets, Ben had thirty-two. Ed counted the baskets and punched out a card with the number. (AK)

*　　　　*　　　　*

The tomatoes in the field were very poor. We were only supposed to pick red ripe ones, and Tom—who was working as a checker—kept repeating, "Only the red ripes, only the red ripes." Everyone, however, was picking pink ones and rotten ones; more or less anything to fill up the basket. There was not much complaining about how bad the tomatoes were, for people said that in two weeks we would really start making money on tomatoes because they would be so thick it would take you all day to finish just one row. "You won't just be checking out just one or two at a time, but twenty-five for each row." (DG)

CORN

There are several techniques of pulling corn. On the first day I held the ears with my left hand and pulled them with my right. This is a very slow technique. The best pickers use both hands, alternating them in a sort of swimming motion. Some ears lean forward and some lean back. The ones that lean back are grasped with the left hand, the ones that lean forward are picked with the right. To get ears that are on the opposite row you reach around behind the stocks and grab, and then with a twisting motion pull them down and around. It is a difficult technique. The ears are gripped near the tassle and jerked downward. If this fails to sever the ear from the stock, a slight twist of the ear is also used. Corn leaves are very sharp, causing abrasions on the face and arms. The greatest muscular strain is around the top of the back and on the wrists, since we have to hold three or four ears of corn and pull at the same time.

Another method of pulling corn involves the use of a knife. The blade is about 12 inches long and straight and square. The corn is gripped in the left hand and the knife is swung downward with the right, cutting the stock and the ear. There appears to be no set rule as to which technique is used: it is purely a matter of individual ability and preference. However, the use of the knife is dangerous in the hands of an inexperienced person. For example, Joe, while using a knife, cut his partner's hand. He required several stitches and was unable to pick. I tried to use the knife several times and found that I could use it in some fields, but when the corn became thicker, there was a danger of slashing my arm. Knives cost from $5.00 to $10.00, depending on the quality. The crew leader sells them.

There are two methods of bagging corn. On some days we went down to the fields in groups of four, three of us picking and a fourth dragging a bag in which we tossed the ears. There is little grading of the corn when you put it in bags; however, there is a great deal of pressure to keep up with each other. The other two men I worked with were experienced pickers and much faster than I; I had to run to get my corn in the bag. The crew usually picks an entire row without stopping. There is a brief rest period of three or four minutes at the end of each row.

Most days, we used a mule train to bag the corn. The mule train is a wheeled platform pulled by a tractor, followed by a flatbed wagon holding

325 crates of corn. Nine pickers pull corn in front of the mule train. They throw it into a hopper, where it is carried by conveyor belt back to be shelled.

There is a hierarchy in the mule train operation. Box (crate) making is reserved for old men and young boys. They are paid 1 cent for each box they make. This involves attaching two ends of a frame together and fastening them with wire. There are two box makers on each mule train. The tractor driver is paid on an hourly basis. Bear, driving one of the tractors, was paid $20.00 (per day). The women on top of the mule train pack the corn and assign it numbers. They are paid 7 cents for each box they pack. Unlike the pickers, who are paid as a group one-ninth the total number of boxes, the packing women are paid on a piecework basis for their individual boxes. Behind the women on the mule train are two men who have high status in the crew. These men are "rick racking," which consists of tying the boxes shut, using a tool that snaps the wire to hold on the lid. Another woman, behind the rick rackers, counts the number of boxes and assigns individual boxes to individual packers to estimate wages. The boxes are then pushed down a conveyor to the trailer, where they are stacked. Stackers earn 1 cent a box, the rick rackers 1½ cents.

Occasionally an agricultural inspector rides around on the mule train. He opens an occasional box of corn, counts it, checks it for grade, and then tells the field foreman whether the packers are doing a good job. Responsibility for sorting and grading the corn rests with the packers. The pickers' only job is to pull the corn, good or bad, and throw it onto the mule train. To keep up with the shelf, which is continually moving, one must pick fast and steadily, and there is no way to systematically control the quality of the work. When, for example, the machine is catching up to me, I will move ahead of it, leaving several ears of corn unpicked. When I was caught doing this, the field walker reminded me that I was leaving corn in the row and occasionally helped to pick the ears left behind. (CL)

Onions

Picking onions requires cutters, liners, and loaders. The cutters top the onions, cut the roots off, and put them in hampers. This is piecework, and they are paid 17 cents a hamper (⅝ of a bushel). A person usually works two rows, straddling one and cutting onions on the row to the right. If two people work together, one cuts to the right while the other cuts to the left, filling up the aisle separating the rows. Most people get down on their knees and straddle the rows, but some sit down, and others stand up and bend over to cut. Some of the old people sit on a hamper and move it along while cutting.

The liners in the crew, two old men in their sixties, straighten up the baskets for the loaders. They string the baskets in rows, allowing room for a tractor to drive through to pick them up. There are usually six loaders working with the tractor and trailer. Some of them walk on the ground, tossing up the full hampers into the crates; others stand in a crate and pick up and stack the empty hampers. It takes thirty-five hampers to fill a crate. Loaders are paid on an hourly basis and occasionally fit in extra hours by loading trailer trucks from 7:00 to 10:00 A.M. The loading in the field starts around 10:00 and sometimes continues until 8:00 or 9:00 in the evening, when the last load is emptied. If there are loaded hampers in the field but not enough to get a complete load on the trailers, they are left on the field.

Usually we work five and a half days a week, but some people also go out on Sunday to do some cutting. Right now, there is only part-time work most days and no work at all on Friday or Saturday. There is an oversupply of onions already cut and stored in the shed. When there are too many onions in the shed, we have to work half days only, for if we work full time we will finish the work sooner. Since the crop doesn't spoil, they prefer us to take twice as long. This is an attempt to keep us at least partly busy so the crew will stay together for the next crop. (LP)

*   *   *

I finished cutting the onions and began the slow process of loading them into baskets. As I worked, the crew leader came over and said, "Don't overfill them." I said I wouldn't. "If you overfill them," he said, "it costs you money and it costs me too." Just this morning, the grower had complained that the baskets were not being filled high enough. (AK)

POTATOES

We drove to the potato fields on the truck, sitting on the floor on potato bags. When we arrived, the farmer had plowed up several rows and was ready for us. The machine plows underneath the potatoes, which come up over some rollers. Everything falls down on top of the ground with the potatoes on top. All the picker has to do is pick them up and put them into hampers. As soon as the plowing was complete, one of the men took about thirty sacks and laid them out along a row. We worked with partners in adjacent rows, stooping over. This allows for faster work than staying on one's knees, but it hurts your back, and eventually most people get on their knees to rest. You put a basket in front of you, right on the row, slanting towards you, and you pick up potatoes and throw them in, moving the basket as you run out of potatoes. While you are picking, you neither grade nor clean the potatoes. The object at this stage is merely to get as many sacks as possible. Occasionally potatoes get buried underneath grass and dirt, and it is necessary to clean the row. Most people will clean about 10 feet in front of them before they start picking, which allows them to work more quickly. Since the potatoes are exposed, you cannot leave any behind you. The crew leader checks continuously. When a basket is filled, we empty it into a large bag holding 60 pounds. Later, a truck comes by and picks these bags up. On each side of the truck there is a man who lifts the bags, and on the truck there are two men who stack them. They then go to the grader.

We generally pack until 11:00 or noon and then go in the shed to grade. When the truck arrives at the grader, it is backed up flush against the machine, and the men on the truck empty the bags. This has to be done in such a way that the grader is not overfilled.

There is a division of labor according to sex. The people who unload the truck are always men, because it is heavy work. On the other hand, women do the actual grading, which is very light work. The baggers are usually men because, after they bag, they must pick up the bags and put them on the scales. The scalers are always women because they just take out or add a few potatoes to get the right amount. The individuals who do each of these jobs, however, change around according to the needs of the moment. (RS)

Strawberries

When we arrived at the strawberry fields, we were each assigned to pick one-half of two adjacent rows. You move down the middle of these rows, picking on both sides. The old people can bend over all day and pick without ever coming up, except to take a completed tray to the other end of the field. I had to get down on my bottom and scoot along between the rows because my knees were raw and my back was aching. A tray holds eight quart containers, and we receive a ticket for each tray that is worth 64 cents. You can cash the ticket in the evening. A fast picker can make around $9.00 a day in a good strawberry field. When we were out, however, the berries were very small. I made $3.60, and $8.00 was the top. While working, people were telling stories, playing jokes on each other, and singing songs. There was a lot of complaining about the condition of the crop, and bickering about "long arming," that is, reaching to pick berries that belong to another person. (GP)

Hourly Work

Besides harvesting, migrants do several odd farm jobs that often serve as "fillers" between the main crops. These include hoeing and weeding, haying, laying irrigation pipe, and driving produce to the plant. These activities are somewhat different than picking, primarily because they are paid for on an hourly basis. Some hourly jobs, in contrast with the individual character of most piecework, require a group endeavor; and some involve small groups in direct contact with the grower.

HOEING AND WEEDING

When we were ready to leave at 7:00 A.M., the truck wouldn't start. We pushed it backwards down a slope, and when it started, we hopped in and rode forty minutes to a farm where we were to weed. There were many delays. The farmer was not there at first, and when he came, we found that the hoes had not been sharpened. Spaceman told us that we were getting a dollar an hour. The hoes finally arrived and we started down our rows. Some rows were less weedy than others, and people would double back and help others with difficult rows. When we are paid by piecework, few people help each other, but when paid by the hour, people will help those with an unusual amount of work. We therefore remained together in our rows, moving at about the same pace. The emphasis was on slowing down. There were some people ahead of us working faster, and Slim said, "If you let those damn fools go on and work hard, we'll have to work a little slower to make up for the speed they're putting on. They want the job to last, don't they?" "I thought you were my friend. Come on, slow up so I can catch up with you and talk to you."

The next day Spaceman woke us up at 5:30 to get out weeding. We started on the long ride around 6:00. Breakfast was eaten on the bus. When we got to the field, it was foggy and damp. There were 25 acres to be weeded, but there were no hoes so we had to weed by hand. The crew was annoyed. "I don't want to do this with my hands. Why can't you get hoes?" Spaceman said that there were none. "Either you do it or get back on the bus." He told us we were getting a dollar an hour for the job. Spaceman assigned us three rows apiece, but later, the farmer came out in the field and said, "Oh, no, let them take one row each." We had started working already and were annoyed at having to come back and be reassigned. In the confusion, a dispute developed when Spaceman assigned someone the wrong row. The man said, "Go to hell. Two times now you have told me what to do—each time it's been wrong. I'm staying in this row. You put somebody else there." They argued for several minutes, and finally Spaceman said, "Well, if you don't want to work, get out of the field. Either you work or get out." The farmer interfered at this point and said, "That's right, I can't pay $1.25 an hour to have this go on." No one seemed to catch the discrepancy between $1.25 and the $1.00 we were promised for the job.

The rows were long. People were telling each other, "Slow down. Don't do it so fast, we're getting paid by the hour. Make this job last a week or so." Actually it is a job we could do in about two days, but the idea was to stretch the work out as long as possible, as we were being paid by the hour and we weren't sure if other jobs would follow. Everyone seemed to like the work. "This is a good job." "It could last all week. Maybe we'll make some money this week." (GP)

*   *   *

Monday I woke up at 5:00 A.M., hearing activity throughout the camp. By 6:00 everyone was ready to go out to work. We were to pull weeds today. After picking cherries for weeks we were to spend the day doing something new, and everyone in the camp was eager to work. There was excitement on the bus and much talk about starting a new job. We arrived at the field, but were not able to start work until 7:00. The early morning wait, the heavy weeds, and the wet and heavy muckland soon dampened the high spirits. We had to work at a very slow pace, almost crawling to get at the weeds, which were very hard to pull. Within a half hour after we started to work, people were complaining. "I thought cherries were bad; now I'm doing this and I wish I were back in cherries." (LR)

HAYING

The farmer picked us up at the camp and took us to his farm to do a haying job. When we arrived, we asked how much he was paying us. "Good men get good pay, poor men get poor pay." We asked again how much we were getting and he said $1.25 an hour. We then asked to be paid at the end of the day. He was furious. "Look, I can give you the money today, but from now on this doesn't happen. You get paid on Friday and Friday only, because I can't afford to make out that many checks."

Red, Larry, and I were the barn crew and we unloaded the hay from wagons when they came in. Two other fellows worked on the wagon. Another worked in the fields, putting rolls of hay in order so the machine could pick them up. As the day went on, things went fairly well. Wagons came in one right after the other and we kept unloading them. The farmer stayed in the barn with us. He showed us how to stack the hay and how to load the elevator. We often switched positions. Sometimes I would load hay on the elevator and other times I would go up into the loft and pile the bales of hay as they came in.

The farmer said that we were going to get a free lunch and would have an hour off. This sounded good and we worked the entire morning without stopping. At 12:30 his wife showed up with the food and we all sat down to eat. At 1:00 we started back to work. We had only half an hour for lunch, not the hour he promised, but work went along well until 4:00, when we needed a drink of water. It was very hot in the loft. Red started down and the man asked what he was doing. He said he was going to get water, but the man said, "We don't have time to stop. Get back in the loft and get to work. You can get water when you finish." Red came back up and went to work again, but he and Larry started talking. They said the farmer would lose more time by not letting them get water because they would not work hard. Larry thought they might cut the strings on the bales, but decided that wouldn't do any good. The man wasn't going to use the hay until late in the winter, and when he started to use it he was going to have to cut the strings anyway. I volunteered to go down and get a drink if they would agree to follow. This would let the man know that we just had to have water. So I went down the ladder, told the man I was very thirsty, and walked over to the barn to get a drink. However, the other two fellows did not follow as they promised. When I came back the man said he was docking my pay for fifteen minutes, although it had taken me only two minutes to get the drink. I asked why. "You weren't working just then, were you?" "No, but I was not gone for fifteen minutes." He told me to go back to work; that he was not going to discuss it any further.

Red and Larry, meanwhile, had decided they were not going to work past 6:30, and at 6:00 Red told the man they were stopping in half an hour. "Well, you fellas stay here and I'll go down to town and get some wine, and then we can work until about 8:00. Will that be all right?" We refused, but he urged us. "You want to earn the money, don't you? We have to get the hay in and we don't know if we will be able to work tomorrow because of the rain." He finally agreed that we could stop, but then said, "I'll give you only $2.00 of your money today because that is all that I can afford." Larry reminded him that he had promised to pay us for the whole day. The farmer replied, "I am just showing you that I can be just as much of a son of a bitch as you can be." He told us there was a wagon, half-loaded, out in the field and that he would finish it himself, but we weren't to get a ride home until that wagon was finished. If we wanted to we could sit there and watch him load it, but it might take quite awhile. We'd get home faster if we loaded it ourselves. The three of us finished loading the wagon, but the man still wasn't sure if he would take us home. Since it was 25 miles back to the camp, we agreed that we would load one more wagon. Finally we got into the back of the truck, and the farmer and two other white men got into the cab. We decided not to go back there to work again the next day.

We arrived at the office to get our money. When we told the man we were not going back and needed all of our money, he agreed and said that he did not want to see us any more. We waited outside the office for twenty-five minutes and finally decided to go in to ask if he could pay us, because we wanted to get home. It was very late by this time. He ordered us out of the office and when he finally came out with the money, said "I can't pay you right now. I have to see your crew leader because I don't know how much money you owe." At that point we said, "It's late. If you are going to give us the money, do so; if not, at least drive us back to camp." He finally paid us for what he considered to be a full day's labor. I received $6.00. (GP)

LAYING PIPE

To lay out an irrigation pipe, you work with a partner and together carry two lengths of pipe, one in each hand. The pipe comes in two lengths, 40 and 20 feet. The 40-foot pipes are laid across the field and connected by joints. The 20-footers are used when the 40-footers are too long. These pipes are aluminum and, when empty, do not weigh more than 35 or 40 pounds. They are very bulky, however, and after you have carried them for an entire afternoon, they begin to feel heavy. It is not difficult work except for the fact that the fields are usually sandy and it is hard to walk.

This week we were moving pipes from an old field where they had been used previously and laying them on another field. This was a problem because the field had just been irrigated that morning and was still muddy. Often we were working ankle deep in mud. Furthermore, the pipes had to be strung out across the field without breaking them apart. Each person stood at a joint and lifted together. We then walked in a line to the new part of the field where the pipe was to be set. This involved ten people and was a very inefficient process. When you have long sections of pipe no one tries to empty the water out of them. The pipes themselves are very light, but when they have water in them, they are almost impossibly heavy and a great burden to carry. This would be true on solid ground, but here we were taking them from a very muddy surface onto a very sandy surface and we sank into both. (AK)

DRIVING

At 4:30 P.M. we stopped picking, and Roy, the driver, had to take the cherries to the processing plant. I went along to help him. We left promptly in the truck with 3 tons of cherries on the back in a giant water tank that keeps them from spoiling in the heat. The grower gave us each a dollar for dinner and we stopped en route to get some food. We got to the town with the processing plant, and had to wait before we even got near the actual building. There were lines and lines of trucks. This was the peak of the season and you have to wait to get your truck unloaded. We waited for fifteen to twenty minutes at the side of the road about a half a mile from the plant. Finally we drove up to the plant. We drove to the weighing house and onto the scale where they weighed the cherries and gave us a piece of paper with a number on it. Then we got in another line and waited until someone came to test the cherries. They take a sample and test it for scalding, quality, and worms. If the cherries are not accepted, you go home; but it is not too difficult to pass inspection.

After the guy took the sample we waited and waited and waited. We were listening to the Yankee game on the radio. About 12:30 A.M. a man came by in a truck and said, "Look, a lot of these guys ahead of you have left their cabs and have gone home for the night. Why don't you just pull on in and we'll get you later tonight." So we pulled around to where he indicated and waited again. At 4:30 A.M., the plant closed down. We went in to wait in the cafeteria, a room with coffee and sandwich machines. It was a wretched place with a lot of flies. At around 6:00 A.M. they were supposed to open the plant again, but no one showed up until 7:00. By this time a lot of the people who were originally ahead of us in line came back and they got to go in before we did. We just sat there and figured we'd be there until 3:00 in the afternoon at least. We sat and waited. We had only a little change and every once in a while bought some ice cream and coke. We couldn't get any substantial food; we couldn't leave. It was hot and humid and rotten, one of the most nauseating experiences I have ever had.

Meanwhile people just moved up in front of us. It was mostly growers driving the trucks, and they would bully the yardman. They looked at Roy and the other black truck drivers as if to ask, "You're not letting him go before me?" It was clear that black drivers would get nowhere until the farmers themselves came.

The process is supposed to work as follows. The truck backs up and empties its load into a metal pan about 3 feet deep. Projecting into the metal pan is a conveyor belt that brings the cherries through a series of metal tanks with water in them to cool the cherries. The cherries are dumped into a tank where the rotten ones are syphoned off the top, and from there they go through a pipe that brings them into the canning plant where they are received and processed. It is a very big operation and, from our perspective, very inefficiently managed.

We had been up all night. We didn't sleep at all because we had to keep awake in case we got a chance to move our truck closer. By 3:00 P.M. nothing had happened. We hadn't moved. We still had twelve trucks in front of us and were completely fed up. Roy went to call the grower but there was no one home, and he returned very discouraged. We didn't have any money left to buy food. A grower can call in and ask the people at the plant to lend the driver a couple of dollars but no one had called in for us. We just sat and sat. Finally at 8:00 P.M. Roy gave up and was going to hitchhike back to camp. We had not slept in thirty-six hours, so we were very tired and dirty. We walked into town and I tried to call the grower again. His wife answered and said that the grower was on his way with some more cherries. I ran out to tell Roy the good news, but he had gone. I looked everywhere in the area and asked a couple of men, but no one had seen him. I decided to walk the mile back to the plant, and on the way met the grower, who had picked up Roy hitchhiking back to camp. He took us back and we arrived at the camp at 10:00 P.M., having been gone a total of twenty-eight hours. (ET)

Part Two

CHAOS AS ORDER

The life-style in a migrant labor camp is often described in anger, dismay, or paternalistically as dirty, degenerate, and, at best, apathetic. Keeping in mind variation within crews and between different crews, Part II demonstrates that migrant labor camps have their own dynamics, their own way of life, their own vulnerabilities, and a style of behavior adaptive to the conditions described in Part I. The life style of any group must be understood within the framework of a particular system: within the context of expectations developing from repeated experience.

Middle-class society expects predictable routines that facilitate planning: we expect to work on a regular schedule or to control its regularity, and to predict most of our relationships. Deviations from expected patterns are highly visible, and we expect to control dissonant elements in order to minimize ambiguity and reassert the "normal." But the migrant labor system has little continuity or regularity that allows for prediction. The impermanence of the crew forces almost total dependence on crew leaders or on growers—that is, on personal, fortuitous, and unpredictable factors. Relations among migrants are short term and tenuous. There are few means by which the migrant can resolve or control the ambiguity pervasive at work and in the camp.

What stands out, then, is the paradox that ambiguity and aberration are structurally intrinsic to the migrant labor system: chaos is order. That is, the migrant's preconceptions of order and regularity, developed from his experience, rest on expectations of continual and unresolvable ambiguity and disorganization. This is reflected within each individual, in his beliefs and personal habits. It is also obvious in interpersonal relationships. It is reflected in leisure-time activities and in attitudes about work. Behavior in each of these areas exhibits tendencies that are consistent, for the migrant's life-style is congruent and adaptive within the framework of an unpredictable and disorganized system.

5

Personal Behavior

Sex, hygiene, health, religion, and superstition are personal matters in which the spectrum of behavior among migrants, as among other groups, defies systematic generalization. The selections in this chapter indicate this variation but, at the same time, point to prevalent tendencies. Common pressures from the social and physical milieu shape personal behavior. Lack of privacy, for example, implies that much behavior normally regarded as personal has little to do with an individual's inner needs but is geared to the ever-present spectator. Similarly, personal behavior is influenced by the fact that there are no differences between associations at home and at work. The strains from one facet of life are carried over to the other. There is no room to maneuver or to escape from relational strains as there is in most groups in a complex, modern society. The difference between personal and public life is minimal, and this has a profound bearing on personal behavior.

Sex and Deviance

The public nature of personal behavior is particularly striking with respect to sex. Intimacy and the privacy necessary for profound relationships are impossible in the available conditions. All gestures and relationships are public knowledge. The preoccupation with masculinity and sex among the men is often a mask, assumed for the audience that is always there. Women are disdained as nothing more than "pussy," and virility is constantly reaffirmed. Discussions about sex are highly ritualized and repetitive and are accompanied by much sexual license. At the same time, there is a high tolerance of sexual deviation; within most crews, there were one or more homosexuals. Deviants have low social status and are often the butt of jokes. On the whole, they are accepted with affectionate contempt. Those who dress as women are treated socially, sexually, and linguistically as such.

Big Betty is exceptionally pretty. Joe was surprised that I, a white boy, should find Betty attractive. His puzzlement had nothing to do with my color—it had to do with the size of the white male's penis. "It's going to take an awful lot to handle that girl. Do you know why it is that black boys have such big dicks? Well, it's because the women are so big." He concluded, "You're going to need a telephone pole to handle her." Joe said that he wasn't very fussy about women and was more interested in "getting fucked than with whom." He told me about his girlfriends. He said he had used a "french tickler" on one of them and she had "screamed for mercy. I got a mule dick and those girls really love it." Joe claimed that sex between a black male and a white female was even more ridiculous than the reverse since an injury was bound to occur. He told about his own experiences with white girls, although in the camp Joe avoids the white girls who occasionally visit and is generally very shy and afraid of white people. (CL)

*   *   *

Longo talked about J.C., an old man who lives in the other bullpen. J.C. is seventy-one but "boy, he sure has a dick on him." According to Longo, J.C. paid a girl $5.00 one night to sleep with him. Longo watched through the door, and when J.C. took off his pants, the girl was really afraid. She shouted, "No, no," because J.C. was so big. Longo claimed that J.C. had done such a good job that, afterwards, the woman returned his $5.00. (DG)

*   *   *

Bo told a joke about a man whose pecker wasn't large enough, so he went to a doctor. The doctor gave him a few pills and told him to take only one. He took more than he was supposed to and went back to see his wife. They went into the bedroom together and went to bed. The man's pecker was getting larger and larger. His wife said, "Why don't I get on top of you?" So she did, and the pecker was still getting larger. The woman then screamed to her children, who were behind the door, and told one to bring in an axe. He asked his mama if he should cut it down and she said, "Hell, no, chop down the roof, I'm going up for old glory." (IM)

*　　　　　*　　　　　*

In the evening Kelly announced he had gotten a "shot of pussy" and was feeling better now. He said that it was from Ben's sister. Ben has taken to calling him "brother-in-law." When they see each other on the street they yell, "Hey, brother-in-law, how are you?" (AK)

*　　　　　*　　　　　*

I have been puzzled by Emma. She said some strange things when we were riding back from the store Saturday night. She is absolutely flat-chested and has a stubble on her face. I assumed she was a little deformed until I asked Longo if she had any kids. He looked at me and said, "You're from the city, aren't you? She and Paul are queer." It turns out that Emma is a boy and Paul is her boyfriend. Paul is the masculine member of the pair. He is large and muscular, while Emma is slight and dresses in a feminine style. Paul is quite henpecked; they argue constantly, with Emma sounding very bitchy and Paul very hurt. The other people in the camp make fun of Emma. Bertha said she used to be kind to Emma, but she wasn't any more because Emma was looking for attention. She used to go into town with Emma but it was embarrassing because Emma always needed a shave and people looked at them strangely. She thought it was funny when Emma came into the outhouse where she was sitting. Emma said, "Oh, excuse me," and Bertha fled.

Honey often leaves her granddaughter with Emma, who she feels takes really good care of the child. Talking about Emma got Honey onto the subject of homosexuals. "Once a man has packed shit, he isn't any good any more and that is just the way he will be for the rest of his life." Honey had known someone when she was younger who was a "muffadite," as she described a person with both male and female sexual organs. She thought of him as a male; "I used to spend all my money on him because he was so beautiful." (DG)

*　　　　　*　　　　　*

There is a standing joke between Marilyn Monroe and the men in the camp. Marilyn Monroe is a homosexual. The men are constantly teasing the women that Marilyn Monroe is better than any of them. A man will sit beside a woman and if she tries to avoid him, he'll say, "I'm going to get Marilyn Monroe. You don't turn me on anyway." Tussy will shake his finger at Marilyn Monroe and say, "You'll have to get rid of your other men or else I'm going to put you down, and once I put you down you've lost a good thing." People are constantly teasing Marilyn Monroe but she makes no bones about homosexuality. She wears her hair long like a woman, walks like a woman, and people normally refer to her as "her." One night she and a guy were having an affair. The woman next door was watching through a hole and called a lot of people to come and look. Finally one man ran in and pulled the covers off of the couple. Everyone was laughing hysterically. (GP)

Personal Dress

Personal attire during nonworking hours varies. There are those who succumb to self-neglect and others who expend considerable effort and money on their appearance. With the dirty work, the low pay, and the often grubby camps with their limited facilities (frequently they lack an adequate water supply), dressing well is difficult. Yet clothes and hair styles are important for many people. Considerable sums are spent on hair processing. In one large camp, almost every woman owned a wig.

Nate was dressed in a light blue, high-rolled-collar shirt, and a royal blue, double-breasted blazer, blue slacks, black shoes and a straw hat—the kind of clothes worn by soft-shoe dancers on television. Like most of the other younger boys, he has processed hair. Most of them have moustaches or are growing them. James told me that a process should be done once a week to stay in shape. What is really good is a "gas job," but that costs $50.00 and up. When he goes to see his girl, he dresses real sharp. When he first met her, she was dressed like "a tramp," but he took her out, bought her some clothes, and taught her how to dress well. (ET)

*   *   *

In the fields, men wear heavy galoshes, baggy pants, and hats. Women wear pants with a skirt over them and kerchiefs. On weekends, most people put on their good clothes. The men wear polished black shoes, good pants, and clean shirts. The women fix their hair and wear dresses. A couple of kids shine shoes for 35 cents a pair. They do quite a job since people really want their shoes to shine. A barber comes to the camp every week and many men get weekly haircuts. (LR)

*   *   *

We discussed the "well-dressed man" and what he should wear. Tee asked everyone in the room what people should wear, and called them "a bunch of dumb, black-assed niggers that have no idea how to dress." "What does it take, nigger, to have a well-dressed man?" he asked. "Well, you need khakis that are washed and clean." "Well, you'd need a suit and a tie." Tee kept shaking his head. "You're all so damn dumb. All you need to be a well-dressed man is a bath and a watch with a big chain." At this point, the argument revealed that Tee was old-fashioned and probably hadn't seen anyone well dressed for fifty years. He is about seventy-five years old.

The men wear khaki work pants. Generally, clothing is torn somewhere in the crotch or on the knee. The pants are almost always dirty. Undershirts and work shirts are worn, and the work shirts are removed when we start picking. Coonie, however, wears loud, sequin shirts, and Gatemouth wears a clean white shirt with short sleeves.

Tuesday night St. Louis put some hair-straightener on his hair and went through a ritual for about an hour, straightening his hair and trying to fix it up. As soon as he started other people came out and also fooled with their hair, using various creams and solutions. It was hard to see exactly what St. Louis was trying to do. His hair didn't look any different when he was finished than it did when he started. However, he seemed very proud of the job he had done and kept asking for compliments. The women, at that time, came out with wigs, which they said cost $30. They combed the wigs and rolled them up in pin curlers. (MR)

*   *   *

Butterman and his wife were seated in front of their cabin. He was playing a harmonica. He was wearing a tan shirt and pants, and three different necktie-sort-of-things around his neck, one with a heart and two with crosses. He had a cross pinned to his lapel, and flashlights and other assorted items sticking out of his pockets. There was also a radio hanging from his belt. Both he and his wife are in their early fifties. He made frequent references to God. He asked if I stayed at the camp year-round. I said no, and he said, "Well, it's for the best, it always is. Jesus always has a plan for all of us, for his people, and you can be sure that you're here because he has a reason."

Flo, his wife, is an exceedingly thin woman with a cataract completely covering her left eye. She always wears very long, shabby, print dresses to the middle of her calf and looks like a stereotype of rural poverty. She wears a rhinestone brooch on a chain around her neck and has extremely thick glasses. The other day, she came walking in with the right arm of her dress covered with mud and a large hole in the back showing a bra that was covered with dirt. She said she had fallen down. She was obviously very drunk and tried to bum a cigarette but no one would give her one. She stood there waiting and asked if she could have a draw. Butterman, his radio strapped to his waist, came wandering up and told her to go back to the room and change into one of her $90.00 dresses. "Don't go around looking like that." She laughed and said she wanted to dance. "Oh, if you want to dance, then we'll dance." He took a quarter out of his pocket and put it in the jukebox. Several people suggested numbers to play. He either had difficulty understanding what they were saying or did not know how to work the jukebox, because it took him a long time to put his money in. Eventually he put on several songs that were very popular in the camp and he and his wife began to dance. (DR)

*   *   *

After bean picking there is dirt and moss in one's hair and on one's face. It accumulates from wiping off sweat during the day. There is a green crust on the nails, which can be picked off with a knife, and a dull, black, saplike substance on your fingers. The dirt goes all the way up to the elbow. If it has rained within twenty-four hours, your pants are mud-soaked from the knees down. Because of this, some pickers wear burlap wrapped around their legs, or the legs from an old pair of dungarees over their pants. Others wear several pairs of pants. In this state of dress, after a day in the fields, we must do all our food shopping in the town. The bus stops at the store on the way back from the fields, and there is no way to clean up beforehand. (IM)

Hygiene

Many migrants express disgust with the conditions in their camp and carefully maintain their own rooms. They find it distasteful to share facilities such as showers and outhouses. The inadequacy and overuse of these facilities are discouraging; efforts to clean up are not considered worth the trouble, for there is no expectation that clean habits will maintain a clean environment. Thus, immediate impulses often prevail over group goals of keeping the camp in shape. Even our researchers found themselves littering.

An unusual scene is first described in which one migrant took it upon himself to replace a broken waterpipe. This event provides perspective on tendencies toward maintaining the camp that are amplified in subsequent selections.

One striking aspect of personal hygiene, found with sufficient frequency that it cannot be entirely accidental, consists of deliberate urination or defecation in odd places. Although the filthy condition of outhouses is unquestionably at the root of their avoidance, the choice

Personal hygiene takes place wherever it can. *Photo by Paul S. Buck.*

of alternatives leads to speculation as to the significance of this behavior. As a recognized object of taboo, feces "out of place" is considered by some to represent a desire to create anxiety. Such behavior reminiscent of Gulliver urinating on Queen Mab's castle, is a pungent symbol of contempt and defiance of order. In a sense, these cases, several of which are described, represent an affirmation of disorder, apathy, and low morale.

Jessie had been complaining to Benny, the farm foreman, about the need for lime in the outhouse to "kill those damn flies" and the need to fix the drainage that was breeding them. There was water standing underneath the outhouse and the shower and around the steps where water drains from a broken pipe below the sink. After we returned from work one day, Jessie found a shovel under the house and started digging a trench. He dug the trench toward a hole in the ground that was intended as a drain or sinkhole. He said, "We've got to get rid of this water. That's where all these flies are living." I asked, "Well, shouldn't the Man take care of that?" He

Outhouses are primitive and photos cannot show the flies.
Photo by Bill Siebert/Glad Day Press.

said, "No, he doesn't live here. We live here. We're the ones that have to put up with it." Other people stood around watching; they neither expressed surprise, nor did they comment that he should or should not be fixing the drain. They were just apathetic as they watched him dig. Benny, the foreman, came over and said, "Hey, yeah, this thing has got to be fixed up. Why don't you dig way down and take out the pipe? If you clear them pipes I'll pay you for it." There was no mention of the price, however, and the foreman added, "Of course, if it stops raining and you have to go picking, but as long as you're not doing anything, you work on the trench." Jessie asked if there was a pick, and the foreman went to get one. I started to help by using the pick along the drain line. Bubba then came over and took the pick from me. There was now some jockeying to get into the deal, as people were interested in getting some of the money the foreman had promised for the job. They moved closer and gave directions about how the job should be done. Jessie just kept on working, unconcerned about whether he would be paid for the job or not. Other people asked, "Well, how much are you going to ask him for?" Jessie said, "I don't know, whatever he sees is fit. What has he got to do with it anyhow? We live here. This place has got to be cleaned up." After we had worked on the job for about an hour it began to rain. Everyone ran inside but Jessie, who continued to work in the light drizzle.

The trench was dug down starting from under the shower, where it was about 6 or 7 inches deep, to about 3 feet deep going down hill, where some stones were placed to catch the drainage. The foreman drove over on the tractor and stopped for a moment to inspect the work. At that time, Jessie asked him if he could get some lime to put in the outhouse. After lunch it stopped raining—and people came out again to watch. Jessie and Bubba lifted the old pipes out and put new pipes in the ground. They did a professional job; both had done this type of work before and they seemed to know what they were doing when they were grading the drainage pipe and getting it placed so it would work. The foreman brought a car radiator hose to place over the broken pipe. Then they were done, the standing water all drained away, even though it was still raining. The last I heard there was still no mention of what the foreman was going to pay for the job. (MR)

*　　　　　*　　　　　*

During the day, when in the camp, men use the outhouse rather than going in the open, although the outhouse is in terrible condition. They do this because there are many children around the camp. One day, while I was walking down to my hut, there was no one around so I walked off the side of the road to urinate. Vance came by and scolded me. "You know better than that." I explained there were too many mosquitoes in the out-house. He said that was true but it wasn't right to piss in the woods like that. (AK)

*　　　　　*　　　　　*

The toilets were all plugged up with cloth and newspaper, and a woman on the bus complained about "people who spend money on wine but don't know enough to buy toilet paper." She said that if anyone didn't have enough money for toilet paper they could borrow some from her. She was very disgusted. Later, I heard Clinton make a similar complaint. "These men who stuff cloth into the toilet are hard-assed grown men and they're really stupid for doing that." (DG)

*　　　　　*　　　　　*

Wolf got up and went to the bathroom against the side of the house. This is not unusual; care is taken only to remain out of view of the women. When I was in the fields one day, shortly after I had arrived in the camp, I was headed for the outhouse but a woman beat me there and stayed in for a long time. Another guy who was also waiting said, "If all you have to do is piss, go over against the bus." (LP)

*　　　　　*　　　　　*

Keeping clean is difficult. The water pump that provides shower water is broken, and there is no time to fix it, as the season is at its peak. Many people in the camp manage to stay clean despite this, but they are bothered by the broken pump and the fact that they can't shower. We take baths in foot tubs that we bought ourselves. Also, several trips have to be taken daily to the drinking-water supply, which is a quarter of a mile from the camp. (ET)

*   *   *

The only person I have ever seen pick up garbage is Slim. He stops to pick up bottles he sees on the ground and will put them in a wastebasket. He is the only one I have seen start fires in the garbage can to burn some of the garbage. He commented today on the peanuts and how shells get all over the juke. Albert was eating peanuts at the time and Slim reminded him to keep the area clean. Though there are garbage cans between each building and they are used, there are still lots of bottles lying around.

Bo, my roommate, is extremely clean. He always wants to sweep out our room and tries to keep the bed clean. He was talking today about cleaning the walls because "we have to live here all summer." To this Albert, my other roommate, said, "Shit, I don't want to keep this place clean. It's a rat trap." To my surprise, I find myself throwing cigarette boxes just anywhere because it seems as if this is what you should do here. (IM)

*   *   *

Bright and early Sunday morning Nappychin came and woke me up to talk. This is the first weekend I have ever seen him sober. I asked what he was doing sober and he said, "Man, I'm working now, got a good job at the plant and I'm gonna stay straight for at least a week." We went back into his room to talk, but when we got there, there was a pile of feces on the floor. "Who put that damn pile of shit down there?" It was Joe, his room-mate. "Joe, get your ass up. You've been drunk all the god damn day and all night, and you shitted right on the floor here." Then Nappychin went over to put on his shoes and found that one shoe was filled up with urine. He and Joe started to scuffle in the hall until Lamb came out of his room and stopped them. Nappychin walked out the door with a shoe full of urine. (GW)

*   *   *

I went to take a shower tonight but I couldn't because someone had defecated right in the shower stall. People get impatient when the two bowls are being used and go into the shower to do what they have to do. Another day, when I walked to my room, I noticed that someone had shit in the hall and also by the side entrance. The old people were really mad because that is where they sit in the evening. (LR)

* * *

About four o'clock I woke up and heard Tee, who sleeps in the next room, shouting, "I'll kill that old son of a black bitch." I heard him loading bullets into his thirty-eight. A few minutes earlier, Jessie had gotten up completely drunk from his bed and had tried to walk down the hall. Tee called out for him to keep quiet, so Jessie turned around and pissed right in Tee's new hat, which was lying on the floor. Tee snatched his hat away and pulled out his gun which, at that time, was unloaded. Then Jessie tried to rip out the screen and jump out the window, and Tee started screaming for Big Time, the crew leader. Jessie finally fell down the stairs. Tee was loading his gun, cursing as he placed each bullet into the chamber that he was going to kill that son of a bitch. Jessie, by this time, had passed out and was lying on the floor at the foot of the stairs. As Tee came down after him, I heard Jessamay scream, "Don't do it, Tee. It's not worth the chain gang." Big Time came out and finally convinced Tee that he shouldn't shoot and that his hat was okay. (MR)

Health

Personal health practices vary widely. Some migrants come north to take advantage of the better medical services available in certain northern states. Others are apathetic and show conspicuous self-neglect about their health. Attitudes in the latter group are fatalistic; doctors and conventional medicine are mistrusted, and, in some cases, "root medicine" is used as a substitute.

About 10:00 P.M. I went to watch television in Pops' room. As I walked in, Red stopped me. "You don't want to come in here." Pops was sick again. "He's got that spell that he always has with the wine bottle. He's been drinking all week and hasn't eaten a thing. Now he's really gone." I asked why someone didn't take him to a doctor, and Red replied that he refused to go. "He just feels like it's his time to die and he wants to die without any doctor around. Look how much weight he lost." Red said that Pops weighed 175 pounds last year but was now down to 120. The Twister wine that Pops drinks ruins your appetite and he hasn't been eating. "That stuff can really kill you. It eats your insides away." Aaron also drinks Twister regularly and doesn't eat much. He keeps swearing he'll quit drinking the stuff and talks about how he needs good food, but every day he drinks wine instead of eating breakfast. (GW)

*   *   *

Jessie takes a lot of pride in never having been sick in his life except when he is drinking. Sickness is scorned; those who get sick are weak and this is not good. Scrap admitted that he had once gotten the flu but that was the only time he had been sick and he said he would never get sick again. This week a young boy in the camp got sick with a high fever. His mother didn't know what to do about it. Someone suggested that she should give him some aspirin. "Well, if I had some I would, but I don't have any." As soon as the child felt like getting up and running around, he did so. There was no attempt to make him stay in bed. His mother, from time to time, would look down his throat but otherwise left him alone.

The other day, Gatemouth cut his leg on a bucket. He didn't try to wash the cut although it was dirty from the rusty bucket. I forced him to wash it, threatening to beat him over his head if he didn't take care of it, so he finally did. However, he didn't seem to care one way or the other. I also saw a guy picking at the palm of his hand with a knife, trying to get at a thorn. He had been to a doctor several times but the doctor just told him there was nothing in there and had "slapped some red stuff on it." He knew it was still in there because every few days it would start to hurt again. (MR)

*   *   *

I developed a very bad rash, so I went to the migrant labor clinic. The nurse commented that this had been a big day for rashes and four migrants had come in complaining about them. All had been working in lettuce. She asked if I had ever worked in lettuce before, and when I said no she shook her head knowingly. My name was called and I went to a booth in the hallway. The doctor took a quick look at my arm, without stopping, and continued walking down the hallway. Then, two young interns looked at me more closely. Both agreed that I had the same rash as the other four people; it was "contact dermatitis." The doctor came by but disagreed with their diagnosis, saying I had hives and that my rash was quite different from that of the other migrants. Later, back at the camp, I told the crew leader that it was hives. He laughed and claimed that hives were only for little children. "Doctors these days just don't know what's going on." He said I had this rash from working in the lettuce field because of the strong insecticides. (AK)

*   *   *

Every night, I put toothpaste on my toothbrush and walk downstairs to brush my teeth outside. I have never seen other adults brush their teeth and most of their teeth are rotten. The young children, however, have toothbrushes. One child of ten asked, when he saw the toothpaste, if he could have some. I said he was welcome to it, and all the other children came running, so I dispensed toothpaste to all. With much glee, they ran out to brush their teeth. They are not used to having toothpaste though they do brush their teeth once a day. (MR)

*   *   *

Many migrants go to doctors, but there is, at the same time, a prevalent mistrust of doctors and clinics that reinforces the use of home cures and "root work." There is a popular belief that if you don't show up at the clinic, they send the troopers after you. This brings many people in, but there are some who refuse to go. One man with a serious leg infection refused to go, and the crew leader's wife explained that this was because the clinic might say it was contagious and give shots to the whole camp. Curtis would not go to the clinic because he wouldn't let a doctor "shoot" him.

Home remedies are common in the camps. Cratchet, for example, had two strings, soaked in kerosene, tied around his little finger as preventive medicine to keep him from catching cramps. Similarly, root medicine is used by some of the older people, who express more confidence in roots than in doctors. Several camps had "rootmen" living in them. In one situation, an argument occurred when a young man claimed that roots are no good any more. The rootman replied that the year before he had predicted snow and, indeed, the cherries froze. He warned against such criticism: "The roots are strong." (LWR)

Religion and the Supernatural

Beliefs about health are not isolated. They are consistently associated with ideas about religion, the supernatural, and general—if somewhat vague and undefined—fears. Some beliefs are ubiquitous among migrants and concern the dangers of snakes. Others are prevalent, but within a more limited group, usually older people.

The first selection suggests the relationship of beliefs to experience. Several common fears and superstitions are then described, and the remainder of the selections deal with religious beliefs and practices. As with medicine, there is common disdain for institutional forms of religion. The religious forms found in several crews offer striking parallels to the social structures of the camps. For example, in one case, the religion is based on a high dependence on a single individual, whose preachings are accepted without question. Various religious beliefs, although differing in detail, deny the importance of the secular, emphasizing that the solution to problems lies beyond the control of the individual. In effect, it matters little what you do; control is elsewhere.

Widely held beliefs must be relatively consistent with experience; otherwise they will not persist. Many beliefs of migrant workers, which appear to be superstitions, are examples of misinformation in matters far from their limited education or experience. One group agreed, for example, that you cannot poison a pig or a chicken because they have no veins. Another discussion revealed a belief that pain rises in the body until it gets to your chest and then you die. Two women discussed whether mermaids have fishtails or whether they just wear costumes.

Beliefs have been observed to change when they do not function successfully in the individual's life. When Amos was ill, he used roots or home remedies, but when these efforts failed, he said he would go to a doctor. Here, his experience with sickness acted to test his belief. But there are many areas of belief that are seldom tested because of the migrant's limited experience and his lack of access to information that might force him to reevaluate his beliefs.

Beliefs concerning God vary, but share common characteristics. It is widely believed that God will literally strike you down with lightning if you sin. Jessie went out to see if there was a storm following some tornado warnings. The next day no one would pick near him, fearing that he would be struck by lightning until he repeatedly said that he had "Jesus in his bones." In another incident, Joe, a supervisor, told crew members to be quiet while there was thunder and lightning because this was part of the Lord's work. In another case, a group of crew members rode past a burnt-down house, and Tussy said that somebody in that house must have sinned. Others agreed that if you don't do what is right, God might make your house burn down or strike you with lightning.

Many older migrants believe in ghosts, "haints," or spooks. They hold their breaths as they walk by cemeteries and believe many noises around camps are caused by ghosts. One camp had a haunted room where people refused to live all season. The members of one crew discussed their belief in ghosts but had no idea of their attributes nor how ghosts are "going to get you." In another crew, however, people described ghosts and their behavior more explicitly. Emma said she saw a ghost with a red face, and Miss Bea said that her mother was given a set of dishes and was told that if she broke any she would be haunted. She got mad at her husband one day and threw a dish at him. From that night on she was haunted and heard footsteps and knocking. (LWR)

*　　　　*　　　　*

People were talking about skin color. If a real black man has a real dark woman as a wife and they have a real bright (light-skinned) son, "well, then you know that something is wrong." This conversation started when Mr. Ed said, "A woman can put a mark on a child when it is in the womb. During that first two or three months, a woman can put a real mark on that baby." He told a story of a kid who used to hop around like a frog. Freddy argued, "You mean to say that woman got frightened by a frog and so the baby jumped like a frog?" Mr. Ed didn't allow himself to be dissuaded and told another story about a colored woman who wanted to have a real light baby so she went out in the middle of July and started screaming for snow. He then recalled seeing a baby in a carnival who was born with one eye in the middle of its forehead. Aaron said that he thought that's what you call a Cyclops. "There is a whole nation of people who are cyclops." Mr. Ed kept asking, "Why did it come that way? Why does that baby have that one eye right in the middle of his forehead? It isn't because of the pox, it isn't because of the gonorrhea." Somebody else entered the conversation and said, "Well, maybe God wanted the eye there."

Another day, Freddy told stories about "haints" and ghosts. He had read a book by a man who traveled around looking for haints. This man was out in an ocean liner, three days from port, and was sitting in a room with another fellow. Suddenly he saw a lady in a white gown come up and kiss the other man, who was asleep. The next day the man got a cablegram saying that his wife had died the night before. In another story a man dreamed that he saw his sister with two scratches on her face. Worried, he called his mother and found out that his sister had died. He told his mother about his dream and about the scratches. His mother said that while dressing the body for the funeral she had accidently scratched the girl's face twice with a pin. Freddy claimed he personally did not believe in haints, "but that doesn't mean that the stories about haints are lies."

Mr. Ed then told how his wife had died in 1958. The doctor had said that if she did not lose weight she was going to die in six months, and sure enough she died six months from that day. Freddy said, "Well, that makes sense, though; doctors are dealing with people like that all the time. Just like you and I can tell beans, he can tell things like that." (DR)

*　　　　*　　　　*

People were telling stories about snakes. They told about one man who could lead the entire crew, picking beans faster than everyone else. He used to sing spirituals while he worked. One day, while he was working and singing, he accidently grabbed a snake by the head with his handful of beans. His voice got caught on one note. All he could do was to stand up and sing that note and hold the snake out at arm's length. He couldn't let go. The snake coiled and uncoiled around his arm. It was dying, but even after it was dead, the man was still on the same note and he wasn't able to let go of the snake. (GP)

*   *   *

Several stories about snakes were precipitated by the forked stick that Geech contrived to hold up the laundry line. Mr. Ed told how he could catch a big rattler with a forked stick. "Just stick it over his head and then grab him by the back of the head, drop him into a sack and hold the sack way far away." While saying this, he acted it out. Then someone told a story about a man who once caught a snake and cooked it up to eat. The next morning they found him dead, all curled up and black. He had cooked a water moccasin instead of a rattler and was poisoned. The conversation went on to snake bites. It was said that a coiled snake just bites into you and nibbles and nibbles. "If you are bitten by a coiled snake, you better have the doctor and the undertaker both in your hip pocket, because otherwise you are going to die before you make it over there," pointing to the platform 20 feet away from where we were standing. Another comment was added. "As soon as that snake bites you, shit, he has to go and suck on a weed or something, because, man, you're as poisonous to that snake as he is to you, and he has to get the poison out of him, too." (DR)

*   *   *

About eight people were sitting in the living room, including the crew leader's seventeen-year-old son, who is called "Preacher" because he is a Sanctified Baptist Church member. At fourteen he had a broken leg and was lying in the hospital. While he was there, he told us, the word of God came to him and he was called to be a minister. This morning he was giving a service in the camp. First, we sang, "The Storm Is Passing Over." No one seemed to know the words except me and the Preacher. Then we said the Lord's Prayer. We then sat down and he said that he was going to speak from Isaiah. He doesn't read well and is difficult to understand, since he mutters. First, he told us that he wanted to make it clear that he wasn't concerned about what church people belonged to, or what religion they had: he only wanted to bring the word of God. He had to do this or he knew he would be sinning. He emphasized that he did not charge for his work. He talked about how people had to come to God, and proceeded to list everything that we had done the night before: drinking, playing cards, chasing after women. People looked very contrite with their hangovers, and were nodding and saying, "Yes, that right, Brother." Later there was a Bible discussion. He would read a few lines from the Bible and interpret them, bringing in recent experiences to explain to the people what they meant. He then talked about preachers "who are not preachers. They are in the preaching business for the money rather than to bring souls to the Lord." People, sitting there with hangovers from the night before, nodded in agreement with everything he said. There was no questioning.

At the end of the service, Preacher asked if anyone had anything to say. It was very quiet for a minute or two; then one of the men, who was perhaps the drunkest on Saturday night, got up and said, "Well, I know I sinned some, but I don't try to be bad all the time," and he confessed for three or four minutes. At the end of the service we all raised our hands, palms up, and asked for a benediction. After this service people were talking among themselves about religion. For several days, Otis kept repeating that he was bad, but he wasn't that bad, and that he knew that he did some things wrong but he really wasn't that bad after all, and the Lord was with him. Some people talked about how they had once belonged to a church but had "back-slid." "I know I had to get out of that church; I was backsliding so bad I had no business fucking with the damn thing. I had to get out of it." It is felt that there is some sanctity to religion. If you believe, then you should behave accordingly. There were some, however, who claimed to have thrown all attempts out the window and were quite open in their disdain for religion. Others take great pride in knowing the Bible. If someone can quote a chapter or verse from the Bible to prove a point, this is considered the final word.

Although the Preacher commands respect on Sundays, he is not well liked otherwise. Perhaps this is because he comes in on Sunday morning to tell everyone that they should not have been doing what they had done the night before. It also may be because he has a car, and people know he visits girls in other camps when no one else is able to do this. He talks about his girlfriends, how nice they are, how much money he spent, and all the great things they did. Once he was challenged: "That's a damn lie." He replied that it was no lie and quoted a verse from the Bible to the effect that he who is with the Lord cannot lie. "Well, when you read from the Bible, you're not lying, but when you talk, you're telling damn lies." A clear distinction is made between when he is preaching and when he is out in the fields picking like everyone else. The other day Big Time and Jessie were shouting from different trees in the cherry grove. They were kidding Preacher about a story he had told about this girl who had "fallen down under him" during the service. He put his hand on her head and she felt the spirit. They gave him a hard time. "So you pushed the girl's head and she fell under you. How do you know it wasn't the devil that made her fall? I think you pushed her." Big Time always seems to be able to trap the Preacher, who answered that he saw her fall down, and he didn't push her. Big Time kept at him. "Yeah, but when she fell down you must have been able to see up her dress." The Preacher denied it, "Oh, I looked away." (MR)

*　　　　*　　　　*

While we were sitting around, there was a commotion outside and we went out to see what had happened. There had been a highway accident involving a migrant labor bus from another camp and everyone was talking about it. No one knew exactly how serious the accident was, but they knew some people had been taken to the hospital. Emma kept saying, "The Lord works in strange ways, the Lord works in strange ways." J.C. said, "Well, it doesn't make any difference, you know. If they had been going 10 miles an hour or 70 miles an hour, it wouldn't have made any difference, they would have been hit anyway." (DG)

*　　　　*　　　　*

People believe very deeply in God, although they talk about how their actions do not fit with the way the Christian religion has taught them to act. One man who said he didn't believe in God was socially in a poor position. The others attacked him verbally and couldn't believe that anyone would think this way. A woman explained how God watches over us, and others agreed that God "prepares the way for us and works in strange, mysterious ways helping us find solutions to our problems." I made the mistake of asking Major how he knew so much about God. He called everyone's attention to my question and asked if I had ever been to church. It was considered disgraceful that I didn't believe in God and hadn't read much of the Bible. But I was told not to worry, that in any case the Lord would look after me. "He works in very mysterious ways." That is the favorite expression in talking about religion and is used to justify almost anything. (GP)

*　　　　*　　　　*

Talking about wine one day, Cory, who was drunk, brought up the story of Jesus changing the water to wine. "How did it happen? We don't know because in the Good Book it doesn't say that the water turned red or brown; all it says is that the guests said, 'He saves the best wine for the last,' but Jesus didn't say he changed the water to wine. You know what it was? Probably all the people were so damn pounded and so damn drunk when

Jesus brought out that water that they thought it was the best wine they ever drank." This got a terrific reaction from the rest of us. Mr. Ed tried to carry the analogy out to changing stones into bread but dropped it half-way through. (DR)

*　　　*　　　*

The crew leader's son asked if I was going to the services of the A to Z Church that night. Deacon, the crew leader, was very active in the church. I went along to the service, which started at 7:30 P.M. There were many children and most of the younger people in the camp were there. The service started with people clapping rhythmically. The women sang, "Thank you, Jesus. Thank you, Jesus," over and over again. This clapping and chanting continued through the entire service. Throughout the evening, young men and women would get up and go into a trancelike state. They rose quickly from their chairs, which sometimes flipped backwards, threw their arms up and lowered their heads, saying, "Thank you, Jesus." Then a man got up to run the meeting. He first asked the junior choir to sing. They sang four songs, most of which had one phrase stated by a solo voice and repeated by the chorus. Then the children's choir was asked to sing.

A young man in his early twenties, not a member of the crew, then got up. He was the preacher and a very good one; his mannerisms were as important as what he said. He walked back and forth, shaking his arms and pointing his finger into the crowd, saying, "It's the Lord I'm talking about, you hear me? You understand what I'm saying? I've never been so sure about what I'm saying tonight. I know something is happening to-night. I've never been so sure. I feel it. I came into this place, I felt it a long way off. I felt it yesterday. It's getting closer. It's going to be here tonight." Meanwhile the women continued to chant, "Thank you, Jesus. Thank you, Jesus," and some of the girls were singing, "Praise the Lord." Whenever the spirit moved them, the women would rise and interrupt the service. At various times, people rose, one at a time, to testify. They would stand and say something like, "I haven't got much to say but I just want to thank the Lord Jesus for my life and for letting me come to the service tonight." Then they would sit down.

After most of the people in the room had testified, the preacher started his sermon. The theme was that there is Christ in every man, and this Christ can be found only if the "self" does not get in the way. He talked about the natural and spiritual worlds. The natural world is the one we live in—this is the world of the self. He then talked about the Christ in every one of us. He said that if we get the self out of the way, Christ will come through because Christ never died and is living in each of us. He then talked about how his beliefs had cured him of several illnesses. While preaching he walked back and forth in front of the room, pacing, jumping, stepping, waving his hand over the audience. At one point he said, "Somebody in here tonight is sick. I know one person in here who has a headache. I feel it. It might be a small headache, probably so small he didn't even notice it, but he's got it, he's got it."

He went on about the spiritual world. If you really believe in it, he claimed, you can go for days and days without eating food. Natural food is poison to your system, but you can live on spiritual food forever. He also professed that he could never die. There was no one who could kill him. The chanting, "Thank you, Jesus," continued during the sermon, and occasionally the preacher would walk around the room and place his hands on people's heads. Some of the women would jump up at this point and go into an ecstatic state. One very excited woman of about twenty jumped up and ran around the room. People had to steady her to keep her from bumping into things. The preacher continued his preaching, interrupting himself every once in a while to repeat, "I've never been so sure, I know what I am talking about. You know what I am talking about. It's here tonight. I felt it when I walked into the room." At the end of the sermon, the excitement began to abate and the preacher started calling individuals to come forward. He called the women first. He would extend his hand, palm turned up. People laid their hands on his. Some of the women fainted or collapsed on the floor. At least several people were no longer in physical control of their bodies. Whenever a woman would collapse, it was regarded as a blessing, a religious experience. They would say, "Lord, thank you, Jesus," thanking him for this experience. One woman got up and said, "I feel a tingling in my ears. I feel it all through me." Then an older man got up and said he agreed with the preacher, that he was a fool for Christ but not half the fool he was going to be. Several other women got up and testified, "I feel it in my ears, I feel it in my whole body." Testimonies were given again, and after all the other people in the room had spoken, the preacher looked at me for a few minutes and said, "I think there is one more person who has got something to say." I realized he was talking about me, so I got up and said that I had met a lot of new brothers and sisters here tonight. This was greeted by a loud chorus of "Thank you, Jesus. Lord, thank you, Jesus." The meeting then broke up into a hugging session. The general idea was to embrace every other person in the room. They hugged everyone—little kids, big kids, grown-ups, old people. "Thank you, brother. Thank you, sister." "I love you, brother," or "I love you, sister." Physical contact was an important aspect of this final part of the service and was unrestrained.

Services such as this one occurred regularly and revealed other aspects of the beliefs. The Elder of the church who came occasionally to the camp was himself worshiped as Christ. The people had complete faith in him and his mystical powers. He could heal the sick, raise the dead, and walk up to you and tell you whatever you had done wrong. Cliff told me that this "faith thing" really works. He told me of an experience when he was speeding on a thruway. While driving, he sang, "I've got heaven in my mind." When he completed the song he said, "Thank you, Jesus," and "Praise the Lord," and as he said this, he looked into the rearview mirror and saw a cop. He knew that he had been speeding, but as soon as he said "Praise the Lord," the cop pulled away from him.

During one service, the wind—which had been variable all day—shifted suddenly and blew from the east, opening the door. Almost immediately someone said, "It's the Elder." The wind then shifted again and blew the door shut. This caused some excitement, for it was agreed that this permitted the entrance of the invisible Elder. When I looked at Bear disbelievingly, he said, "Yes, that's what it was, that's it. The door opened just like a man opened it." Cliff confirmed it; "Yeah, the wind has been blowing from the opposite direction all day. It wasn't the wind, it was the Elder that opened it."

Another aspect of the religion is its literal interpretation of the Bible. The preacher frequently quotes passages from the Bible as the literal truth. However, unlike other forms of organized religion, this church claims that its members are already in a state of grace. The Elder says that other churches prepare people for life with God after this present life; they had none of what he called "the living God." He was concerned with the spiritual in this life; others prepared people for the deathbed. He called the preachers of other denominations, "DD," not for Doctor of Divinity, but for "Dead Dog." He said they went to "theological cemeteries" not seminaries.

In one sermon, the Elder picked up a chair, asking, "Are there any people in here who follow the Ten Commandments? Are there any Christians in here?" No one responded. He held the chair over his head. "If there are any Christians in here, come on up and I'm going to beat your brains out. You're a bunch of hypocrites, lopsided, pigeon-toed, knock-kneed, brotherless liars and fools." He said that if one believed in the A to Z Church, the chair was not a threat, since believers are immortal and physically invulnerable. But Christians, as members of the outside world, and missing the "living God," were vulnerable. Related to this was his emphasis on faith healing. All humans suffered the same ailments but they could be cured through religious faith. He could separate the faithful from others by finding out who had faith when confronted with physical illness. Those who run to the doctor have no faith. To achieve the "living God," according to the Elder, requires a focus on spiritual rather than secular problems. On this basis, the Elder criticized such men as Martin Luther King for misleading people into thinking that social power is relevant. (CL)

6

Interpersonal Relations

Mistrust and tension pervade the atmosphere of migrant labor camps. People are with each other twenty-four hours a day, at work in the fields and in the limited physical setting of a camp. Moreover, migrant crews normally include many people who were strangers prior to the season and who have little expectation of seeing each other subsequently. There are some crews who are mostly kin; but others have only a small core of people who move regularly with the crew leader each season, and many who join temporarily for one summer. Most relationships exist, therefore, only in the present, having no reference to the past and no plans for the future. These relationships, different from more permanent associations, have considerable effect on the social atmosphere in the camp. Understandings between migrants, for example, are exceedingly vague in contrast to those in permanent groups, where social relations are regulated by an extensive network of norms learned over time and clearly recognized by all members; migrant labor crews, with their temporary structure, have few such understandings. This leads to ambivalence and uncertainty, for it is often difficult to predict the behavior of others, particularly as new people come and go during the season. The lack of privacy and the inability to escape or avoid people compound this ambivalence. Similarly, boredom, dependence on the crew leader, limits on mobility, and social exclusion from the local rural community serve to shape patterns of interaction between crew members. To reduce the potential for misunderstanding under these strained circumstances, a leveling mechanism underlies most social interactions; differences *between individuals are reduced, bringing all group members to a common level. In implementing the leveling tendency, exchanges between people have a ritual aspect that resembles dueling, as individuals pit themselves against each other. These exchanges, however, through their ritual quality, balance and maintain the system and minimize friction.*

Marriages, Muck Marriages, and Mother

In some cases, men come north on the season alone, leaving wives and children in Florida. In others families come up together, living and working as a unit in the camp. The predominant pattern of family relations consists of temporary liaisons established for convenience during the season. These are labeled by migrants derogatorily as "tramp" or "muck marriages." Conditions in most camps encourage the formation of these relationships. Both parties benefit: the women have someone to help them pick; the men can save money if they have a woman to cook for them. Despite the derogatory name, muck marriages are accepted and, even among persons with spouses elsewhere, are regarded as legitimate. The intricacies of these relationships, however, are common meat for daily conversations.

Two characteristics of family relations are striking. One feature is that, even where there is relative stability over the season, husbands and wives maintain separate social groups. Men seek male company most of the time, although they will often pick with their wives. Second, the often discussed matrifocal pattern of southern Negro families is only occasionally evidenced because there are relatively few women. It is suggested indirectly, however, by the norms about providing financial support to "mother."

Checker Bill asked me to read a letter for him. It was from his wife, asking him to come back to Florida. She said that his children needed new clothes, that they missed their father, and that she knew that he was running around with other women. The handwriting was very poor and the English was so difficult that I had to reconstruct it as I went along. She kept saying she wanted him to come back, but he should do what he wanted to do. Checker Bill was visibly upset. He claims he has not been fooling around with anyone in the camp and has sent money home. I have seen him in town getting a money order.

He asked me to respond to his wife and he dictated the letter to me. He wrote that he was not fooling around with other women, that he cared for the children, and that he would return home as soon as possible; but the work was bad, and there wasn't much money. He said that he didn't know who could have told her that he was fooling around up here because he wasn't. He said he loved her and that he wanted to come home to see her and the children. A few days later, Bill came up to me with another letter from his wife. She had written to say that she had received his money, but again accused him of going around with other women; and she threatened to go to Miami to seek work. This frightened him. He didn't want her to go to Miami, because this meant leaving the children. He asked me to write a telegram to tell her to stay home. After I sent the telegram, he bought me a beer and asked me to come to his room to write another letter in order to straighten out a few more things. He had previously written that she was to have his car fixed, and now he wanted to make sure that she paid for the repairs in installments. He again mentioned that he had saved money and put down payments on the children's clothing and that he missed the children very much. The letter ended, "Kiss the babies for me." On Monday, he received another letter. It was a little nicer. His wife didn't accuse him of adultery, but said that she was getting the car fixed and that the children missed him. (LR)

*   *   *

Hump talked about his wife and how "she is probably fucking guys in Florida while I'm fucking girls up here. But that don't matter none because she told me I'm welcome back whenever I come." (AK)

*   *   *

Sam asked me to write a letter to his wife. This is what he wrote: "My dearest wife, I don't feel so good because you're not here. All I do is sit around and look at the walls. Why can't you come up here and go to the doctor? There are good doctors up here. Sorry I cut you off the phone the other night but I did not have any more money to talk longer. Been expecting you for some time; however, you fooled me. You told me you were coming but you didn't show up. You must have another man in Florida and he won't let you come. If you wish to come, please answer this letter immediately. I will send money for you to come. Tell your mother hello and kiss the kids for me." (HH)

*   *   *

Ben has two children in Florida, staying with his wife and his mother. This was his first time in this crew, but he has come north on the seasons five times. He talked about his wedding. He had to take three blood tests before he got married because they are good for only thirty days. He had left Florida after each blood test and they all expired. Finally, one day his girlfriend came to him at work and told him that he had to come with her immediately; that her mama had something for him. Ben didn't know what was up, but he could tell from her look that it was important, so he told his boss he was leaving on personal business. When they got outside his girlfriend reminded him that it was the last day of the blood test. It had completely slipped his mind as usual.

Figuring he had nothing to lose, he decided to go ahead and get married. He showered and changed his clothes and went to the justice of the peace with his mother, his wife's mother, and his future wife. He was so nervous that when the justice of the peace said, "You may now kiss the bride," he had to hold her tight to avoid falling over.

He was always talking about his wife in camp and how much he loved her. He called her two weeks ago because she didn't know where he had gone. She wanted to come up and be with him, but he told her that she shouldn't because there was no work. She has a good job in Florida and can't afford to leave it. He talks about his wife, even in front of Flo, with whom he sleeps here in the camp. Yet he has also said a number of times that he loves Flo, and from the way she kids around with him, it appears she likes him too. (AK)

* * *

Roy's family occupies two rooms. He and his wife sleep in one bed with a child, and the other four children sleep in the other bed. A small gas-burning stove is set up on the floor of the second room. While Roy and I were eating a meal of rice, collard greens, and pork chops with a thick gravy, a girl of twelve walked in the door. She was Roy's oldest daughter. I asked what a young man like Roy was doing with such an old daughter. He replied "I may look young but I'm twenty-seven." Roy's wife looks older than he does, and he is teased about his baby face. This child came from another liaison when Roy was fifteen years old.

Roy and his wife are affectionate with each other. I have seen the two of them walking through the camp arm in arm, although public displays of affection are rare. He claims to be a real sport and brags that he chased a lot of women before he and his present wife started running around together. (CL)

* * *

People believe that, regardless of how little money one earns, one must financially support "mother." They may disrespect their wives and women, but mothers seem sacrosanct. George sends his mother $20.00 every week.

He says his mother is much more important to him than his fiancée because "you can have lots of wives but you only have one mother." He feels it is right for him to support her, though he doesn't feel he must see her. Talking about his mother, Tee said he would want to die if his mother died. He claimed his three sisters and four brothers were very close to their mother and to each other, conspicuously omitting his father from the list. He criticized Clint for not sending money to his mother. "Clint doesn't send nothing to his grandma or his ma. He doesn't do anything for nobody but Clint. He just doesn't care for nothing." George asked Patterson, an orphan, if he sends money to the woman who raised him. He was quick to reply that the reason he didn't send her money was because she did not need any since her husband had a good job. (LD)

*   *   *

While we were talking in between the trees, someone asked Curtis if he sent money home to his mother. He replied that he cared first and foremost about himself and wanted to preserve himself more than any other person. People were shocked. James said even though he couldn't stand his mother, he sent her $20.00 each week. "My mother was the one who brought me into this world and I owe her for it." Curtis answered, "Well, I think my father had a pretty big part in it too." "That's not important. Your mother is the one who brought you in and you have to send her money." Jessie was also criticized for the same attitude. "Does he ever send any money at all to his mama? That boy is a disgraceful son."(LR)

*   *   *

During a crap game the father of the Florida family walked over with a beer, sat down, and talked of his marriage. He wasn't married until the age of thirty-seven. That gave him plenty of time to make up his mind. "When you get married you just have to be a man about it." He had been married to the same woman for thirty years and had ten children. The four younger boys and the littlest girl, age five, came north with him. He explained that they pick together as a family and whenever they get paid, they pool their money and everybody gets a dollar a day, putting the rest aside. On Saturday night, they all count how much they have earned and put it into the bank. (DR)

*   *   *

One of the pickers complained he was having trouble with his wife, who was a packer on the same crew. Packers have more status than pickers; they earn more money and do less physical work. They get a penny less per crate, but there are only four packers on each machine and they pack the corn picked by eight men. The job is always held by women if they are available. This man was picking on the same machine on which his wife was packing. All day, he said, his wife had been looking down at him. Every time he was picking corn, he'd look up and see his wife looking down. It was as though she disdained the fact that he was a picker. He has worked for seven years picking corn, in Florida in the winter and here in the summer. His wife brings home more money than he does, but he ends up paying for more of their expenses. Yet, she resents the fact that he does not make a lot of money. He said that he wasn't sure if he should have married this girl or not. She was more trouble to him than she was pleasure. (CL)

*   *   *

Everyone was talking about Sleepy and his wife. He had been having an affair with some woman in the camp and his wife caught him. She was going to beat the woman, but Sleepy got mad and he beat his wife first. Her brother then got involved, claiming that his sister had caught them red-handed and that Sleepy shouldn't have beat her. It would be different if she had not caught them. If she had complained on the basis of a rumor, Sleepy would have reason to beat her. One of the women agreed, "You know, if I have a man and he's out with somebody, I'm not going to say anything to him unless I catch him at it. It's stupid to say anything because if he's not doing anything, then he's going to go out and do it anyhow." This is the pattern with Major and his wife. He goes out with a lot of girls but his wife never says anything to him. Red accused Major of not respecting his wife, but Major claims he does respect her, for he gives her all his money. "Respect" means that a man must not let his wife know he goes out with other women, and that he must give her all his money.

There are several norms involved here. One has to do with the legitimation of adultery, which is accepted if secrecy is maintained and there is no financial involvement. Another is that a woman has to catch her man in order for a violation to be believed. Suspicion alone is no grounds for complaint. (GP)

*   *   *

The younger men were taken from the crew to another camp several hundred miles away, where we were to work for several weeks. The women were left behind. The major topic of conversation while we were driving to the new camp was adultery. It was agreed that it did not make any difference whether a person was a man or a woman: "While men are screwing different women when they are away from their wives, you can be sure that the wives are doing the same when the men are not around." Brown said he had heard some men claim that their wives behaved themselves when they weren't there. He never believed it. "These people are either lying or they're fools. If a man looks at a woman thinking how much he'd like to sleep with her, more likely than not the woman is thinking the same thing." Brown thought adultery was all right as long as you did not get caught. He saw no reason why a woman should not sleep with someone else other than her husband as long as the husband did not find out.

There was one man in the car who had been conspicuously reluctant to leave his wife back at the camp. He did not expect his wife to be faithful to him while he was away. She might be faithful for a few days, but after that she would start looking around. This did not especially please him, but he accepted it as a fact of life. (CL)

*   *   *

Aaron came chasing after his wife between the two barracks, swearing at her while running. He then left camp for the afternoon. That evening, the fight between them resumed. He had taken her beer from her and she demanded it back. They argued and yelled at each other right in the middle of the juke. She retreated toward a corner and he followed her. Other people watched and laughed, avoiding them as they darted around the juke. Finally, when his wife struck him, Aaron said, "Okay, you win. I'm through with you, woman." He chanted this over and over again, and she responded, "No, I'm through with you." Aaron, however, kept coming back for more. Later, when I went out to brush my teeth, they were carrying on the argument outside. He was now singing a song, "I'm through with you, Babe." There were still several people watching, including a lot of younger children. They laughed and said it was kind of like a Broadway show and that we would have intermission soon. (DG)

*   *   *

Pete told a joke about a schoolteacher who wrote the word "dear" on the blackboard and asked if there was anybody in the class who knew what the word was. No one raised his hand, so the teacher thought a little while and then said she was going to give a hint. She asked the little girl in front of the room what her mother called her father when he got home. The girl said, "My love." The teacher said, "No, that's not it." Then she asked another little girl in the class what her mother called her father when he came home. She said, "Honey." "No, that's not it either." Then a little boy in the back of the room waved his hand frantically. The teacher called on him and asked what his mother called his father when he came home. The boy said, "Hello, you motherfucker." (IM)

*   *   *

Red was not out in the field today. The girl he lives with had gone off on Sunday night with some other guy and had not yet returned. He was waiting in front of his house in the car with a gun. He had been there since 6:00 in the morning and at 4:00 P.M. he was still there. Frank, the crew leader, said he didn't want to be there when she comes. "There's going to be blood." People discussed whether she was right doing this. They were not married, but did that mean that she could leave him at will? Pops pointed out how she had stopped Red when he wanted to go for another woman; now she turned around and did this to him. The question was raised as to whom Red should get—his girl or the man who took her away. Most agreed that it was the girl's fault. Sam said, "I don't know what our colored women are doing now. They just run off and do anything they please. They don't care about us at all any more." It was agreed that no man, unless he had a gun, could force a woman to go with him. Pops felt that Red should kill both of them. Frank told a story about a girl who had liked him but couldn't stay with any one person. He told her to "cut the whole thing out right now." James then offered his personal experiences with his wife, who was "really wise and had to be straightened out." He was forced to beat her in order to keep her in line. "That's the only way colored women can be handled." He and his wife are often fighting and hitting each other. Sam agreed, but he is a very mild and nonviolent person and unlikely to practice this. (LR)

*   *   *

Aaron complained he hadn't eaten breakfast because his woman hadn't gotten up on time. She didn't cook lunch for him either. Amos baited him, "You've got this lady back in camp who you're spending your money on and who is supposed to be cooking for you, yet she doesn't get up on time to fix your breakfast or your lunch. I saw another man down there last night with her. He must have stayed with her all night because I saw him come out this morning when I got up at five o'clock." Aaron did not want to believe what Amos was saying, but he began to wonder what a fellow would be doing coming out at five o'clock in the morning. Then he began to worry about all the money he had left with the woman to buy groceries. "I'm spending all my money on this woman and haven't seen any results. I even go home in the afternoon from the job and she isn't there to cook." He concluded that he was spending $20.00 a week on her and her four children and was getting nothing out of it. (GW)

*   *   *

People say that one should not fall in love with a woman on the season. "At the end of the season she's going to go back and you're going to go back and you'll probably never see each other again." Johnny said that he was crazy and could never be quite sure of what he was going to do. He might fall in love anyhow, even though he doesn't want to, having already been married five times. (AK)

*   *   *

It was 9:30 when we arrived back from work, and a woman who has been at the camp now for three or four days started to talk to me. She wanted some man to live with her to help with her expenses. This is the second woman in the camp who has approached me in this way. I told her that I wasn't interested, and asked where the man was who had been living with her before. She told me that was her husband and he is now in Rochester trying to get a job. I asked, "And you want me to live here with you? He just might come in at any time." She told me I didn't have to worry about that. She finally persuaded Hart to live with her and to give her money. When we go to the cherry field, he always helps her pick cherries. (GW)

Communication

Migrants communicate mainly about present events. Stories about the past may be volunteered, but there is considerable reluctance to probe into the past. A person's history is his own affair, and curiosity is not encouraged. People often know little about one another, including names; as a result descriptive nicknames, which identify individuals but preserve anonymity, are prevalent.

The most conspicuous aspect of communication in the camps is its bantering and argumentative character. Boredom and wine generate long conversations that develop into arguments over trivial matters. There are many migrants whose relations are ritualized in this fashion; they relate to each other almost exclusively by continual bickering. The ability to argue effectively, to have a ready and clever answer, is admired; the objective is to "put down" one's opponent in an argument. The subject is often less important than the relationship between the participants. Bickering not only ritualizes and stabilizes relations but displaces more serious conflict by focusing on a level that can be managed or shrugged off as trivial. This ritual quality is indicated by the repetitive nature of arguments and the fact, not entirely accidental, that they occur where there are spectators.

The tendency to exaggerate and to lie is another aspect of communication in the camps. Lies may reflect personal problems but also have ritual value as does bickering. Here, however, it is important to examine the content of lies, for where lies are considered to be more auspicious than the truth, areas of anxiety may be found.

I asked Ben how long he had known his roommate. He said they had once stayed in the same boarding house in Florida but had known each other only casually. When they rode up north on the bus together, they got to know each other pretty well. I asked him his roommate's name. He said "Names don't mean anything to me; I just call him 'Buddy.' " (AK)

*   *   *

Clinton was sitting right behind me on the bus, and about halfway through the trip he leaned over and asked where I was from. "Well, I don't want to be nosy or anything like that. I don't want to pry into your business. . . ." He was very apologetic about asking questions. (DG)

*   *   *

The camp was quiet and boring. Raymond was sitting in his car, dozing with his head on the back of the seat. Other people were sitting in front of the kitchen or beside the barracks, not saying anything and staring into space. The expression on their faces was similar to the look people have riding the New York subways. It was 3:30 P.M. and Shorty and Bobo were both drunk. They began to argue about the longest road in the United States. Bobo insisted that it was Route 13 and Shorty insisted that it was Route 41. Both insisted that the other did not know what he was talking about. "What do you know? You've only been to three or four states in your whole life." Bobo, who had been in the army in Korea, said that he had seen more countries than Shorty had seen states. This argument went on for forty-five minutes. Shorty went into his room and brought out a map of the eastern United States. It was not a road map; it was a hurricane map. They argued the length of highways when they actually were looking at the border of a hurricane. Then Raymond said you don't have to argue about things like that. "Just look it up. You guys will argue just about anything."

The conversation shifted to parachutes as Shorty talked about how you have to use a parachute to jump out of a plane. Bobo said Shorty didn't know anything about parachutes. Shorty then asked each of us whether we had been in the army, saying, "Well, I ain't been in the army and I ain't going." Bobo said he couldn't get into the army because he has a record. Bobo argued that he had a record before he went into the army and a record didn't mean anything. This started a new argument, which was never resolved.

Another argument developed about the number of states in the United

States. Some insisted it was fifty-two; others insisted it was forty-eight. Shorty again went to his room and this time brought back an old almanac with about twenty or twenty-five pages left in it. It did not have the information that he wanted. He returned and brought out a book entitled *George Washington*. It was a children's book, with colored pictures, concerning the Revolution. He went through it to find a flag in order to count the number of stars.

Another argument concerned divorce. The question was whether you remained married to someone if you never divorced them, but just left. Bobo insisted that you would be married as long as you weren't actually divorced. Shorty argued that if enough time lapsed you were automatically divorced. The subject shifted to friendship and love, Bobo saying that there was no such thing as a friend. "When you have money in your pocket, everyone is your friend." Shorty disagreed, but didn't back himself up. As to love, Bobo said that you'll always love best the first girl you ever loved. Although you might care for others, you will never love another. Shorty claimed that Bobo didn't know what love was. He said that he had been married for twenty-six years and seven months, and he turned to me and asked rhetorically, "If you had a million dollars and were married to Jay Gould's daughter, would you be happy?" Shorty and Bobo always argue together. In a sense it seems to solidify their friendship. They have what may be called an "arguing relationship," which is a bond even though it appears to divide them. (IM)

*   *   *

Aaron and his wife were talking about the same things that they always talked about: their son back in Georgia and his $150.00 motor bike. Aaron talked of his past work experiences. Often they would speak at the same time, sort of at one another, neither one really listening to what the other was saying. (DG)

*   *   *

At 6:15 A.M., Ben, Shock, and Bull were drinking a pint of Tiger Rose together. Before drinking each would tell a story or a poem. Bull recited a little poem about jungle animals. Ben told jokes about preachers. In one joke the preacher wanted to sleep with the beautiful wife of a parishioner and succeeded by telling her that it was the will of God. Bull and Ben talked about their experiences in jail, including intricate details as to how the guards would wake you up by shouting into your cell and rapping the bars with a stick.

Suddenly a heated argument broke out between Shock and Bull. It started with a disagreement about the depth of the Rhine River. Shock said the Rhine was so shallow they forded it, and Bull said they had to build pontoon bridges on it. Each started to prove he had been in the army and was an expert on this matter. Shock pulled out his papers, but Bull said his had been stolen in Czechoslovakia. Nevertheless, he insisted that he had served in the European Theater and at Guadalcanal. "Anyhow, what's in the head is important, much more so than what's on paper." Clinton, overhearing this comment, told us a long story to prove how things in "black and white" are more important than what is in the head. When he went into the hospital they wanted his Social Security card. He had the number memorized but they would not let him in until he actually showed the card. When Clinton contradicted him, Bull started to get wild. Shock baited him. "Well, let's hear you give marching directions," and Bull said, "Hup, hup, hup," and leaned back on the bed, pounding his feet on the ground. Shock laughed and asked, "What's the difference between 'at ease' and 'at rest?'" Bull got up and stood at ease (I don't think he could have stood at attention then if he wanted to), and then sat down to show "at rest" and bumped his head hard against the wall. (DG)

*   *   *

During a game of whist, a heated series of arguments took place. Pete said, "President Kennedy came into office when he was over forty years old." Several minutes later someone replied, "Hey, Pete, are you out of your mind, you know he was younger." Big Time added, "He was thirty-six." Pete then claimed, "I never said he was over forty." A long discussion followed over whether Pete had or had not said that President Kennedy was over forty. This kind of arguing went on all night and occasionally led people to push each other around. (MR)

*   *   *

There was one group in the field consisting of the winos and five or six others. This group was engaged in continual conversation, most of which was a patter requiring very little thought. Everyone joined the conversation, telling of experiences or observations, and occasionally offering opinions. As soon as a person stopped offering information, he was not addressed by others and was excluded from the group.

The talk included a lot of boasting and exaggerating. For example, Nate and Junior would boast how many beans they had picked the previous day. They boasted about their fighting ability and sexual prowess, and continually accused each other of lying. Lies were a perfectly acceptable form of conversation here. The best lies are the biggest ones. For example, Nate claimed he had picked 50 bushels of beans in one day. This was greeted with a great burst of laughter. Another kind of conversation is called "rapping," a kind of insult also called "scoring" or the "dozens." Raps are often delivered against an opponent's mother. Joe, age seventeen, got into an argument with Junior by saying he could do anything better than Junior. He could swim better, play basketball better, and have better luck with women. He could sing more songs and talk better. Junior objected, saying that no one could rap better than he could. Joe then reeled off a list of insults: "Your mother eats hooks, your mother likes pulpwood, your mother drives the tractor, your mother drives the bean picker, your mother's a lumberjack, your mother drives a truck. She is a tractor with big flat, fat motherfucking wheels." Everyone thought these insults were very funny.

Once Junior had been effectively put down, Joe turned his scoring powers on Nate, who also came out second best. Nate knew only one or two raps. Joe had a repertoire as long as his arm. Junior and Joe continued to argue about other abilities, and it turned out that Junior's only claim to fame was that he could eat "more than any other human being in the world." He suggested they have a marathon eat, set in a room with five turkeys, four gallons of milk, and several apple pies. The first person to emerge would be the winner. (CL)

*   *   *

People in the crew exaggerate and lie to each other about how much they have picked or about their personal adventures. Scrap tells fantastic lies about where he has traveled. He makes up stories to embellish events in his life. People criticize Scrap, "He thinks he's so damn hip. He thinks he's the only one that knows anything around here. He must think we're all farmers." They don't believe his stories, but enjoy listening to them as entertainment. Most people lie only occasionally, but Otis and Gatemouth are chronic liars. Otis tells elaborate and inconsistent stories about his relations with women. He claims to have been married to four women, but never can remember which of them died or whom he had run out on. He also forgets the names and ages of his children. "I've got a girl half as old as you and she is not the oldest one; I've got one older than that." "Well, how old is that one?" "Well, thirty-seven, she's as old as you are and she's not the oldest one." He'll go on along these lines very seriously, getting everyone confused. Once Otis starts lying he is unable to stop. He can be kidded into saying he was born in 1800. He once said, "I don't tell any more lies than the rest of you." And Scrap replied, "Yeah, but you sure tell them faster."

The other chronic liar is Gatemouth who, on a number of subjects, is unable to tell the truth. If asked about his productivity, he immediately doubles the amount he has picked. Someone walked up to him early one morning before he had started working and asked him how much he had picked and he replied, "Ten." One day we were on the way back from the plant and he stopped to talk to a girl along the road. She asked him how many buckets he picked, and he said, "I don't pick no damn cherries." His immediate reaction is to make up a story which makes him seem different than he really is. (MR)

Reciprocity and Exchange

Another aspect of interaction is concerned with reciprocity and exchange. Generosity characterizes many relationships. Despite the scarcity of material resources, people expect to share what they have. Accumulation of goods without sharing is suspect, except among those with heavy family obligations.

Reciprocation is expected for favors, though not necessarily in kind. Tussy, a wino but a skilled picker when sober, often helps others finish their baskets as insurance against those times when he is too drunk to work and needs assistance. Unlike many societies where sharing wealth is a means to build up long-term social obligations, in the migrant milieu goods are shared with the expectation that reciprocation will be prompt. The nature and content of the exchange is usually verbalized; seldom is it taken for granted as understood. That the terms of exchange must be expressed suggests that exchange serves to implement the leveling tendency referred to earlier. Except for the crew leader, gifts or favors are seldom offered in exchange for deference. Although giving a gift establishes prestige for the donor vis-à-vis the recipient, such cases mainly involve the crew leader as the donor. In contrast, among crew members sharing serves to equalize and to prevent any one person from standing out.

People often ask each other for food, and, if a man has money in his pocket, he will normally share his dinner if asked. If he is broke and doesn't know where he will get the next meal, he will refuse. The most common items regularly shared are cigarettes and wine. Sharing is, in a way, like banking. When someone has borrowed cigarettes from me, I can borrow cigarettes back when I need them. Others have offered me wine, and when I have wine I offer it to them. One day, Major approached Red saying, "You're just going to have to change. You've got no heart." Red asked, "What are you talking about?" "You sat there and ate four slices of baloney without offering any to anybody. You're no soul brother. Man, you got no heart, no feeling. You've got to get out; you've got a heart like a white man." Everyone joined him in heckling Red, for those with a lot of food are expected to offer some around. One night, I was eating and a man came up and asked for part of my meal. I had worked hard all day, this was my first meal since breakfast, and I was not about to share it. "You're going to keep it all to yourself?" "Yes." He took the food and dumped it in my face. As I stood up to get the food off, he thought I was going to fight. He took two quick swings and missed, and I picked up a bottle and shot it at him. He ducked and came back a second time, when someone came over and stopped the fight. Actually, neither of us had touched each other. (GP)

*   *   *

Shock had just come back from the hospital and was on the bus. Before we left, Geech, who lives in the bullpen, came on and said that everyone in the bullpen was going to chip in some money so that Shock would not have to work. So Shock got off the bus and didn't go to work that day. (DG)

*   *   *

When I came back from the toilet, Ann said that she wanted to talk to me for a minute. "I did that favor you asked me to last night. I told Jessamay that you wouldn't be there for dinner." I thanked her and she repeated, "I did that favor for you. Could you get me a pack of cigarettes from Jessamay?" I said okay and asked Jessamay to give me some Kools and gave them to Ann. (MR)

*   *   *

Junior was talking to a fifteen-year-old girl. He said that he was twenty and she should listen to him. "Didn't your mommy always tell you to listen to your elders to learn something?" They exchanged a kind of cursing banter that is common between young couples. He called her a bitch and a whore and the girl responded, "Goddamn motherfucker." He was annoyed at her because he had been helping her pick and had given her several pounds of beans. As we walked back across the field, he turned to me and said, "I don't know what's wrong with that girl. She wants help picking but she isn't willing to fuck." (DR)

*   *   *

Nate came in and asked what I was cooking up. I had some stew and he said, "Give me some." I told him that I would have some left over and he could have it. As I left for the cookhouse, Nate suggested, "Why don't you cook up some rice, too?" At dinner that night, I ate some and gave the remainder to Nate. He then promptly offered me his peanut butter. (CL)

*   *   *

Bo told a story about a hobo he met many years ago. The hobo was hungry so Bo gave him $2.00 to buy food. The man returned with change, but Bo refused to accept it, telling him to use it as he pleased. Fifteen years later, Bo was loading cotton and the same man approached him; but now he was manager of the plant. He remembered Bo's kindness and did many favors for him.

The obligation to share is strongly emphasized in the camp. One day, when I went in to wash, Albert was at the sink. He asked if I were done working. I said, "No, it's a lunch break." "Good! You work the whole day long because *we* are going to need that money." "We?" "That's right, buddy. We." If one person has more money than his friends he is obliged to distribute it in some way and eliminate the discrepancy.

Some forms of exchange are more socially fluid than others. Cash, for example, is not normally useful for social exchange. It cannot easily be distributed without raising questions of status. So, cash is often converted into softer "currency," such as alcohol or food. For example, Shorty is a forty-one-year-old migrant who lives in the camp but works directly for the grower, driving a tractor. His weekly income is higher than that of the bean pickers with whom he lives. Each week, upon receiving his check, Shorty stocks his refrigerator and, with the remainder of his money, he drinks and plays craps. He gives quarters to kids to play the piccolo and buys beer for his friends. He often will cook pork chops for anyone that wants them. At the end of each weekend Shorty is "dead broke." These gifts do not give him greater social rank; they merely remove the discrepancy of "wealth" and permit him to be part of the group.

What would happen if Shorty did not share his goodies? A partial answer is suggested by the case of another man who works directly for the grower and lives in the camp. Unlike Shorty, however, he does not liquefy his paycheck but translates it into hard goods: he owns a car and a television set, and does not share those possessions with others. He also operates a beer concession. This man's status is high in that he enjoys the distant respect of the others, but this is at the expense of social rapport. He is relatively unusual. Others in the camp who earn extra money seek to prevent the development of status differences. For example, the man who sells the hard liquor liquefies some of his cash by giving out free food. I have seen him cook pigs' ears or pig tails for himself, while distributing pork chops and ham hocks to others in the crew. He often runs parties, cramming eight or nine people into his small room. Likewise, Peanutman has a peanut concession. He keeps his price low enough so that he accumulates only enough money to live just like everyone else.

In contrast, exchanges between the crew leader and crew members are intended to increase the gap in status and to maintain dependency. Favors, such as giving rides to town, offering extra coffee, cashing tickets before payday, are provided selectively as a means of control. These services build social obligations where deference and obedience are expected in exchange for favors.

Giving of gifts incorporates the notion of reciprocity. In the case of the crew leader, payoff is in the form of deference. Among peers, reciprocity is often explicit. In the same breath that Pete asked me for a ticket or two, he mentioned he was cooking up some hamburgers later on and I might join him. Bo offered to give me a ticket worth 70 cents the next day if I would give him 50 cents today. Moe offered me his radio until he paid back the 55 cents he owed me. The importance of reciprocity is dramatized in the following incident. It was common knowledge that Albert begged and borrowed without feeling any obligation to reciprocate. One day, several people decided to try and embarrass him. Albert was eating crackers in front of his room, so Moe walked up and asked for one. Albert ignored him, walked into his room, and closed the door. Then Bo came up, knocked at Albert's door and asked him to come out. Afraid to antagonize Bo, Albert opened the door only to be confronted by Moe who again asked for a cracker. The group watching the incident broke up laughing, and Albert retreated into his room.

If a person wants to avoid providing loans, he can demand excessive reciprocity. A visitor cut off a request for a beer "for old times' sake" by demanding some sweet milk in the morning. This was impossible to provide, so the exchange never took place. Conversely, the offer of reciprocity can force an exchange. Pete tried to borrow liquor money from Shorty, who refused because, he said, he needed his money for dinner. Pete countered with an offer of food from his freezer. Shorty was left with no reasonable alternative and handed over the money.

The tension that often accompanies exchange suggests the tenuous character of the rules about exchanges. The promises explicitly made in each transaction indicate that exchanges do not occur as a means to build up long-term obligations, as in permanent groups. Reciprocation must be concrete and prompt, since it is understood that social relationships are temporary. (IM)

Tension and Mistrust

Migrant labor camps are tense and potentially explosive despite mechanisms to minimize conflict. Tension and mistrust are significant aspects of all social relations. Tension among roommates is common. Many single men live in "bullpens," with four to eight people in a room. But even where there are single rooms, it is difficult to get off alone. Tension sometimes develops from proximity and extensive contact. In other cases, a disruptive individual may be the source of problems. In most social situations such individuals can be isolated or ignored; in the camp they grate incessantly. Tension is greatest when work is scarce, stimulated by frustration and excess idle time. It is expressed in many ways, but primarily in the prevailing mistrust. Knives are carried by most men and many women and doors are always locked. People regard each other as unpredictable and suspicions and accusations create an atmosphere of hostility in which arguments begin easily and playful gestures develop into serious incidents.

Around 11:00 P.M., I went back to the room with Pete to get some sleep. We got into bed but our third roommate, Albert, did not want to go to sleep and was sitting on his bed playing with a deck of cards. He announced, "I'm not ready to sleep yet and I'm leaving the light on." Pete said, "Come on, man, I want to get some sleep because I'm going to work tomorrow." But Albert insisted, "Man, I'll go to bed when I am ready to go to bed. I do what I want." Pete asked me to turn off the light. Albert then got up, put the light back on again, and sat down saying, "I'm not ready to go to bed yet; I'm going to play with my cards." After some arguing, I got up again and turned off the light, and Albert got up and turned it on again. This continued for forty-five minutes, when I finally got up, took out the bulb, and brought it to bed with me. At that point, Albert opened the door saying he needed fresh air. Pete got out of bed, closed the door and climbed back in; and Albert opened the door again. I finally left and went to sleep on the kitchen floor. At 5:00 A.M. Raymond came in and commented that he had heard all the noise last night and it kept his whole family awake. (IM)

*   *   *

Ben complained that Johnny, his roommate, is constantly talking and never shuts up. "You can ask him about the weather and he will give you a forty-five-minute speech about everything he knows." Later, in the afternoon, we left for our weekly trip to town. On the bus, Johnny complained about Ben and how he always wakes him up in the middle of the night. Ben then claimed he hated living with Johnny because he sleeps naked, and Johnny replied he could sleep any way that he wanted to. (AK)

*   *   *

Jessie and his roommate, Clyde, both drunk, were arguing about whether Clyde's home town was a "good city." Neither of them was taking the argument seriously until Clyde suddenly got mad. Jessie tried to avoid a fight, saying he did not mean to be insulting, but Clyde threatened him. Jessie walked away, but suddenly he turned, picked up a brick and called Clyde a drunken black bastard. If he wanted to fight, he should fight now because he was going to break his skull open. Neither man could stand up very well, but every time Clyde made a move, Jessie moved his brick as if to strike him. Finally Clyde walked away and went into the police station, which was only a block away. Jessie, still anxious to avoid a fight, put on a sport jacket and said, "Maybe if I put on this sport jacket, he's so drunk, he won't recognize me." About three to four minutes later Clyde came back from the police station and sat down to wait for the bus. When the bus came, they both sat down and fell asleep. Later Jessie said he never got along with his roommate because he was dirty and he couldn't even get him to sweep up the room. He said he didn't like fights but "I like myself better than anyone else in the whole world and if someone is going to challenge me, I will kill the other guy first." (AK)

*   *   *

Some people returned from the field early and were in the juke talking about how Jessie was spreading rumors about everybody. He had been saying that Pope was trying for Pat and that James was after Emma. Each person added something about Jessie's stories, and they got increasingly agitated as they talked, claiming his rumors were ruining people's lives. "You shouldn't interfere with matters between people, you should only worry about yourself." When Jessie came back from work, at least five people approached him with accusations. (LR)

*   *   *

Frank's wife was furious. Several girls were sitting outside the juke talking about what had happened. Willy Wine, while drunk, had said that Frank's wife was fooling around with Sonny. Both she and Frank were very upset about this. When Willy Wine appeared again, Frank's wife went after him with a butcher knife, threatening to slit his throat for what he said.

Later, still in a rage, she told us how Frank couldn't eat because he was so mad and she was going to "kick Willy Wine's motherfucking ass in. That damn wino is wrecking other people's lives. He shouldn't interfere with married people." She left and everyone was very quiet on the porch. After about twenty minutes, Frank drove up, said good morning and went inside. He and his wife could be heard arguing. Willy walked up shortly afterwards, still drunk, and sat down, saying that nobody around here could take a joke. He was warned that if he kept joking like that he'd get his throat cut. Soon, Willy's wife made him get back to his room. "You're only causing a lot of trouble." She walked over, grabbed him by the collar, and pushed him down the hall like a little kid. (LR)

*   *   *

Jessie and Johnny were arguing about who was the smartest. Johnny said he would throw Jessie out the window if he didn't stop being so nasty. "Ain't nobody gonna throw me out the window because I'm Jessie and nobody takes advantage of Jessie." "Well, this boy will." "You can throw me out the door. Ain't no one gonna throw me out the window." Jessie tried to show how smart he was by saying he knew every president in the White House since he was born. He called Lyndon Johnson the "worst motherfucking, cheating, lying man that's ever been in the White House and Humphrey is a motherfucker too." Johnny said, "Hold on, he's a Democrat." Jessie insisted, "He's a motherfucker." "No, he's a Democrat." Then they argued as to whether a song was by B. B. King. Jessie was using "motherfucking" as a prefix to every noun, and Johnny told him not to "profane" so much. Jessie said the word was "blaspheme," and that started another argument. Jessie finally announced, "I came in here to talk to you. I liked you but I found out you are motherfucking stupid." He got up to leave. Johnny told me that Jessie was the cause of a lot of problems among his roommates because he never sits down and talks to anyone decently. "He always has to be so damn smart." (AK)

*   *   *

There is no work and everyone is very tense. People snap at each other and arguments develop about nothing. Everybody is in a sour mood. The only time this mood disappears is in the juke when music is playing. At other times, people curse at each other much more than earlier in the season and there is hostility in the air. A few weeks ago, if you asked to borrow a cigarette, people would share willingly. Lately, when people share, they complain about it. We stay up much later than usual. Late at night, people wander around the buildings and there are many threats. "You think you're smart, don't you. Come on over and I'll knock you on your ass." "I'm not going to let anyone walk over me. This has gone far enough." Things are building up for a fight. The tension is from lack of work. Everyone is wondering how he will ever get any money and is anxious for the bean season to begin. Some of the tension focuses on women. "When they told me I was coming up here, they said there were a lot of pretty girls in this camp. When I got here, there was nothing but these snuff chewers." There are a lot of young, active men in the camp and it is hard to imagine them sitting around bored for another five or six days without something happening. The women are not as tense as the men about the lack of work; however, I heard a couple of women talk about trying to make money through prostitution. "If worse comes to worse, I guess I can do that." "There's nothing wrong with it. These babies have to eat." (GP)

*   *   *

On Sunday, the atmosphere is strange. Friday night, people start drinking and by Saturday they are drunk. Sunday they have been drunk and things get messy and sloppy. There are a lot of provocations and many potential fights. As I went to sleep Sunday, I heard James threatening Jessie, calling him a "black bastard," and telling him he was going to cut him to pieces. It seems like everyone is ready to explode on Sundays after a hard weekend of drinking and gambling and the realization that they are broke and must go back to work to make money again to live for the week. (LR)

*   *   *

Junior and Joe share a double bed in a room where there are four of us. Joe has a talent for what he calls "flagging." He was pestering Junior about talking in his sleep and tossing and turning on the double bed. He said that Junior woke up this morning and started turning over toward Joe's side, claiming that Junior had homosexual tendencies. Junior, at first, didn't get offended and laughed it off, but later Joe picked it up again and began to get on his nerves. A few days later, Junior came back to the cabin at 10:00 P.M., picked up something, and walked toward the door, saying he was going to the bathroom. This is the last we saw of him. He left camp, leaving his clothes and toilet articles. He had taken a pair of shoes that belonged to Cliff and $35.00 that he had borrowed earlier from Joe. The next day, Joe was called a fool for loaning the $35.00. The flagging that he usually gave to others was returned. Joe took it in good humor. When he was teased that he had lost his money and was betrayed by a friend, he laughed and admitted he had been a fool. "I'm going to catch that motherfucker and beat his head in if I ever find him." He told a story about a man who hit a six-foot man with a stick and reduced him to three feet. Junior was going to catch some of that, too! (CL)

*   *   *

Shorty was in the juke, Friday night, extremely drunk. He had a roll of money in his pocket, which he took out every once in a while to show off. Bobo said he was worried that someone was going to take it. He wanted to get Shorty out of there but was afraid to take him back to his room because he thought he might be accused of taking the money if someone else came and stole it later. Bobo finally did take Shorty back to his room and locked the door. Someone asked if he had taken the money and he denied it. Then what Bobo feared actually happened. Later, when Shorty woke up, he found his money was gone. He accused Bobo of taking it and pulled a knife on him, cutting his left ear. (IM)

*   *   *

When I got back to the bullpen after being gone for a few days, James, my roommate, asked if he could borrow a dollar from me. He promised to pay back a dollar and a quarter. While I was gone, he had cleaned up our room, although I had told him that I would clean up my part. He followed me back to the room and told me he had been very honest and had not stolen anything from me; that I would find all my stuff if I just looked around. As I was getting my money to loan him the dollar, he suggested that I keep it in another place. I usually keep money in a brown paper bag in my duffle bag. He suggested a safer place would be my pocket. He kept insisting that he was not a thief and didn't take anything that I owned. (DG)

*   *   *

Roy was repairing a broken window that had been removed from the cabin the night before. Whoever took it out had cut the screen outside the cabin. Roy said that the noise made in cutting the screen woke him up. When he went to investigate, he found someone outside, but was unable to identify who it was. The man who was out there said that he had also come out to investigate, but Roy was convinced that it was this person who had attempted to burglarize the cabin. He replaced the glass with another he found in the field and nailed both windows shut. He also hung a light bulb outside the door. (CL)

*   *   *

I went across the hall to Pops' room to talk. The conversation concerned the "jitterbugs," five new boys who had just joined the crew. He was complaining about "all the hell those boys raise every night talking about fighting with each other, whose ass they're going to kick, and all that kind of stuff." Pops said that the boys had informed him they would steal anything they could find, and people had begun to miss some things. Before these boys came, we left things lying around. Now we are locking our rooms. Nappychin said he slept with his clothes on last night and hid everything. While he pretended to sleep, the boys searched his room and said, "This bitch doesn't have anything. We'll try him some other time." During the day the jitterbugs stay around the camp and don't do much work. This caused so much concern that the crew leader finally told them that they had to go out to the fields. (GW)

*   *   *

The rooms in the camp are always kept locked, but those people who sleep in the hall or the living room are unable to lock their possessions. I generally lock my door, although on occasion I have left it open for an entire day and nothing has been taken. I don't have anything of value that anyone would be interested in stealing. However, Tee told me that "a nigger will steal your underwear." (MR)

Violence

Tensions often explode into fights. There are several characteristics common to most violent incidents. Participants are usually drunk. Most fights start easily and spontaneously; they are like brief explosions and, although often sparked by competition for women or by specific arguments, are seldom focused or goal directed. Fists, bottles, and knives may be involved, but considering the number of incidents, there are relatively few that require police interference or that end in hospitalization. Even where knives are used, damage is usually minimal. Weapons are employed mainly as a threat and, when actually used, people will slash rather than stab, thereby limiting the seriousness of the consequences. Even in one extreme case, described below, Bull's 100 stitches kept him out of work for only a week. Another characteristic of fights between individuals is that onlookers seldom interfere. Although most fights have observers, few want to be involved. Finally, fights end almost as quickly as they begin. There is sometimes an obvious winner; other times the parties simply stop. In either case, anger is temporarily dissipated and those who fight one day may be good friends the next day. Grudges cannot last where close daily contact must be maintained.

Fights do not, by any means, occur in all camps. They are most prevalent where there is a large percentage of single men and where few people knew each other prior to the season. In these circumstances, fighting is a mechanism to regulate and control relationships. Where there are few institutional mechanisms for social control, the threat of violence has its own power. Minor scuffles between individuals serve as rituals, breaking boredom, dissipating tension, and sometimes preventing major breaches. Fighting also serves as a leveling mechanism, controlling deviant individuals. The prevalence of violence is an inevitable consequence of the tension that develops in the unstable and unpredictable environment of the camp.

In the juke, people were playing a game similar to bingo except with a deck of cards. There were two full tables of ten people each and one small table of five people. In the far corner there were eight people playing craps. There was also a group around the piccolo, listening to music. The younger people, the fourteen- to sixteen-year-olds, danced once in a while. They encouraged the winos to put quarters in the piccolo. I saw twenty bottles of wine sold over the counter during the first hour that I was in the juke, until I stopped counting. By midnight there were around fifty people crowded in the small room. The camp custodian is supposed to put the lights out at midnight, but he has chosen to ignore this rule made by the camp management. The crew leaders may have pressured him to ignore the rule, since they made more money when the juke stays open late. Around midnight, a Negro man pulled up in a Cadillac with three prostitutes: two Negro girls and one white girl. The word passed that these chicks were on the block, and one of the guys I was sitting with called a girl over and asked, "What do I have to do to get you, honey?" The girls were very frank about what they were doing; they wanted $7.00 apiece.

The night wore on this way. I was talking to two young boys who were north for the first time. We were watching a couple dancing when, suddenly, the boys jumped on the man dancing, and he went sprawling all over the floor. Suddenly, everyone started grabbing everyone else. As soon as the boys jumped this guy, a girl jumped on them and then others joined in. The next thing I realized, someone was reaching for me, and at that point, I stopped observing. The man who was hit was well defended. It was his sister and her boyfriend who had joined the fight first, and once three or four people were involved, it got out of control. I tried to sit quietly on the sidelines but someone I did not know came up and took a kick at me. I ducked under a table and saw someone in the corner threatening a kid with a hatchet. Then I heard shots from somewhere. I managed to get out the door and ran down to the edge of the camp, where I sat in the woods for about ten minutes before going back to my room. With all that row, nobody was hurt that evening. (GP)

* * *

Flo complained that Ernestine, her neighbor, was making too much noise, and Ernestine replied, "Just because you have a grandchild don't mean you have to protect him like that." Angry words were quickly exchanged as Flo walked away saying, "Well, I'm going to leave because I don't want to have to whip your ass," and Ernestine shouted, "You can't whip my ass. Hell, you can't whip my ass at all." Then Flo replied, "I'll have to get me a pair of glasses before I hit you." At that, Ernestine jumped up and handed her glasses to somebody. "You ain't going to say that." The next thing I knew the two women were fighting on the ground. They weren't punching or pulling hair—it was more like wrestling. Flo quickly got on top of Ernestine, who was on the ground on her back. Ernestine's little girl came and tried to pull Flo off her mother, and a crowd of people gathered around the two, laughing and joking. Finally, Flo just got up, and brushed herself off. She sat down on her doorstep. In a few minutes, Ernestine came by and said, "Those people over there are saying you whipped my ass. That ain't true. Hell, no! We weren't punching or hitting or scratching or anything like that; I mean we weren't really even fighting; they're saying you whipped me. You didn't whip my ass." Flo smiled and nodded her head. "We weren't fighting that much. We were just kind of pushing each other around." Ernestine walked away. (DR)

* * *

Florida Joe and Geech, both drunk, had been arguing, and Joe siphoned some gasoline from the bus and threatened to throw it on Geech. Geech took out his knife and the two men stood there threatening each other. Geech finally slashed Joe and ran away from camp. When I saw him, he had just come back. Cory had called the police, and they bandaged Joe's neck and hustled Geech off in a car. People in the camp discussed the incident for days. Some said it was self-defense, others disagreed. Some guessed that both would go to jail since "it takes two to make a fight." Others said Geech would go to jail and Joe would get off. Johnny took two different positions. First, he said Geech would be locked up for a long time. Later, he thought that Geech would be in Florida by the time everyone got back. "New York don't want to pay all that money to take all those people from Florida to bring them up to New York for the trial. Don't tell me. I know all about laws. I got a book." He came out of the room with a large red book. It was the book of *New York Criminal Procedures*, 1936. Johnny turned a few pages and told a story about a guy who cut someone a few years ago at this camp. "We got back to Florida, and, shit, he was already there."

Later, Bean was chatting with J.B., the crew leader, and Florida Joe walked over, his neck bandaged. A word or two was passed between Joe and Bean. Then suddenly Bean ran over to the side of the building and grabbed a thin iron rod, about 3 feet long. He came charging at Joe, the pole raised over his head, and brought it down on Joe's shoulder. Joe stood there stunned. I heard J.B. cry out, "Hit him again." Joe turned around and ran, with Bean on his heels. It was an amazing scene; Joe running through the parking lot onto the road and Bean in hot pursuit, waving his iron rod. Everyone was excited and followed them as far as the lot. Nothing came of it, and once people had quieted down, the story came out. Joe had tried to borrow a cigarette from Bean, who refused. He then threatened to burn down Bean's cabin that night.

The incident prompted a series of stories about other fights. J.B. related one about a fight in Florida when he had been attacked by three guys. They all had bottles and knives. He said to them, "Well, if you're going to do something, why don't you do it now?" Then he ducked and they almost killed each other throwing the bottles. J.B. turned to Fats, and said, "I'll give you four bottles and I'll keep only one and I'll kill you, man. Shit, yes." Fats said he could throw the bottle at J.B. and hit him just right so he would be killed, but J.B. kept saying, "Shit, man, you don't know how to fight. You're just a little kid. I'd just wait 'til you threw all your bottles at me, and when you didn't have any more, well I'd break my bottle and stick it in your face." He was holding a Pepsi bottle at the time and acted out the scene. Fats was trying to defend his fighting ability and then told J.B., "You should meet Daddy. Jiminy, you are two of a kind. You're both real mean. Real bad motherfuckers." (DR)

*   *   *

Emma cooks breakfast each morning. This morning, Ben walked in and started kidding around with her. Hump interrupted, "Don't kid around with her this morning. She ain't in no mood." But Ben needled her about taking so long cooking his breakfast. Hump again warned him not to make trouble because Emma wasn't in a good mood. Ben said, "It's okay 'cause I used to be married to that girl. We used to live together down in that shack over there. It was nice, but I had to leave her because she never would cook for me." He continued in that vein, clearly kidding, but Emma took him seriously. "I ain't never been your wife. I ain't never lived with you."

"Sure you have. Come here and give me a big kiss." "I'll give you a kiss on your fucking, black ass, I'll give you a kiss." "That ain't no way to treat your own husband." Ben continued teasing and Emma kept saying she would never be the husband of "no fucking winehead nigger." Finally she said, "You come one step closer and I'm going to pull out this big butcher knife on you." Ben took a step closer and Emma came at him with this knife and they started wrestling. He grabbed her arm and finally made her drop the knife. Then he grabbed at her breasts a couple of times and she slapped him. Hump tried to stop them by saying, "Come on, don't fight, he's just kidding around," but they weren't listening to him, so he just sat back and enjoyed the scene. Finally Ben picked up the knife and Emma went in to get another one. This time she really came at him. Ben tried to grab the knife from her but cut his finger. It was bleeding badly. She still wouldn't put the knife down until he finally forced it away. By this time the fight had lost all of its joking aspect and they were slapping each other and pulling hair; Hump continued to laugh and enjoy the spectacle. Finally, Ben just stopped and they both walked away. (AK)

*   *   *

For no apparent reason, Robert and Albert started fighting. Both were drunk and they would take light slaps at each other and then walk away, standing about 20 yards apart. They both kept talking about how they were going to whip each other. Every few minutes they would make a move and take another slap at each other. Then they would walk away again and talk about how "nobody is going to whip my ass." This happened about ten times. It was almost like a dance. Then Shorty, who was also very drunk, picked up a stick and started waving it at Robert, who said, "Why are you messing with me, man? I didn't do anything. I have nothing against you." Some people held Shorty back, asking, "Why can't you all be friends?" Slim also tried to break up the fight but was not successful. Eventually, it stopped and everyone acted as if nothing had happened. (IM)

*   *   *

I heard some noise near the juke and saw Albert running for the road, Shorty hot on his heels. They ran up the road about a quarter of a mile before they stopped about 50 yards apart. I could see by the motion of Shorty's head that he was yelling at Albert. Albert had asked for food, and since he is always borrowing, Shorty refused, upon which Albert threw a beer bottle at him. The chase lasted over an hour. Shorty had two rocks in his hand and later ran into his room for a knife. As Shorty approached him, Albert would back up; then Shorty would turn around and Albert would follow until Shorty turned again to chase him. People in the camp, watching from a distance, were unsympathetic to Albert. "Someday someone is going to kill that nigger." Bo tried to mediate, and an agreement was reached whereby they would fight without rocks and knives. They wrestled and Albert managed to throw Shorty into a ditch and jumped on him. Bo pulled Albert off and we all walked back to camp together. Although Albert won, he looked shaken up and didn't talk to anyone. He had been bitten on the arm. Shorty conceded that he had lost, but, at the same time, insisted that if he were sober he would have won. (IM)

*   *   *

Cookie told Hart, her husband, that she was ready to go into town but Hart would not leave. She started pulling at him and finally swung a bottle at him. Hart said, "Go on, woman, don't bother me," and continued to ignore her, talking and joking with the men. Cookie kept insisting until he said, "Go on, woman, you're not any good. You can't work." At this point she hit him with a bottle. Blood poured all over the front of his shirt. Then he began beating her and threw her to the ground. Just then, a man from a bottling company drove into the camp and asked why we didn't stop them from fighting. "The cops will come up here and put you all in jail as material witnesses." No one wanted to interfere and stop the fight; even the crew leader refused. He said he didn't want to get involved. While the fighting was going on, Raymond and I had a bottle of Tiger Rose and walked around by the tree where we couldn't see the fight. Raymond said, "I didn't see anything." Meanwhile Cookie got a knife and was swinging it at Hart. She wasn't trying to cut him because if she really wanted to she could have. Hart finally simmered down and they stopped fighting without anyone having interfered. (LP)

*   *   *

The other night Bull slept with some woman in the camp. Her boyfriend heard about it and waited outside until Bull appeared at 5:30 in the morning. He invited Bull to have a drink and they drank together for an hour. Then the man accused Bull of drinking too much. He used the whiskey as an excuse to fight so that people would not think he was fighting over that particular girl, who was known as a prostitute. Bull said he would not take insults and they started to fight, at first with their fists. Meanwhile people were gathering around, and when Bull started to win, the other man pulled out a knife. Bull didn't have the sense to run away and was badly slashed. No one stopped them. Someone eventually called an ambulance because Bull was slashed very badly. He required almost 100 stitches, but the wounds were superficial and he was back to work in a week. (GP)

7

Leisure Time

Life in a migrant labor camp is monotonous: The minimum facilities, isolation, and the limited range of personal contacts contribute to the monotony. There is a great deal of time to be killed—days with no work and times when crops are delayed due to weather or poor planning. Often growers and crew leaders bring crews up earlier than necessary to be sure they are available at the peak of season, and there are slack periods between major crops when work is scarce. Even when there is work, long daily bus rides and extended waiting periods must be endured.

What do people do? They sit around telling stories and jokes, gamble or play other games, listen to the piccolo (jukebox), and particularly on weekends, when they have money, they drink.

Migrants work, play, and live together twenty-four hours a day. Where, for most of us, recreation provides a change in activity as well as in social relationships, there is no alleviating context for the migrants: they must take their leisure with those with whom they work and live.

Pastimes among migrants are literally means for passing time. Few leisure activities are directed to special goals; they merely "kill time." But if time must be killed, leisure time activities have importance beyond their simple recreational value. The fact that games, storytelling, and drinking always take place in a public context suggests their social importance. Leisure provides a means to express individual differences that cannot be expressed in the work context; whereas work norms tend to level all workers, leisure permits individuals to assert themselves. At the same time, leisure activities serve as control devices to sanction idiosyncracy and deviance.

149

Stories and Jokes

The bulk of leisure time is spent sitting around telling stories and jokes. Requiring no money, equipment, or space, storytelling is an important diversion, and good storytellers have considerable prestige. Able to capture an audience by the content of the story and the manner of telling it, they play an important role in the camps. Since stories and jokes are liberally sprinkled through this book where their content has been appropriate, this section is dedicated mainly to analytic material. The role of the storyteller and his techniques are described. One selection provides a content analysis of all jokes and stories collected from the camps studied. Another probes the function of humor beyond its value as entertainment. Some stories suggest the reliance on chance. Others emphasize "beating the system." Since migrants are impotent in actual ways of beating the system, verbal forms, often with a Paul Bunyanesque quality, substitute. Humor becomes a way of releasing tension, permitting temporary detachment from immediate problems and the working out of socially permissible aggression that would be intolerable under other circumstances.

THE STORYTELLER

Bear often tells "down home" stories. He also tells long stories about the familiar romantic triangle. One day, he said, he went over to see this woman. He brought a fifth of alcohol with him. They drank and he screwed her all day. When her husband came home he found her drunk and was real mad. When Bear came by the house later, the husband said, "Hey, boy, come in here." Bear knew the guy carried a pistol. "Well, I braced my feet. One mind was telling me to hit him and the other mind was telling me to run. The mind that told me to run won, so I went charging out the door. He was coming after me with that pistol and I was zigzagging down the road and he was chasing me and chased me all the way to J.C.'s camp. Finally, I stopped and said, 'I ain't running no more,' and I got out my knife. The guy turned around and walked back and I vowed I would get him." The next night, Bear claimed, he looked in the guy's window and the only thing that kept him from shooting was that the husband was holding a baby. A couple of days later he was laying for the husband behind some bushes, but when he caught him the husband said, "Oh, I've forgotten everything. I thought we were friends." So they talked it over and Bear said, "You don't mess with me and I won't mess with you." About a month

Yard scene—storytelling and just talking.   Photo by Paul S. Buck.

later, when Bear was sitting in front of a store, someone came up and put a hand on his shoulder and said, "Hi, Bear, how you doing?" He turned and saw it was the guy and he jumped 5 feet in the air he was so scared. "Boy, if that man was ever fixing to get me that would have been the time—I'm just lucky, he wasn't."

Frank, a crew leader, told a story about a time he and a friend were in a field and heard a rattling noise. They began to wonder if rattlesnakes were around. They walked on and the rattling continued. Finally they fled, whereupon Frank discovered the rattling was simply some liver pills that he kept in his pocket.

"Strong man tales" are popular. Many tales are told about a southern hero called Hercules whose feats of strength are legendary. Bear often talked about "Samson," a man of twenty-seven, who neither "smoked, drank, nor messed with women." He swore he saw Samson pull his truck out of a ditch with one hand.

Storytellers captivate their listeners with physical and verbal techniques. In a story about plowing, Bear imitates a mule by taking the index finger of each hand and putting them up on the side of his head to make mule ears. Big Time was able to control his voice to sound like a screaming woman or a little child. He imitates all kinds of stuttering and includes sound effects in his jokes and stories. He moves around, using his body to explain how things happen. Describing an FBI agent, he got down on one knee in the middle of the room, firing an imaginary gun. Stories are told as if they are personal experiences, as if the storyteller was actually there when it happened.

One rainy day three or four of us were sitting around, and Roy came down and told a story about shooting dice in the tomato field. A guy accused him of cheating and pulled his knife, and Roy had to run across the field. Just then, in the middle of the story, Roy stopped abruptly and said, "I've got to run." We were bored, but the story had revived us. We were all let down when he left the room. (ET)

*   *   *

Cory pointed to Joey, who was visiting from another camp. "Here's a man who can really talk that shit." And Joey began to talk. He could pick up a comment somebody else had made, and for five minutes create a verse from the phrase with every second line rhyming. For a half-hour he went on. He moved from one person to another, picked up something about them, and made a rhyme. "I knew your mother when I was a boy. She was real pretty and she was real coy. She fucked all the guys from the front and the back. And that's why your face is so goddamn black." In response to Whiskers, who tried to challenge Joey, he quipped, "You talk real cool and you talk real fast, but I saw you kiss that white man's ass." This was greeted with loud cheering and laughter. As soon as Joey stopped, Cory goaded him to start all over again. He pointed out the yardman. "He's a funny bastard, he has only one tooth," at which point Joey picked up the idea of one tooth and made a rhyme about the yardman, who loved being the object of Joey's jokes and laughed very hard. "Boy, that Joey, he can really talk that shit. Nobody can talk shit like Joey." (DR)

*   *   *

Slim told us a story of how he was out drinking in a juke 3 miles out of town. He got drunk and decided to walk back. He started out down the road and the cold air sobered him up. As he was walking he saw an irrigation ditch and walked down to get a drink. There was this old dog down there, drinking too, so he walked down, pulled his hat off, and said, "Get out of here, dog. Git. Git." Then, he reached down to get a drink. When he looked back up, "There was this mountain lion looking me in the eye. So I got up, got my hat, ran up to the road, and got in the wind. I got up to 50 in no time at all. I looked back and this mountain lion was just loping behind me, just loping, loping, loping. So, I shifted into another gear and moved it up even faster. And I looked back and that mountain lion was gaining on me." Slim went on about how the lion kept licking his lips. He ran for at least 3 miles until some fellows came by in a pickup truck and stopped to give him a lift. He wanted to get in, but he was unable to stop and he ran another 4 or 5 miles. They finally pulled him into the pickup. He had a knife in his hand and couldn't let go of it until they pried his hand open. When Slim tells stories, they are funny and, no matter how fantastic, they seem almost true. (LP)

THE CONTENT OF HUMOR

Sixty-five jokes and 148 stories were collected in the migrant labor camps and analyzed according to their themes.

Jokes were differentiated from stories if they provoked laughter, though this criterion was, at times, unclear. In classifying the material into themes, the same categories were used for jokes and stories: sex, violence, snakes, other animals, environmental manipulation (getting away with something, escaping a dangerous situation, beating the system in some way), "put-down" (denigrating someone), superhuman feats, "super" (concerning the character of some nonhuman object), and institutions (referring to experiences that occur in any institutional framework such as that of the army or prison).

THEMATIC ANALYSIS OF JOKES AND STORIES*

Theme	Jokes		Stories	
	Number	Percent	Number	Percent
Sex	10	13	21	11
Violence	—	—	28	15
Snakes	2	2	9	5
Other animals	8	11	3	1
Environmental manipulation	—	—	44	24
"Putdown"	37	49	26	14
Superhuman feats	5	7	23	12
"Super"	4	5	10	5
Institutions	—	—	11	6
Other	10	13	13	7
TOTAL	76	100	188	100

* Totals are more than the number of jokes and stories, since some contained several themes.

Note the difference in what is considered appropriate thematic material for each of the two media. The most significant type of joke is the "putdown." In each case, the person put down is someone other than the narrator: a white man (usually the employer) in twelve cases; a Puerto Rican or other outgroup in seven cases; a Negro in eleven cases; and "people" without specification as to group in two cases.

> This white man went under a pine tree and prayed every day for the Lord to kill all niggers—big niggers, little niggers, and medium-sized niggers—to kill them all. So one day this Negro man overheard him and said, "If he comes back out here again tomorrow, I'll fix him." So he climbed the tree the next day and sure enough, the man came back under the same tree and said the same prayer, and when he asked the Lord to kill all big niggers, medium-sized niggers, and little niggers, the Negro in the tree shot a brick down and hit the man in the head with it. Then the man jumped up and said, "Good God, Lord, can't you tell the difference between a nigger and a white man yet?"

> There was a guy who was real drunk once and went into a cracker's [white man's] grocery store down in Georgia and he took a can of dog food off the shelf, thinking it was a can of meat. He gave it to the storekeeper to have the top taken off. The cracker looked around and didn't see any dogs there but he took the top off of the can anyhow, and that nigger was so drunk that he just ate the whole thing right there, said how good it was, and walked out.

In the "putdown" stories, white men are belittled in six instances, outgroups other than whites in one, the opposite sex in four, Negroes in three, and "people" in general in eight cases. Four items are vague in that their point is to build up the Negro, putting down others only by implication.

Environmental manipulation themes are by far the most numerous in the stories. Of the forty-four environmental manipulation themes, thirty-two are told in the first person about personal exploits. A typical example is the man who told a story about how he never got caught when he stole, although one time it was hard to get away since he had taken so much. Like the "putdown" stories, these build up the protagonist, who succeeds, by cunning, in beating the system, manipulating the environment to accomplish something unexpected. Not one joke fit into this category.

Of the twenty-three stories involving superhuman feats, ten were about personal exploits. One man talked about how he jumped a brook 8 feet wide to escape a snake; another told of outrunning a mountain lion. Superhuman stories about other people include the story of an Indian who could see things many miles away, and a German who could load cabbages in shorts in freezing weather when everyone else was cold. (LT)

The Social Functions of Humor

Examples of migrant humor suggest four ways in which humor is related to social conditions. First, there is humor which touches on conditions of the migrant relative to the larger society. It establishes a "we–they" dichotomy recognized as common to the group. Second, some humor relates to concrete situations that migrants can not control. Third, there is teasing or "scoring," which neutralizes strains inherent in social relationships. Fourth, humorous games are used to control deviant individuals in situations where social avoidance is impossible.

"WE—THEY" HUMOR

There was this nigger out in the front of this white woman's house down in Georgia. He was starved; hadn't had anything to eat in three days. He was trying to think of a way to get something to eat. He saw the woman come out on her porch so he said to himself, "I bet if I go up there and start eating the grass she'll give me something to eat." So he ran to the lawn and started chomping on the grass. The woman looked at him and said, "Oh my God, look at that poor nigger out there eating the grass." She said, "Sir, Sir!" The man looked up, "Ma'am?" "When you finish with that short grass there, there is some longer grass in the back if you want it."

Jokes and stories relating to the callousness of white society are often told by older men who have inherited a repertoire of traditional lore and capture their audience with their skill in acting and in voice control. Listeners participate by commenting and by adding stories of their own. It is common to hear the punch line of a joke repeated for several days.

Many jokes and stories of this type have a similar pattern. Situations are developed where the white man's words or actions backfire and he becomes the fool. Or a situation is constructed to appear plausible, but is then twisted to highlight the absurdity of the white person's response. Many jokes are variants of the "Old Marster" folktales. The black man is characterized as clever and crafty, outwitting the white man, making him appear ludicrous in the end.

In such jokes, a dichotomy is established between "we" and "they." Harassment backfires and the last laugh is at the expense of the oppressor. Like many "underdog" stories, humor of this type often assumes Aesopian form.

A rat fell into a whiskey barrel and was swimming around until a cat spotted him. "Hey brother cat, get me out of here." The cat said, "Why should I get you out? I don't have time." "Look, brother cat, you get me out of this whiskey and I'll let you eat me up." The cat agreed, got him out of the barrel, and put him aside to get the whiskey out of him. Finally, the cat said, "Okay, come over and live up to your promise to let me eat you up." Brother rat said, "You must be kidding." "Brother rat, aren't you a man of your word, you said you'd let me eat you up." The rat responded, "Brother cat, a man might say anything when he's in whiskey."

Migrants recognize and appreciate the humor out of common sensitivity to prevailing attitudes. In case there is any ambiguity, many storytellers employ the names of individuals who are present—a technique that explicitly brings to the surface the relation between personal and collective experience.

SITUATIONAL HUMOR

Humor relieves uncomfortable situations by permitting an expression of dissatisfaction that could never be made seriously. The situations most evocative of this form of humor revolve around work. Migrants are often forced to work in fields that have already been picked over, a slow and discouraging proposition for those paid piecework. The system of dependence however, precludes serious protest.

> Do you think I'm going to pick here most of the morning and then break my day in half and go up there to try and work too? If you ever bring me out in another field like this, you son of a bitch, I'll cut your goddamn throat!

This was expressed to a field man with clear indication that it was to be understood as joking. He, as well as other migrants within earshot, laughed and continued to work. The humor in this situation channeled dissatisfaction through a harmless outlet and helped to make bearable a situation that could not be avoided.

Migrants are unfamiliar with the northern environment, both culturally and geographically. In strange surroundings, vague fears and anxieties are easily aroused and these become a source of spontaneous humor. The exaggeration of danger allays anxieties by expressing that threat in a form that is patently ludicrous. This technique is often used in the fields, for example, in stories relating to snakes.

Eating is a perpetual source of banter. Persons who eat a lot are the butt of practical jokes: a plate of food is sometimes snatched away when its owner temporarily leaves the table. Exaggerated stories of long periods of hunger are appreciated with laughter. Hunger is a situation well known to many migrants. In some cases crew leaders use the threat of hunger to force productivity; a man who does not work runs the risk of being denied food on credit. Eating as a specific source of anxiety becomes a subject of raillery.

Humor as control

Who does he think he is? Why does he come over here anyway? He must think he's the boss over the entire field. Why doesn't he go back where he belongs? You give people a pencil and they think they own the entire world.

Reece, whose authority was ambiguous, had told a few people to work faster. Comments made in a joking manner enabled the group to handle authority and yet avoid antagonism.

It is intrinsically difficult in a migrant labor camp to avoid conflict. The limited setting precludes keeping peace through physical or social avoidance. One way to dissipate hostility is to sanction mutual disrespect if it is carried on in a playful context. Practical jokes, popular among adults, serve this purpose. A man substitutes water for wine in his wife's bottle when she leaves to get him some food. The wino's shoe laces are tied when he is sleeping and then he is aroused with cold water.

Such pranks impose physical or psychological indignity on the victim, often a wino, a homosexual, or an exceptionally naive person. They adjust relationships, in some cases reinforcing the pecking order, in others preventing any one person from asserting authority over others.

Many crew leaders use a humorous supervisory style, particularly at times when conditions are poor and people are upset. In the case of one particularly exploitive crew leader, a bantering, humorous style—utilized judiciously in moments of tension—reinforced control over the crew. Mock punishment is a technique used primarily by crew leaders to exercise authority. A crew leader pulled off his belt and, swinging it around his head, chased a migrant who was not working. The migrant bowed as if to a king and went to work, mumbling audibly, "A man can't get a little rest around here, what kind of a life is this?" It was known that this crew leader never actually beat his men so the situation was laughable; yet the element of threat held real meaning, since force is often a serious means of asserting authority.

Joking may substitute for fighting. For example, two individuals once had an unresolved fight, but have since kept peace by a mutual exchange of banter in public.

"Come over here and I'll give you a dose of what I gave you back you know when." "You're lucky that knife was grabbed away because I was about to kill you." "You knew your days were almost over." "Your teeth were chattering."

Laughter allowed the participants to withdraw without losing face. There is a great deal of overlap between this humor, used primarily where people jockey to assert their own position with respect to others, and the following type, used to control specific acts regarded as deviant.

HUMOR AND INDIVIDUAL DEVIANCE

Larry commented while working, "This isn't a bad field," to which Pinochle replied, "Shakespeare said, 'All good things come to those who wait.'" Tussy noted, "Well, I've been waiting a god damned long time and nothin's come to me yet." Larry then baited Tussy, "All the damn wine you drink, if something good did come to you, you wouldn't see it anyways." Tussy stopped and said very properly, "I'm sorry, sir, but I don't allow myself to engage in conversation with a white man." At this, the entire group broke up into laughter. Larry said something about Tussy's mother: "For all you know I may be your daddy. If you don't believe me, why don't you go and ask your mother." Tussy again repeated, "I'm sorry, I can't talk to you. I don't talk to crackers." Everyone around was laughing and started to get on Larry, calling him a white man. At this point, Tussy, compounding his advantage said, "When the crew leader gets here I'm going to ask him to kick this white man out. I don't believe in working in a crew with white men, especially white men who don't do any damn thing." Larry couldn't get out of the situation. He would attack back at Tussy. "So what! Your mammy works down there in that packing house on the muck and you know the salesman, the milkman, and all those men who go by . . . most of them are white aren't they? What do you think your mammy does? How do you think she pays her bills?" Tussy switched to this theme. "Your mammy sold herself in the corn fields for a shot of whiskey." "So what, I slept with your mother and for all you know I could be your father." Larry also accused Tussy of sleeping with Marilyn Monroe, the homosexual, but Tussy had clearly won the game since the group continued to attack Larry as a white man.

In this example of the verbal game called "the dozens," colorfully phrased aggressive insults are exchanged until there is no further effective rejoinder or until the situation explodes into violence. The game is always played for an audience, which acts as a sounding board, the response determining subsequent patterns of expression. The observers respond with laughter, increasing with the biting quality of the insults. Drunkenness, homosexuality, age, physical characteristics, dubious parentage, and sexual activities of mothers and girlfriends are all fair subjects to employ in "the dozens."

The game, as observed in the camps, has several objectives. It helps to establish the pecking order by enhancing the personal prestige of individuals skilled in creating entertaining insults. And it is a means to bring group pressure on individuals who jeopardize the group. This becomes clear in observing the context in which the game is played and the kinds of incidents that precipitate it. If a person brags or "mouths off," he becomes the victim of the first jab. If he then scores back as a defense, the game is under way. A person who works conspicuously faster or slower than the rest of his crew is "scored," for it is understood to be better if individuals do not stand out. A person who asserts his authority or acts in an aggressive manner becomes a target, but only if he clearly carries no legitimate authority. A person who changes his style of speech is regarded as "putting on airs." Others will mock him for "talking pretty like a cracker." Vigorous scoring is applied to those who act "niggerish," or in a manner that will reinforce the white world's image of the Negro.

> The only thing you know is to get behind that mule when the man says go. You get up early and say, "Good morning, boss." He says, "Get to work!" When lunch time comes you say, "Lunch time, boss." He says, "Hurry back!" When it's time to knock off, you say, "Quitting time, boss." He says, "Be there early in the morning!" And that's the only thing you know. That's the only way you know how to come on to people. Other than that you don't know a damn thing.

Humorous techniques of control are utilized so often in the migrant labor camp that they have a ritual quality. As a form of expressive behavior, humor in migrant labor camps is shaped by the concerns generated by social conditions. Jokes provide a necessary release, a means of collective confrontation with these conditions. They are a device to adjust precarious relationships and to control those who deviate from the expectations of the group. Humor thus helps to define the limits of appropriate social behavior. (DN)

Games

The games popular among migrants reflect many aspects of the migrant social system. Many involve forms of gambling that are more dependent on luck than skill. Craps is a regular pastime, and card games that depend on the fall of the cards, such as Pokina or Georgia Skin, are popular. Numbers runners also find business in the camps on payday.

Gambling is not solely dependent on luck, however. In some cases, highly developed skills are manifest, particularly in the speed of playing; in other cases, attempts are made to control fortune through supernatural beliefs. Cheating is often expected and seldom severely punished except when gambling for high stakes. Those who "beat the system" and get away with it are admired. On the whole, however, the games that predominate are consistent with migrant experience, where strategy and planning are largely irrelevant. The popularity of games based on chance are thus related to personal beliefs and attitudes discussed in Chapter 5.

Many games such as baseball are popular but uncommon because of space limitations or equipment shortages. When social workers and others made such equipment available in a few camps, these sports were taken up enthusiastically. One striking feature of such games is their impact on adjusting relationships and redistributing prestige, suggesting the need for more such adjustive mechanisms in migrant camps.

The crap game involved five people and lasted from six o'clock, when we got back from work, until midnight. Among all of them, there was only about ten dollars exchanged during the whole evening. In the end, nobody won anything, nobody lost anything; however, it was played with great passion. (GP)

*   *   *

Several young people, ages between fifteen and twenty, were playing craps on a blanket. Joe was winning regularly. He claimed he was just lucky and there was no skill involved. He won about thirty dollars. I later learned how the game was played. Bets were made, as in ordinary craps, on whether or not a person makes a point; however, the dice are shot only once. If a point is made, the opponent wins. If a seven or eleven comes up, the shooter wins. On the blanket the dice can be arranged so that with a little skill a seven or eleven will come up most of the time. You line up the six on one die with the one on the other, and a four and three and a five and two showing on the side faces. The dice are held in one hand, loosely, so that when shaken they will sound like they are rattling, but actually they do not rotate. They are rolled simultaneously across the blanket so they roll at the same speed. With skill, the results are somewhat controlled. Joe had learned this skill and was in the process of cleaning out three people. He won between three and five dollars from everyone with whom he played. Later he had difficulty finding people to play with him.

Another time, when I was in the cookhouse, I found Joe there with a pot and his dice. He filled the pot with water and placed it on the stove to boil the dice. Several people were in the cookhouse, but no one commented on what he was doing. After the dice boiled, he left the cookhouse to find a pair of pliers. He returned a few minutes later and put the dice back on the stove to boil again for three or four minutes. Joe put the dice between a pair of pliers, squeezed them and flattened the dice; then, he threw them against the wall, saying either five or deuce. These two sides were the sides that were flattened and they came up each time. The holes were no longer round and the shape of the dice was obviously altered, but Joe thought no one would notice for the same reason that cheating in the blanket game was not noticed. He felt that the only people who would play against him with such dice were chumps and were bound to be fooled. (CL)

*   *   *

Junior, Bear, and Roy were shooting craps. Every time he rolled a ten, Junior said, "Tennessee Tom born half-white and half-freeborn." For an ace, "Eddie Ross walked a fast hoss." Before playing he announced, "All right, line up all you women, line up, cause here I go," or, "All right, all you whores, you start screwing cause here I go." Junior asked me to put some money down and I said, "I ain't got enough to play these kind of games." "Oh, shoot, man, you can win, anybody can win. Come on, baby." (ET)

*   *   *

Sam uses roots for gambling. "I went to this rootman and he gave me some little beans that I put in my pocket. I played some Georgia Skin and every time I would get ready to choose a card, if it was not the right card the beans would kind of nudge me in my pocket. I walked away with about four hundred dollars that night, using the beans." (HH)

*   *   *

Bean, Geech and his wife, and Florida Joe were playing cards in the juke. Bean did something strange to the deck. Without looking at the cards he took the card from the top with his thumb and forefinger; at the same time he took a card from the bottom. He pulled them both off the deck and placed them on top of each other. He did this to the entire deck. People remarked how he was setting up the deck so that he and his partner could get all the good cards later. (DR)

*   *   *

Saturday night, five different people, two women and three men, appeared at different times during the evening to sell numbers. I decided to try my hand at it. That night, after I got paid, I bought some numbers from a woman who had been there before. She asked me what number I wanted. I picked 51 and she asked if I wanted to "back it up." "To back it up" means to also take the number backwards. I agreed and took 51 and 15. I could put in anything from 25 cents up, so I put a dollar on each number. The crew leader bought numbers with all five people who came in to sell them. There were also several others in the camp who bought different numbers from different sellers. The numbers people know when everyone is paid off and they come around each week at just the right time. (GW)

*   *   *

People talk about numbers constantly; which numbers came in, how they just missed, what they'll play next time. In the kitchen is a book that has numbers with little pictures next to them, suggesting certain feelings on certain days. There is a number that is to be played depending on how each individual feels. Many people select their numbers this way. Yesterday someone bought a copy of the *Pittsburgh Courier* and was going through it with a magnifying glass. There are supposed to be numbers in this paper that indicate the winners. I haven't heard of anyone winning as yet. (LR)

*   *   *

I had been watching the fellows play checkers and noticed they had, what seems to me, an odd style. They move very quickly, almost before their opponent puts his checker down.

I decided to play a game with the camp champion. He was going to give me odds, so he bet me two dollars to my dollar that he could take me three straight games. I didn't believe he could beat me three straight games; in fact, I didn't think he could beat me at all, so I agreed. As I sat down, he moved a piece immediately. I sat there and thought about my move. There were a group of spectators and they all urged me on. "What are you doing? Are you going to play? Come on, come on. What are you doing, man?" I said, "Look, when he moves, he moves; when I move, I'll make my move—now don't bother me." Then someone said, "The cat's trying to fuck over you, man." And I said, "What are you talking about? It's my move, let me move." Then, my partner said, "If you're gonna move, move. Now we are playing for money. Either you're going to play right, or you don't play at all." I replied, "Well, I'll take my money and get up." "No, all right, we'll play your way. Go on, I'll beat you at any rate no matter how you play." So I took my time on my moves, and he moved in a split second after I moved. I eventually began to move faster because there were eight guys around watching the game and urging me each time not to take so long. He beat me in three straight games and I lost my dollar.

After the three games he wanted to play me one more. This time he said that if I got one man into the king's row I would win. He took the money he had won from me plus his two dollars. He put three dollars up and wanted me to put up 50 cents. I figured that it was a good bet, but he kept me so tied up, I couldn't get a man over the line at all, let alone into the king's row. By the time we were finished, there were fifteen people watching us. Beaten so badly after taking so much time about moving, I am teased as the worst checker player in the camp. (GP)

*   *   *

A basketball game of "21" was played between Moe and Albert. Moe, from the beginning of the game, teased Albert that he didn't have a chance in the world of beating him, "The only way that you're going to beat me is by getting the outside shots. You have no chance of driving at all." Moe began with a very strong lead and then let up quite a bit to show that even by playing sloppily he could win. Albert tried to play very hard—in fact, he tried so hard he played badly, being very tense during the whole game. Finally Moe became lax and Albert won. Winning the game, however, was little satisfaction because Moe continued to tease him for being a bad player. Even after having lost, he effectively used the game to put Albert down. (IM)

*   *   *

A social worker brought in some baseball equipment one night, and after that we played every day. Not only were those who played involved, but almost every man, woman, and child in the camp either coached, played, or cheered. It soon became apparent that baseball was more than a brief diversion, it became an important feature of camp life.

When the social worker told us we might play a team from the Puerto Rican camp, the reaction was enthusiastic. There was a big, grassy field to the left of the barracks used for a baseball diamond. Practice was held every evening. We played the Puerto Ricans and lost, but the enthusiasm grew, and avenging this loss became a matter of primary importance. Frank, the crew leader, surprised us by building a backstop and benches and by having the grass mowed on the field. We practiced every night after a long day's work, and the older men and women came over to watch. The girls decided to form a softball team of their own and soon everyone was involved.

Baseball provided a break from boredom and satisfactions that were not forthcoming from other activities. Baseball also offered a chance to acquire prestige, often for those who could not acquire prestige in other activities. For example, one of the winos came to the field to play. Everyone laughed, but, as soon as he showed he could play fairly well, jeers ceased and feelings toward him changed. On the other hand, James should have been a good ballplayer. He had experience, he practiced a lot, and was an excellent athlete; but when it came to the games he rarely played well. James was generally resented. He was the kind of person who talked a great deal about his feats, but was more an object of scorn than praise. His awareness of his status seems to have affected his performance, which in turn reinforced his position. Checker Bill was respected, well liked, and a good picker. When baseball was initiated, he decided he would like to pitch, but he caused the team to lose. People criticized his performance and excluded him. He and

James became good friends and eventually both lost interest in baseball.

Finally, baseball affected the solidarity of the crew with respect to the Puerto Ricans in the nearby camp. Relations between the black migrants and the Puerto Ricans were strained. The latter would come to the camp with fancy cars and money and take the women out to "show them a good time." The migrants resented this. They made fun of the Puerto Ricans—the way they talked and the way they dressed. They tried to goad them into fights but rarely succeeded. The baseball diamond became the center of competition. The desire to beat the Puerto Ricans led to a solidarity that was not evident in any other activity. (LR)

The Piccolo

In most camps, there are "piccolos" (jukeboxes) operated through arrangements between the crew leader and a concessionaire. They contain popular records, including a selection of soul music. The piccolo is played continually during weekends when money is available to feed it, and occasionally during the week. Despite the variety available, there is considerable repetition in the selection of records. The same few numbers are played repeatedly, and the choice often reflects the mood in the camp at a particular time. What is most striking, however, is the noise level. Music is usually played at a deafening pitch, precluding conversation. It was not by accident that official-looking visitors to the camp were often led close to the jukebox, where they had to compete with the music to make their business known.

After dinner, Big Time dominated the conversation, telling stories. The kids were outside playing a game with rocks. Upstairs in Anna's room the radio was playing and downstairs the piccolo was blasting away. The piccolo has many soul songs: "How Sweet It Is to Be Loved by You," "Come to Me Baby," "Respect," and other hit numbers by Aretha Franklin, Sam and Dave, and Wilson Pickett. The content of almost all piccolo songs is "love," "lost love," "women who have run out," "come back baby," "please don't go," "it will be better when you come back," and "things will work out."

Spaceman, like most of the older people, usually selects blues-type songs: "Baby, You Don't Have to Go," "I Gave You All My Money and My Cadillac Too, Now You're Running Off and Leaving Me Behind, That's a Pretty Rotten Thing to Do."

In the juke, playing cards and listening to the "piccolo."
Photo by Paul S. Buck.

After he finished some stories, Big Time played a song by Sam and the Shams on the jukebox. He played it over many times, and pointed out to people that Sam is white, but that he must have lived around colored people. "He really knows how to go." Everyone seemed to enjoy the song and, as it played over and over again, remarked that it was really amazing that Sam could be white. The piccolo is played in the morning when we are waiting to go out to work, in the evening before dinner, and right after dinner before TV is turned on. On the weekend it is played continually.

Songs sung in the field are similar to the choices made on the piccolo. Tee makes up his own songs to the piccolo melodies to sing to himself, putting together lines from very sad songs about how much he loves his baby and he can't get to her: "Baby, I miss you, I haven't seen you so long, Oh, when I get to you, the touch of your hand, Oh, you set me on fire, Oh, I wish I could see you again."

Ann likes spirituals and sings them in the field along with her daughter. They sing a first verse and the chorus of a song, which they will repeat five or six times, occasionally trying to make up new words that fit into the melody to substitute for those they do not know. People usually sing individually, although occasionally groups will join in together. When they do, it is ragged, and there is no attempt to make harmony. (MR)

*   *   *

Everyone has a favorite song on the jukebox that he plays repeatedly. Junior's is "Maggie's Farm," Bean's is "Laid on the Water," and Nate's are "I Don't Need No Doctor" and "We're Going to Make It." James plays the same song over and over again, "Keep a Light in the Window 'Til I Come Home." One night I went to bed around 10:30 and was about to doze off when I heard "Keep a Light in the Window . . ." played five times straight. (ET)

*   *   *

There is a change in the mood of the music played on the piccolo at different times. When there is work and a lot of money around, selections are fast and peppy. There is always music on and everybody dances. In contrast, when there is no work, the music is played less frequently and is different in character.

At about 9:30, after a day with no work, the juke was empty except for some winos. I walked to the side entrance where a group had gathered. They had one of these portable, battery-operated record players and were playing old blues records. Joe was sitting there very depressed. He said he missed his son in Florida. Everyone was listening to the music quietly. They occasionally referred to old times in Florida and to their families and talked about the old soul singers, the old blues. (LR)

*   *   *

Sonny was working on the next tree and had his radio with him. The radio was blasting and he remarked that there weren't any good stations in the north like there were in Florida. "They don't have anybody like Rocking Big Daddy." A lot of the songs were psychedelic music. Then, James Brown came on. James, who was far away, called to Sonny to turn the volume up even louder. He stopped picking and a few other people came over to listen to the James Brown song and they danced right in the field. Pops called over, "That's my man, that's my man." As soon as the song stopped they walked back and started picking again. (LR)

*   *   *

To the left of the kitchen is an open shed—a platform with a roof on it. It is used as a dance floor. There is a piccolo there that only works on quarters. It just eats up dimes. This causes a bit of hardship; several times a day somebody is trying to poke a hanger through the coin slot to retrieve his dime. There is some terrific dancing, and even the tiniest kids dance. The only men who regularly dance are the bachelors and those who have left their wives in the south. When these men dance, they sometimes dance alone or in a group of men. Partners are not required. Good dancing is admired. "How that little kid can jive." (DR)

*   *   *

While we were sitting out on the back stoop, James took the lower part of a broom and unwound the wire from it. He went into the hallway and stretched this wire out from the top to the bottom of the wall. He put a can at the top and a flask bottle at the bottom end. Then he started playing it, using a knife as a pick and a glass as a fret. This creates a buzzing steel sound—almost like a steel guitar. He plays blues with good rhythm and he has a very pleasing voice but can only do about three songs, which he plays over and over again. He learned the songs when he was doing time in jail. Later James was showing somebody else how to play the "one-string," which is what everybody calls his instrument. The guy was kneeling beside James, looking at him admiringly. "God gave you that gift," he said. James, as well as his instrument, is now called "One-string." (DG)

Wining Up

Drinking is a major pastime. Despite this, many migrants regard drinking with ambivalence or hostility. When sober, they will denounce alcohol, but those who criticize alcohol when they are sober, may, on weekends, become drunk to the point of incoherence.

Alcohol, like so many other features of their life, brings relationships between migrants to a common level. Alcohol is not something to be hoarded; it is to be shared among friends and acquaintances. A person earning more than others has his earnings redistributed in this way, for those with money cannot drink alone.

Excessive drinking has other implications. Alcohol permits deviant behavior in contexts that might otherwise be unacceptable. Being drunk is both an escape and an alibi for changed behavior; this becomes extremely important where people cannot seek change by manipulating personal associations. This underlies the tolerance shown by migrants for the "winos" who are a conspicuous group in most camps. While they are often small in number, the limited confines of the camp inflate their importance in establishing an atmosphere. Migrants regard winos as harmless: like homosexuals, they are disdained and the butt of teasing, yet they are accepted and tolerated. Where a sizable number of winos are found in a single camp, they form a distinct and isolated group.

As far as the outside world is concerned—to the extent that outsiders come into the camps—it is the winos that constitute the most significant social group. And alcoholism is viewed as the predominant problem by migrants themselves. Heavy consumption of alcohol is a fact, yet it is overexaggerated. Not only do most migrants have insufficient funds for serious alcoholism, but the fact that they must, with their relatively meager incomes, pay double the retail price to buy their alcohol limits the amount of drinking.

Today I went to town with George. He bought six cans of soda, four cans of fruit juice, seven six-packs of beer, and a pint of Scotch. I jokingly asked, "You sure don't want to run out of that stuff, do you?" He replied, "When you've been around here another two weeks, you'll be living on this stuff too." (LD)

*   *   *

This Saturday drinking started early. The old men hit the bottle first, and by 9:00 A.M. beer and wine were flowing freely. Suddenly, Willy Wine, who had been drinking all morning, keeled over on the floor. No one did anything; no one moved. I finally went over and picked him up, put him over my shoulder, and carried him to his room. Last week Red vowed he would not touch a drop of alcohol for two months, but he was dead drunk this weekend. Sam also vowed to turn over a new leaf. He had learned the "recklessness of his ways" and was going to cut down on drinking. People were talking about what they liked to do when they were drunk. Red said when he's drunk, he likes to dance. James said he likes to talk—a fact that is evident. Sam said he could drink at any time of day. Wine is better at night, but sometimes in the morning, when you have a bad hangover, a shot gives you a real kick so you can go to work. (LR)

*   *   *

"Man, you know I drink whiskey once in a while though my old lady doesn't like for me to drink, but I'll never touch wine because it makes you crazy in the head." When Junior said this, Bear told a joke about a wino who went to the doctor one day and the doctor said, "Man, if you don't stop drinking that wine, you'll lose your mind," and the wino said, "Really?" The doc repeated, "You've got to stop or you'll lose your mind."

The wino looked at the doc and said, "Come here wine, go away mind, don't take no mind to drink no wine." (ET)

*   *   *

I stopped by Raymond's house to get a bottle of wine and took it back to the room, where I found Wolf asleep. I knocked on the door and he got up, and we passed the bottle back and forth until it was gone. Then Wolf pulled up his mattress and said, "I had forgotten this," and he brought out a wine bottle that was underneath the mattress.

Wolf keeps wine, his onion knife, and a can of insect killer under his mattress. He also has a coat there, raising the mattress to make a pillow. He sleeps under only one blanket because he has given me the other. We passed the bottle back and forth and he pointed to three empty Tiger Rose bottles, on the floor, which he had already finished. Of the $28.00 he had received Saturday he had spent $23.00 on wine. This left him enough to carry him through until next week. He usually doesn't work if he has enough money to buy wine, tobacco, and a little something to eat. Last Saturday he told me he didn't have money to buy any groceries. "I can't stop smoking and I can't stop drinking so I'm gonna stop living." In about thirty minutes he started coughing and heaving. Finally, he vomited in a little can he keeps near his bed. After that he got back into bed and both of us went to sleep. (LP)

*   *   *

Every person in the camp has discussed the evils of drinking. They say alcohol is terrible and that bad things happen when you drink. On Friday night, however, after we are paid, everyone, except for one family, gets drunk. Junior, an easygoing guy, drank two fifths of rye on Friday evening. Saturday morning he was up early to go to town. He was drinking wine when I saw him there. Later, back in the camp, he continued drinking. He was so drunk he knocked over a case of beer bottles in Nate's room and broke them all. Nate was not angry. "You're drunk now. Go in and sleep it off and we'll talk about your paying back later." Nate had all this beer in his room because he was going to start selling it, but he decided after this accident that it wasn't worth having the problem of these guys being drunk on him. (HG)

*   *   *

Nappychin asked me to bring him some wine. I refused, but he got it elsewhere. The crew leader told me he was drunk all the time because "he's not very stable and that's the only way he can make it." Pops is about fifty-five and has been coming to the camp for eighteen years. He is a good worker but was laid off the job at the fertilizer plant last week and has been drinking ever since. When he's drunk, he talks all the time. Sometimes he sits and laughs and curses at himself. Aaron came to work after having wine for breakfast—so weak that he fell. He keeps promising not to drink but also says, "I like my wine more than I like my food." He told me about a time he spent $80.00 to get rid of a hangover. "I sat down and drank for three days straight and then had to drink more to get rid of the hangover." It cost so much because "you have to buy for everyone else too." Wednesday night, Joe, one of the winos, was walking around drinking from a large bottle of soda. He couldn't afford wine or whiskey any more so he had mixed rubbing alcohol with orange soda. "Aren't you afraid of what it will do to you?" "No, Nappychin drinks it all the time. Why don't you take a drink?" (GP)

*　　　　*　　　　*

Late in the morning, Shelly, a ten-year-old boy, and I walked to the store down the road. On the way back, we were talking about what he wanted to be when he grew up. As we passed the Maple Camp, across the street from the camp where we lived, he told me how he didn't want to grow up and be like the people there. He told me that they were all a bunch of winos, which is why they don't pick as well as we do. "They're never sober enough to even get out to the fields; man, they can't pick worth a damn." He told me he had never tasted any booze and never would. He wanted to be a preacher or a policeman, preferably the former, and thought that wine was very bad. He said that the kids in his class down south had already begun drinking but he wouldn't because he wanted to keep getting good grades. (AK)

*　　　　*　　　　*

Of the eighty-five migrants in my camp, twelve were referred to as "winos." Most of them had to have alcohol every day. Shock, who had fits after a three-day drinking bout, had to be taken to the hospital, where the doctor ordered him not to drink for a while. He avoided liquor for about a week. James was considered a wino, but he was drunk only on weekends. During the week he worked regularly and drank only a beer or two at night. It is not only how much a person drinks, but what he drinks and how he behaves when drunk that defines his position as a wino. Ben, Bertha, and Aaron all drank as much and as regularly as the winos, but they were not considered winos by the rest of the crew. They usually drank Seagrams Seven whiskey, or beer, while the winos drank cheap wine like Tiger Rose or King's Port. They also had a different style of drinking. The winos drank anywhere. When the bus stopped at a liquor store, they would buy wine and start drinking immediately. Others were more discreet. They drank from cups instead of bottles, and only in the camp or in bars. The winos were conspicuous when drunk. Shock and J.C. would come to the juke and dance wildly. When James was drunk he would stand out in the yard and preach a sermon.

Most of the winos worked in order to drink. Weakened by liquor, they earned just enough to pay off their debts and to provide themselves with more wine. They were the poorest people in camp. Their clothes and shoes were ragged and they seldom changed when they got home from the field.

The winos were the older members of the crew. Their average age was fifty-four and only one was less than forty-five years old. They were all male and single, although several claimed to have wives in Florida. They were physically isolated from the rest of the camp, all living in the two bullpens; and since each bullpen had its own cooking and food storage facilities, they did not mix with the rest of the crew during mealtimes. This separation was partially maintained even during the working day. They usually sat together, talking and sometimes drinking, in the back of the bus, and picked together in the fields.

Since the migrant labor camp is small, there is bound to be contact between all groups if only because of physical proximity. The winos were teased and their inferior status emphasized. On the way to the fields, Honey kidded Shock about what a poor picker he was. Shock just laughed and admitted she could pick sixteen before he could pick six. Then Honey said she could beat him in other ways as well. He made a move, pretending to come forward on the bus to attack her, but she just laughed and said, "If you try it, I'll knock the rest of your teeth out."

Buying beer and wine involved problems for the winos that reaffirmed their low status. J.C. and Clinton were the only two winos who had a steady source of income, since they were both receiving Social Security. As a result, the crew leader, who sold wine, was ready to extend credit to them. The other winos were forced to wheedle credit and were usually refused unless they had cash. They borrowed from one another, but occasionally went to other members of the crew. Paul, a fifty-year-old wino, came into the juke one evening and tried to borrow 25 cents from several men. When he failed, he went over to Honey and played with her grandchild. He soon asked Honey for a quarter, but she also turned him down. Finally he went over to the crap game and tried to scrounge a quarter by telling Reece he was bringing him good luck. Reece pointed out that he had just lost a hand, and everybody laughed.

Longo, one of the most frequent nonwino visitors to the bullpen, enjoyed talking to the winos, but he baited them. He told them their drinking was convincing the farmers that human bean pickers were no good. Because of them, all the workers would soon he replaced by bean-picking machines. He told Clinton that the "shit he drinks" has made him lose his sexual powers.

The winos were aware of their low status. When asked his home address, J.C. replied, "My address is the sticks." Clinton once said, "A man with a suit thinks he's better than me, just because my pants are dirty and his pants are clean. But God doesn't judge that way." One day, a state inspector went through the camp and found fault with many things, but found nothing wrong in the bullpen. For weeks Geech repeatedly made the point that the tables had been turned. "They think we're no good, but there ain't nothing wrong with us—it's them aristocrats up there—those millionaires on Wall Street (meaning the rest of the camp) that are messing up."

In the face of camp disapproval, the winos remained close to each other. James dramatically told Ben how much he loved him because he was always willing to share his liquor. Shock and Bull made up stories about their adventures together in the west. Clinton talked about sharing, "One good turn deserves another and if a man lends you a dime, you should lend him a dollar if he asks you." Despite claims of loyalty and generosity, however, the winos kept track of their few personal possessions and did not trust one another. No one kept food in the communal refrigerator in the corridor, fearing that it would be stolen, and, when they were not drinking, they hid their wine. (DG)

8

It Cut My Spirit
and I Can't Pick a Thing

A migrant labor crew operates as a unit both at work and in the camp, and each situation affects the other. Although the specific conditions of work described in Chapter 4 are reflected in productivity and work attitudes, other aspects of crew life are equally relevant. For example, the leveling tendency evident in the camps carries over to work, where supervision is resented and unusual productivity is suspect. Even more striking is the erratic and disorganized condition of the system as a whole, which is reflected in extraordinary fluctuations in productivity. Athough attitudes and morale affect productivity in every occupation, they are particularly salient in this group, where piecework is an individual enterprise and there is little effective supervision and control. It is the "spirit," highly sensitive to conditions in any given situation, that affects productivity. Just as conditions fluctuate from day to day, so does the "spirit." Widely divergent tendencies are therefore evident; some people manifest considerable pride in their skills, others pick out of necessity. Attitudes also fluctuate in the same person at different times. High productivity will be used under some conditions to demonstrate superiority in much the same way as rapping or teasing; on other days, the same individuals are apathetic, picking the minimum required for their sustenance. When crops were poor, when brought to fields for second pickings, when long periods of time were wasted, workers not only showed little interest in work, but actively discouraged others from picking.

Attitudes exist, however, that are potentially supportive of productivity. These attitudes are diffuse, for there are few camps where this potentiality is systematically encouraged. Work is viewed by the migrant as a balance between the cost of working—the submission to an unpleasant routine—and the potential reward—wages. This balance is perceived as precarious and, when earnings will be predictably poor, it is not considered worth the trouble to work. Whatever conditions may be, they are usually accepted fatalistically. Poor conditions "cut the spirit" but "some seasons are bad." There are hopes of regular work, but no expectations. Unable to alter conditions, migrants bend with them, extending themselves only when prospects of success seem likely.

The Image of Work

Beyond the momentary satisfaction of a good day, there is a general sense of shame and lack of satisfaction in migrant work. This is graphically expressed with reference to work in general or, more specifically, to the northern context. Migrant work is described as "dirty work," as a "bad deal." Migrants refer to themselves as unessential or easily replaceable. Yet, some manifest pride in their skills and their ability to take the rigors and hazards of work in stride.

I got up early in the morning and found there was no work, so Tina and I sat on the steps and she told me the story of how migrant labor began. Some time ago everyone, north and south, used to grow string beans and corn, and a few greens and maybe a few onions and things like that, in a garden outside their own homes. She said, "There were no people like us traveling up and down the road to pick beans or corn. Everybody had their own gardens. Life was good then; you would have your own pig, you would kill it and smoke it, and you would have the food from your garden. You could live a good life that was much better than the type of life we are living now." She went on to explain how somebody got the idea about making money, so they started growing beans and corn in large plots. Then they needed people to pick it. Once they got people like us to do the picking, they could sell food at prices cheaper than we could grow it ourselves. "So, then what happened was that we decided it would be better to go to work and earn money so we would have more time. So, we would go out and work for a little while to earn more money to buy the beans and corn that we no longer planted." But then, she said, "They pulled a dirty trick. Once they got us out there working a little bit, then they had us working for other, bigger things. We started working longer hours so we could get more and more things. Pretty soon, we didn't have any garden at all. Pretty soon, we didn't have a little pig, and they just got people working and buying. Now we get the same things that we had before, only we must work longer and we don't have as much and we don't enjoy it as much. That's how the gardens became farms and how we began working the season." (GP)

*   *   *

People often ask each other, "What are you doing here?" or "Why did you fall for this?" "Why did you come up here on the season; can't you do better in Florida?" No one seems to have an answer to these questions. Several people quit good jobs when somebody told them they could make money on the season. "That's okay for the first time but you keep falling for this stuff year after year." Lamb has been up every year for the past seven years, and each year he knows it's no good but he just can't stop coming. Last year he swore that it was his last season, but he ended up here again. He advised me, "You do better to just stay in one place. This traveling stuff is no good. You can't predict the weather, you can't predict what's going to happen. You can't predict the good days or the bad days, so nine times out of ten you end up with some kind of complication and no work. You do pretty good for a week and then have no work at all so it just doesn't add up to anything." He told me about Florida, where "you get a steady job and a pretty good break because you work all the time. It gets hot, it rains but it doesn't rain that long for a person not to go right back to the field within a couple of hours or so. Here it rains almost all the time. You don't get a chance sometimes to work no more than two days out of the whole week, and then you're working in the rain when you do that." (GW)

*   *   *

Joe was talking to an old lady. He said he had fourteen kids and he wanted to raise them and take care of them as best he could—just like everyone else. He hated to see the people doing this kind of work. "This isn't a man's work. This is just too dirty. I'd like to see people doing other work —not like this." (LR)

*   *   *

While we were out in the field, a school bus came by with the children from camp. They waved and laughed and called us "bean pickers." The parents of the kids talked about this for quite a while. "Wait until I get home. My own little boy riding by in a school bus laughing at me. I am going to wear his hind end out when I get home." Some people were amused but one woman, very upset, said she never let her children know what she did for a living. She didn't want them to know that she worked on her knees. She didn't know what she was going to tell them when she got home that evening. Actually, her children, living in the camp, must realize what she does each day and may even help her to pick. But she was ashamed of the work she was doing, and tried to dramatize her condition and express the conflict it created in her by imagining that her children would ask, "Mommy, what were you doing out there on your knees today?" (GP)

*   *   *

We discovered that other crews were earning more per pail for cherries. I tried to bring the resulting gripes around to the fact that farmers need migrants to pick their cherries, trying to gather if the people were conscious of the importance of their job. They allowed that, "Yeah, they need us to pick these damn cherries." After a while, however, Bubba said, "Wait a minute, don't get stupid. They can always get someone else." "Yeah there must be a million damn niggers around here out of work who need some kind of a job." (MR)

*   *   *

Freddy was boasting how he could lift a hamper and tell us the exact weight. "The only reason that I carry the scales is cause folks might not believe me. I lift them up and say, 'This one is too light' or 'this one is too heavy,' and they think I might be stealing beans from them. When you work in a field a long time, like me and Mr. Ed, you get to do that kind of thing. Now Junior here picks real fast and throws those beans right in there. They all stand up one end and he can have his bushel real high and it won't be the right weight. But if you lay them in real careful, with no leaves, it might not even be full and it's still the right weight." Mr. Ed then told about how in the early days, when he first learned how to pick, he used to put his beans in the hamper standing up on their ends. He would fill the hamper up and, even if you pushed on it, the beans were placed so that they would break before they would give. This was before they started weighing beans. "That's something colored folks taught white folks because the colored folks were out in the field and they were doing the picking and they knew what the tricks were." (DR)

*   *   *

Falling out of cherry trees is a common hazard, but accidents are regarded as humorous. Gatemouth fell out of his tree twice one day, and for several days people talked about "doing the Gatemouth." "Watch that limb or you'll do the Gatemouth." Gatemouth hurt his knee and bruised a shin, but each time he refused to act as if he were in pain and walked around cursing the ladder. When asked if he was hurt, he denied it. Many people fall out of trees and are usually laughed at as people comment about their ability to balance on a ladder. The reaction of those who fall is to make light of the accident and to laugh at themselves. They will sometimes blame the tree, claiming that the limbs were rotten, although the usual cause of accidents is carelessness in reaching too far. (MR)

Attitudes toward Supervision

Supervision is often resented and undermined, especially if the supervisor or field walker is a member of the crew. Some crops, in fact, are preferred over others because of the difference in autonomy. The most acceptable style of supervision is one where the field walker exerts no pressure, acting as "one of the boys." He is often the focus of blame for delays and other immediate problems, but inevitably passes responsibility to the crew leader or the grower. "He told me to do this." The supervisor at work assumes, and in fact possesses, only limited power and control. Accordingly, his status is seldom recognized by the pickers as differing appreciably from their own. The northern white grower, however, is viewed from a different perspective, particularly when contrasted to his southern counterpart.

Flo was asked if she were going to hoe lettuce on Monday. She said, no, that she preferred to pick tomatoes. "When you pick tomatoes you can sit down and rest whenever you want to and you can pick as many as you want to pick. You don't have to worry about anyone pushing you or telling you to keep on working." It was explained that we were going to work lettuce with a long hoe, which was easier than short hoe work, and that there was good money in it. She still preferred tomatoes, even though she knew she would make less money. She is her own boss when she picks them and doesn't have a foreman hanging over her, telling her what to do. When you hoe lettuce, there is a man who walks around and inspects the job you are doing, telling you whether you are cutting out too much lettuce or leaving too many weeds. There is also pressure about speed from the group. It is your responsibility to keep up with others. Otherwise, they have to help you finish your row and they resent this. (AK)

*　　　　*　　　　*

St. Louis spent a lot of time on Thursday riding people, trying to get then to pick faster, to do a better job of picking, to work harder. "You want to make some money so you can get that 'man' (bottle of wine).

Let's get to work." People resented him. Whenever he passed they would mutter under their breath, "Motherfucker." Except for specific directions, field supervising seems to have no effect at all on the people other than to make them angry—it doesn't get them to speed up or to pick fewer stems. (MR)

*   *   *

The crew leader shook his head and said, "Colored folks are just not right. All these people asking me for work, and I try my best to give them something better than anyone else and they just don't appreciate it." He had placed some of the crew in a canning plant; but for some reason almost everyone had quit. He was trying to figure out what had gone wrong. He felt that people had left because the boss at the plant had hired a black foreman. The crew leader explained, "Negroes don't trust other Negroes. They just don't like to have one guy raised above everyone else. They asked me to find a black foreman, so I did, and now the crew doesn't like the idea of this person being over them and telling them what to do." He tried to explain why this happened. "They all feel they can all do the same thing. When you find a Negro in a position like this, other Negroes at the place want his job and they will try to do anything to get this person fired."

The conversation continued late into the night and others added their opinions on the matter. Paul told us of an experience he had when he worked at a plant where there was both a white foreman and a black foreman. Every time the white man said something, everybody in the place jumped; if the Negro foreman told them to do their work, they did nothing. Lamb, from Florida, experienced the same situation in a packing house in Florida. "The people don't like to take orders from other Negroes. They just don't like to see Negroes in the position of giving orders."

An example of this occurred today at work. Our crew was split up into three different fields, and the crew leader and his son could manage only two. Paul, who is usually a picker like everyone else, was given supervision of the third field. He was to assign rows and grade cherries. The pickers resented his being a supervisor. Paul was just another picker, and there he was out walking around telling other people what to do. "Grading the cherries and sitting on his behind all day." Red said he could have done the job as well as Paul. "I'm going to have to whup his ass." Paul tells everybody to watch their rotten cherries. "I don't like it. You put a nigger in a position like that and he thinks he's some kind of damn fool that's supposed to be running around the field giving orders, and I just don't think that he can give me orders." "What are you gonna do about it?" Red replied, "I'm not going to pick any more cherries." (GW)

*   *   *

We were first told that we could quit at 4:30; later this was changed to 5:00, and then to 5:30, and then to 6:00. It turned out that we weren't brought back on the bus until 6:20. People were annoyed. "Trouble with colored people is they say they're gonna do something and never do it. That's why we're in the position we're in today." "This isn't slavery time. We're not slaves." The blame focused on Reece, the crew leader's son, who was supervising. People criticized him for bossing them, saying he wasn't the boss over the entire field so why should he act like he was boss. One group quit before 6:20 and called the others "hill niggers." "55 cents or 85 cents won't make or break me." (GP)

*   *   *

Joe, the foreman, goes around talking to people, helping them, talking about old times, telling them how good they are working and how bad other people work. Then he goes to another person and tells him exactly the same thing, making everyone feel good. He does his job well, and doesn't alienate anyone. He supervises by trying to act like one of the people. They identify with him to the point where they don't think he is bossing them around— that he is just one of them with the same sort of problems. (LR)

*   *   *

People were comparing farm owners in Florida with farm owners up here. Farm owners in Florida all have hired hands to drive the tractors and work in the fields, and they don't do anything. Once in a while they come around to see how things are going, but then all they do is drive around in a Cadillac in their good clothes. In contrast, the farmers up north work all the time. Migrants do not interpret this as admirable. Rather, they think the farmers up here are greedy and do not want to spend the money for extra help to drive the tractor. They admire the farmers in Florida who do absolutely nothing themselves and hire other people to do all the work. (HG)

The "Spirit" of Work

The enthusiasm with which people approach each day's work determines their behavior at work. This enthusiasm or "spirit" varies from day to day, and even within a given day. People talk about what "cuts" or "raises" their "spirits": the condition of the field, delays, or the style of supervision. The initial reaction to a field when people first arrive in the morning may affect attitudes for the entire day. If the crop looks thin or if time is wasted waiting for equipment, people become apathetic and this mood dominates the day. Boredom with unchanging routines also has significant effects on "spirit." A change in crop always

Waiting to begin work. Photo by Roger Smith.

elicits excitement and anticipation, regardless of the crop; productivity is often higher during the first few days at a new task than later, when the boring repetition of daily routine palls. When fields are good and there is a possibility of earning money, people settle down to work, setting themselves high objectives. The contrast beween the apathy when conditions are disappointing and the energy evoked by more promising circumstances is striking.

We arrived at the field early on Thursday, expecting to pick the whole day. As soon as we started to work, however, we were told we would be picking for only a half-day. It cut everyone's spirit. "Spirit" is often talked about as if it is a tangible or measurable thing. It is as if a person has twenty units of spirit, and disappointments can cut off eight or ten units. Jessie, for example, said he came out with a lot of spirit this morning but when he found out that he could pick only until noon, it "cut his spirit." He claims he "makes it" on some days but picks poorly on others. "It sort of depends on whether I'm left alone or not. If I'm left alone and nobody bothers me then I can go, but if somebody comes around and messes with me, telling me I can't pick past twelve, or if I can't get started on time, it cuts my spirit and I just can't pick a damn thing." (MR)

*　　　　　*　　　　　*

We were told on Thursday that we would not get paid for Friday's work until the following week. This raised much concern. St. Louis walked up and down the rows several times, trying to reassure the crew, explaining why we had to wait until next week to receive Friday's pay. People were still upset, however, and did not want to work, so he promised to get some of the buckets picked Friday morning on the week's payroll. Reassured, we went back to work; but that night, people were talking through the walls after they had gone to bed. "Well, if they are not going to include Friday's work this week, there is no sense in my going to work at all." (MR)

*   *   *

As we were finishing the field Thursday afternoon, we heard we could not start the new field of sour cherries until Monday. No one argued that we should start the sours on Friday or Saturday and get out of this bad field that was yielding so little. They accepted the fact that sour cherries would start on Monday without question. Although they complained, they did not blame Big Time or the grower for the inefficiency and the delays, but rather nature in general. Cursing is generally directed against the trees and the cherries—even when the fault clearly lies with a particular individual. (MR)

*   *   *

We left on the bus from our field at 4:30 and drove to another field to pick up the rest of the crew. They had not completed their picking yet and were still out in the rows with their bushels uncounted. We had to wait until 6:00 for them to finish up and get their money. During this wait on the bus, people were passive. No one was upset that we had to wait over an hour. (DG)

*   *   *

It threatened to rain in the morning and this had slowed people down. When the clouds cleared away, we sped up and it appeared that it would be a good day to get a large number of buckets. The field was good and people were working quietly, trying to get as many buckets as possible. I think people picked more today then any other day—between 25 and 30 buckets each. At this rate they could have made a good wage for the week had they been able to keep it up each day. Coonie picked 29 buckets. This amazed the other people. "Well, he must pick with his damn toes. I saw him taking his shoes off." (MR)

*   *   *

When we arrived, the cherry trees and the grass were dripping wet. There were no buckets and no ladders. We stood there and waited for half an hour, but when we finally started to pick, the trees were very full. People started picking very quickly. We worked for about forty minutes and then it started to pour, and we drove back to the camp. At 11:30 it stopped raining and Big Time came to drive us back to the field; but on the way it started to sprinkle again. People were dejected. "Man, we ought to go home, we're just going to get soaked again." They wanted to get back at those good cherries and were unhappy because it looked as though we would have to give up the field. However, we finally did get to work about noon, and people really worked hard. There was little conversation except talk related to picking, "Boy, you really shifted into third gear now. You're really starting to get them. Better slow down, you're going to burn up the fields." People would shout between the trees, "Let's get 'em boys, bring 'em in, let's go. Talk to those cherries, get 'em, boys." Considering the short day, productivity was very high: Jessie got 16, Pete 14, Bubba 16, Gatemouth 12, and Spaceman 21 pails. (MR)

*   *   *

This is a celery crew, although we work in cherries since it is still too early for celery. Everyone looks forward to the celery season. James describes the process of cutting celery as a great art. He talks about it in the same tone as he talks about drag racing. "It's beautiful to watch." Pope challenged James to a contest, saying he could pick and stack more celery. This started a game; people called out to each other, "How many can you pack in a day?" James said 3000; Pops said 5000. They talked of famous celery crews in Florida, and the superhuman feats of a picker reputed to be the strongest man around. (LR)

Productivity

Productivity is affected by many factors: the immediate conditions in the field, supervision, and social relationships within the camp. There are attitudes among migrants potentially conducive to high productivity. Men with families, for example, are expected to be more productive than single men. The individual who regularly optimizes his earnings is admired. At the same time, there is an underlying current of resentment concerning ambitious individuals who threaten less productive workers. Conversely, those whose productivity is too low are perceived as threatening because they may call attention to the group. Both extremes meet considerable social pressure, forcing them to at least appear as if they are producing at the same rate as the others. Thus, there are norms governing how one works and how to not work while in the fields.

When we got out to the field in the morning, a large family was already there. They were still working when the rest of the crew left. Everyone in the family was working, even the small children, who were carrying hampers and filling them up. The father was moving from person to person, watching them pick and yelling at them if they did not keep up steadily. Sugarmama was on the bus, watching the family at work. Her reaction combined admiration and resentment. That they could work that hard was admirable; but Sugarmama thought it was sort of foolish to stay out there that long after everyone had come in. (DG)

* * *

Last week Spaceman picked 62 buckets. His high production was discussed. People claimed that the reason he picked so well is that he is part Indian. Jessamay said, "No nigger would work so hard." (MR)

* * *

Married men in the camp worked harder and were out to work earlier each day than the singles. Married men worked on Saturdays, and there were

Although children are not supposed to work, it adds to family income.
Photo by Paul S. Buck.

many times when they would be working while the singles were sitting around talking. It was the married men who complained when they were unable to work. "This waiting ain't no good." "I wish they would tell us whether we are going to work." "You can't just stand here and make money." In contrast, the single men often hoped it would rain so they would not have to work. When the storage plant was closed down, there was no work. Singles expressed relief; married men griped. "When you have a family, you gotta work. If you got bellies to feed, you don't have a choice. When you're single and nobody depends on you, then you can do what you want, because all you need is money enough to feed yourself." One married man was teased because he worked hard. He answered that he had to because his grocery bills were so high. He had four dependents and had to feed them all.

Payroll data indicate the extent to which these voiced attitudes were reflected in actual productivity. The following figures summarize the earnings for single men and married men (sometimes with the help of their wives) for a six-week period.

	Range of total earnings	Range of average weekly earnings
Singles (13)	$180.00 to $457.00	$36.00 to $ 76.20
Marrieds (12)	$361.00 to $997.00	$60.08 to $166.13

Since wives often pooled their earnings with their husbands, the higher earnings of the marrieds in some cases reflect the total earned by husband and wife. The women, however, responsible for cooking and child care, did not go into the fields for long periods of time, and while there spent considerable time watching the children and talking. Also, most women lacked the stamina to pick well, particularly if the trees were high and ladders were used. In most cases, the man himself earned the bulk of the family's income. Assuming this to be the case, the differences in income between marrieds and singles remain significant.

In the six-week period, the thirteen singles put in 1420 hours of work (on hourly pay) on tasks such as weeding, and also picked a total of 2549 bushels of cherries (for which they were paid piecework). The twelve marrieds put in 9 hours more in hourly work, but picked twice as many cherries. The figures below summarize these differences.

	Average hours worked per person	Average number of bushels per person (piecework)
Singles (13)	109.2	196.0
Marrieds (12)	119.0	413.6

That married migrants in the camp had attitudes conducive to productivity was reflected in their output. In this case, a relatively efficient management permitted those with tendencies to be highly productive to earn a commensurate income. Indeed, management in this case was so efficient that, even for singles, productivity and income were approximately double that for most crews that were studied. (LD)

*   *   *

Aaron said he could have gotten a good job at the packing plant but he wasn't willing to work hard to rise to a position where he could be "like some of the white men at that plant, walking around just doing a little bit of nothing." However, he felt that the work was too hard for the $1.50 he was getting and that he was going to start saving money to leave. Amos told him, "You can't save any money. I've known you for three years and every time that you get a big roll in your pocket, you go out and gamble it and lose it and drink it all away." (GW)

*   *   *

By the end of the day my back was hurting from bending, and since I was pretty well up in my row, I lay down and decided to wait until everyone caught up with me. It was at this point that I caught all hell from the crew. It was all right to slow down but not to lie down. Someone said, "I wonder why Spaceman doesn't say anything to him. That punk is over there on his back and what does Spaceman say? Nothing! Yet he's on everyone else's back." Slim picked up a stone and threw it toward me: "Get up off your ass. Who the hell do you think you are?" I picked up the rock and shot it back. Then Slim called Spaceman: "How does this guy get to lay down when everyone else has to work?" Spaceman yelled, "Get up off your ass. What makes you think you can get on your back?" I explained that I was ahead of the group and thought I would rest. He said it was okay to rest, but I had to stand up and rest. I complained, "My back hurts," and he asked me how old I was. "Do you see these old women working here? They aren't lying on their backs. If anyone should be complaining about their backs, it should be them, not you." A couple of others joined in, "All he needs is a good ass whipping." "No, he doesn't need a good ass whipping. All he needs is a wife and about five kids at home and that pain in his back would disappear." Everyone broke up into laughter. I started working, but was teased all through the day.

Another day a similar incident occurred. Three of us got about 30 yards in front of everyone else, and Major, who was supervising, called us back and told us to help other people with their rows until we were all at the same place. He wanted us to stay together. We went back and helped the other people. Then he reminded us that we were working by the hour and to work slowly. I decided to sit down for a while and wait for people to catch up. "Don't do that. Stand up and keep the hoe in your hands all the time. I don't care if you only chop it once in five minutes, but just keep that hoe in your hand in case the Man comes out." I stood up and chopped once every two minutes or so at an extra slow pace. It was worse chopping slowly than working fast. It was boring, but to stop to rest would have threatened the others. (GP)

*   *   *

While waiting to check our buckets, four of us started a card game. When the truck arrived and we dumped our cherries, we didn't feel like going back to work. We were sick of picking cherries, so when everyone started picking again, we continued to play cards. There was immediate pressure for us to get back to work from the crew leader, the foreman, and the workers themselves. As we played cards, people would pass by and say, "Oh, the gamblers, they're too rich to work." Joe said, "You guys will come on payday, and after you pay your debts you'll have a quarter left to your name." The crew leader came around and commented, "Oh look at this, we're having labor troubles now, too. My people would rather play cards than go out in the field and work." Finally, after a lot of ribbing, we decided to go back to work. (LR)

Wages

For most migrants, work provides no intrinsic satisfaction, and the trip north is tolerated only out of economic necessity. Many sustain themselves during the season as "$3.00-a-day men," intending to earn only enough money to keep themselves in food and wine. They have no long-range goals and think only of their daily needs. There are others, however, who come north with plans to save money, often having a specific goal in mind, such as a car, or, in one case, a set of false teeth. Saving money in a migrant labor camp is difficult, and such goals are often reduced to "breaking even." The selections below suggest the plans, goals, and frustrations relating to wages, and conclude with descriptions of payday. Although migrants know how much they produce and therefore what their wages will be, the tension and mistrust evident during the actual process of payment is striking. The atmosphere surrounding this routine weekly event vividly illustrates the ambiguity the migrants feel about the relationship between work and its rewards.

"What are you going to do after the season is over? What are you going to do with the money you make?" "All I want is money and I'll be okay." Earnings are a major concern, but few people make money and most spend it immediately. Hart earned $100.00 during the week and a half he had been at the canning plant. This seemed to him like a lot of money, so he decided to take off a few days and go to Rochester and just "cool it." Other people talk about doing the same thing at the end of the season. "I'm going back to cool it for a while."

Amos said, "Last year, out of the whole summer I was here, I only saved $45.00." He spent his money on wine and women. He managed to save $45.00 only because he was picked up by the police and accused of something he didn't do. At that time he had the $45.00 on him, and they kept him in jail until they found out who had actually committed the crime and then turned him loose. This year was going to be different: "I'm going to have a large bankroll in the bank by the time I get back to Florida." Later, when he received his money for the week, Amos walked by bragging, "I've got enough money to choke a hog. I'm going to really put it to some good use. I'm not going to drink any more . . . that stuff is messing me up." However, later in the evening, there was a crap game going on and I found Amos at the crap table, gambling and drinking up his paycheck. (GW)

*   *   *

There was no work and everyone was lying around. Clinton was talking about the Social Security money he was going to receive and how he would spend it. Last year he didn't have to use the checks and sent them to his sister, who banked them for him. This year he has to use the money "cause there is no guarantee that we will even pick tomatoes." On these days when we don't work, Clinton spends his days just lying around in his room, occasionally reading papers or detective stories. Shock was reading an article in the newspaper and he started talking about "three million motherfucking dollars." "People are doing everything now for money," he said. "It's the root of all evil. What makes it so hard is that I can't get enough of it. With two or three thousand dollars I would be all right." Geech commented, "I don't know how I'll eat tomorrow," and Shock replied, "Damn right." Clinton added, "It happens in this business. I got caught with my pants down," meaning that some seasons were slow and you couldn't make it. Shock agreed, "Yeah, yeah, it sure happens. Every damn year is getting worse and worse. It's a bad situation." "Yeah, it's a sorry-assed world." (DG)

*   *   *

People's aspirations for their summer's earnings aren't very high. Junior said, "Well, I just want to have enough money so that even when I have paid everyone and done everything, I'll have about thirty bucks left over." Bear wants to save fifty bucks to get an old car. (ET)

*　　　　*　　　　*

"Here I am, trying to save money, and all he does is borrow from me and get on that card table and lose it all. I can't save at all. All that I've saved I've given him to gamble, because he's done so much for me I couldn't really turn him down." (GW)

*　　　　*　　　　*

After we had been picking for about an hour, Jessamay came out and joined us. She, as well as everyone else, was angry that we were getting only 55 cents a pail. She wanted to save only a hundred dollars or so, so she could buy a set of false teeth. She said she wasn't about to let any damn man buy her teeth for her, implying that if Big Time bought her teeth for her and she wanted to leave him one day, she would be unable to keep her teeth. With the exception of Jessamay and one family in the camp, no one seems to be saving money for any particular thing. Most of the others in the camp live from day to day. When people first came to the camp they said, "Well, I at least want to make enough money to get out of debt." Since then it seems to be, "I want to get enough to get a 'man' (a bottle of wine)." "I'm going to earn me a half a man today—a half a man relieves you." "No, it will leave you hung-up. Get a whole man." There don't seem to be many long-range goals or aspirations. The family from Selma was saving to buy a used car with the money earned picking. Their goal was $350.00. They didn't realize they would have to get insurance for the car, which would also cost them quite a bit. In any case, by midseason they no longer talked about it, and seemed to have forgotten completely about getting a car. (MR)

*　　　　*　　　　*

Clinton is able to recall dates and facts exactly. He spoke about when he was working on the railroad in 1962 and was getting $1.68 an hour. Now they are getting $2.10 an hour, he claims. Exact wage scales are very important to most migrants. They talk of exactly how much they have made at various jobs. They can remember what years they went to what camp and what crop they picked. Some of the people talk about details as far back as 1957. (AK)

*　　　　*　　　　*

It was about 8:30 P.M. and we were waiting to be paid off. The grower had come to the camp to give us our week's pay. The variations in earnings were enormous. Some of the earnings were as follows (the first number is the total amount earned for the week; the second is what was taken home after all the debts were paid):

$38.00 – $ 3.00	$30.00 – $30.00	$19.00 – $2.00
14.00 – 2.00	19.00 – 5.00	10.00 – 4.00
10.00 – 10.00	5.00 – 3.00	

While we were getting paid there was a small incident. Florida Joe thought that he had not been paid honestly and asked to see the figuring. People started to make disapproving noises. "What is he doing, asking to have it checked?" However, the grower respected the man's right, and they spent about ten minutes figuring it out. No mistake had been made. Joe said he was sorry to have bothered him, but the grower said it was perfectly all right; a man had the right.

I went back to my room and Junior was there, trying to figure out on paper how much he had really earned. He wrote down the number of baskets he had picked every day and multiplied it by 70 cents. He was having trouble with the arithmetic, but finally said, "Well it looks right, but I still think that they cheated me." He had been coming up here for twenty-seven seasons. "Once, back then, it was pretty good—enough to make a living picking, but it's getting worse every year. You can't make a living in this no more." (DR)

*   *   *

When you bring cherries up to be graded, they dump them in boxes and then punch your ticket. Each person has a long ticket, with 100 numbers on it in four rows. The person grading has a copy of it on a big ring. They put the two together and punch them both. Payday is usually Saturday at 2:00 P.M. and takes place in the kitchen. While people are being paid, there is complete silence in the room. The only sound is an occasional whisper. There is no real talk. People are depressed and nervous. Many of them remain in the room after they are paid, for there is a fascination in watching each person go up, one at a time, through this five-minute spectacle.

Each person, when his name is called, walks slowly around the kitchen to Jessamay, who tells him the amount of money he owes. He then slowly turns and walks three or four steps to Big Time. Big Time pushes his pay envelope across the table. He then picks up his pay envelope and walks back four or five steps, turns away, looks at his envelope, rips it open, and gives Jessamay some money. She gives him his change. Description can hardly convey how awkwardly and slowly events take place. No one is in a hurry. When it came to my turn to receive my envelope I too was in a similar frame of mind. Jessamay called my name. I was to receive $10.00. I received my pay envelope from Big Time. It contained $9.60, with a deduction of 40 cents for Social Security, although Big Time does not know my Social Security number. I owed Jessamay less than a dollar. Some people had as little as $3.00 or $4.00 left in their pay envelope after they finished paying their debts.

As soon as this process was finished, Big Time walked into another room and left Jessamay alone in the kitchen. As he left, people came up to Jessamay, quietly calling her names, cursing her food, and generally taking out their frustrations on her. Occasionally Big Time would wander back into the kitchen and everyone would be quiet.

One week it was announced that Friday's wage would not be included on the week's payroll; that it would be held over until the following week. People felt this was an attempt to stop them from paying their debts. "I can't put up with this; how am I going to pay off my debts at that store? What's he trying to do?" The crew leader explained that the bank closed early that day, and if he waited to see what people picked on Friday, he would be unable to get to the bank on time and there would be no money until Monday. He would include Friday if they wanted, but it would be their own tough luck if they didn't get any money until Monday. People grumbled but agreed. Later he made a compromise. We would be paid this week on Friday instead of Saturday as usual.

At 2:00 P.M. on Friday, people tensed up about not getting their money, which they expected in the early afternoon. There was an air of restlessness. People were sitting in groups talking calmly, when suddenly someone would stop and shout, "I want my damn money" at the top of his lungs. It was as if, all of a sudden, they couldn't take it any more and had to shout what they wanted. This was also an attempt to communicate to Big Time, who was in his room. He could certainly hear these outbursts, which continued at irregular intervals. At about 2:30 Big Time left and people said, "He must be going to get the money." While he was away the same outbursts continued, with no effect other than perhaps relieving frustrations. Big Time finally arrived with the money, and the usual payday scene took place, although there was a little more talking than last time. People began cracking some jokes and singing some songs. There was more money made this week and people were able to pay off their debts and they felt better about getting their pay.

People guard their envelopes very carefully. Otis, for example, takes his envelope from Big Time, steps back a couple of feet and holds it very close to his face, with both hands around it so that no one else can see what he has made. Although people often know how much he has picked, once he gets his money he does not show it to anyone. Occasionally a person will snatch his envelope from the table, and go to the side of the room, turning his back on the group to count his money in private. (MR)

Part Three

PERSISTENCE OR CHANGE

A migrant wants and needs money from regular employment, but his experience with work is such that he defines liberty as the freedom to do what he wants, when he wants. He has goals influenced by the outside society, but his experience has told him that they are not within his grasp. He feels that the gap between his ends and the means available to him cannot be bridged. Although cohesion and organization are traditional avenues of social change in American society, the migrant crew is riven with dissension and mistrust, and normatively rejects the hierarchy necessary for successful organization. Humiliated and conspicuously deprived, the migrant is hostile and resentful; but, more than his deprived urban counterpart, he is almost totally dependent and is therefore afraid to express his needs. Where participation and individual effort are required for social change, the migrant, in his position of impotence, has learned to withdraw and avoid problems, or to depend completely on others. These are the contradictions and dilemmas that confront and frustrate the efforts from within and without the system to "do something" to change migrant labor. Indeed, the norms that make life viable in the camp are useless and, in fact, disreputable from the viewpoint of the larger society: the very accomodations necessary and adaptive to the migrant labor system limit the potentiality of social change.

Part III explores the relationships of migrants to the world outside the camp, beginning with their perceptions of the outside society and major events. The obstacles to change are sharply focused by internal efforts to "beat the system." Occasional attempts to organize for the purpose of improving conditions and efforts by individuals to simply

193

escape are described. Often, aspirations for change, unable to crystallize into immediate action, are concentrated on children; therefore, selections concerning the raising and education of children in the camps are included.

9

The Migrant
and the Outside World

Migrants' perceptions of the larger society are based on an extraordinary lack of knowledge about events outside the camp. It is not that this knowledge is unavailable. Influences filter into camps through television, social work, educational programs, growers, and shopkeepers. But most information is simply not received because, in its inconsistency with personal associations and experiences, it is not regarded as relevant. Relevant associations with the outside world are dominated by fear, suspicions, and mistrust. These evoke a varied response among migrants, ranging from anger to apathy, from belligerent antagonism to passive acceptance. The response varies from that of the urban ghetto only in the greater predominance of apathy. Angry and apathetic people alike perceive the world as polarized. There are "we" and "they," black and white, poor and rich. This is apparent in their views of white people, of social institutions, and of national events. The polarized lens through which migrants perceive the present system helps to maintain it; for, in many respects, the migrant labor camp is a shell protecting and isolating its occupants, allowing them to withdraw from a world seen as dangerous and exploitative.

Black Folks, White Folks

"KICK THEIR ASSES"

All migrants are aware of and resent their position relative to the rest of society, but it is only the younger people who express resent-

ment overtly. Their heroes are those who dare to put defiance into action. Although they talk of anger and aggression, it is rare, even among the most belligerent of younger people, to express this anger directly. It is more often revealed in jokes and stories, several of which appear below.

We were working in the packing house and Amos walked over to me saying, "Hey have you noticed anything?" I hadn't, and he said "Look at us! Look who's working together! Why didn't they put one of us down there in the tank and one of those white men up here? If you notice, they do this everywhere up here. It's just like it is down south. Look at the other plant! Didn't all the blacks work together there too? You never worked with a white man over there did you?" He was right, and he added, "Well, it shows you one thing. The same thing that goes on down south is right here too." (GW)

*   *   *

Preacher was talking about "those white people" and how they try to take advantage of black people. "Those white people must think that we blacks are pretty stupid." A white car salesman had tried to sell him a 1956 car, for $400.00, that wasn't worth $10.00. The man kept insisting that it was worth the money and tried to convince him to buy it, saying that some other black guy would take it and he would just feel sorry. Preacher complained that white men down south treat their mules better than they treat Negroes. He told about an Alabama man who got three weeks in jail for beating his mule and also had to pay for its medical treatment. "If some guy beat a nigger, he would have a medal pinned on his chest. He wouldn't get any punishment at all." (AK)

*   *   *

On the bus Flo was telling Reece that there are parts of Africa that aren't yet civilized. Reece asked, "Where?" "Oh, in the Belgian Congo and places like that." Reece replied, "Oh, you damn fool, most of Africa is pretty well civilized. Anyhow, what is civilization?" Flo looked kind of vacant: "Civilization is civilization, don't be so damn stupid." "No, it isn't. You take us here in the camp, for instance. You consider yourself civilized?" Flo looked at Reece and said aside, "He's a damn fool. No, I am not civilized," and Reece replied, "You're right, you're not civilized, and you want to know why? Because if you go listen to some of these people around here, some of the white people, and they talk about the way we live in this camp, they consider us uncivilized, so you have to define what you mean by uncivilized. Even some of the Pygmies would consider some of the people around here uncivilized, so you have to know what you are talking about when you say civilized." Flo then said, "Then I don't give a damn about the people around here. As far as I'm concerned *they* are uncivilized." She started talking about an incident in the store: "Damn man tried to cheat me out of my money, trying to sell me some rotten meat." "You know why he tried to cheat you?" "Yes, because he was a damn fool trying to mess with my money." Reece replied, "Because he thought you were uncivilized and stupid, and wouldn't know the difference. Like I said, there are people around here that consider you uncivilized and that proves it." (GP)

*   *   *

A migrant who was friendly with one of the white social worker girls living in the camp was resented. "She should have her ass kicked. There she goes, looking up to that white girl as if she's some god or something." "What the hell is the matter with her? What does she think these white people are? As far as I'm concerned, they're just shit like everyone else." "She just saw that white girl and went running after her like a little dog. Somebody should take her and kick her ass and teach her a thing or two." People also were down on a young boy who had been hanging around another white girl, also a social worker. One day a group of guys said that he should "set her up for a gang bang." The boy replied, "No, I wouldn't do that to a dog." "Look, if she was a black woman and we were all white, that's exactly what would happen and you know it. Why not do the same thing?" When he refused, they asked what was wrong with him, calling him an "Uncle Tom." They talked about things that white men had done to black women during slavery time and things that go on in the south now. Blacks should stop letting whites step all over them and stand up and fight like men because "This nonsense has gone far enough." There was agreement that blacks should start acting, but no suggestions as to the form action should take except that "We should start kicking asses because that's what people have being doing to us for so many centuries." (GP)

*   *   *

Nate told me that in Tuscaloosa there were five all-white theaters and two black theaters. Some white people wanted to come into the black theaters one night to go to the movies and they wouldn't let them in, so the town closed down the black theaters and integrated the white theaters. Now the whites sit below and the blacks have to sit up in the balcony. One time this friend of his, half-drunk, was up in the balcony. He unzipped his fly and, as he walked across the balcony, urinated down on the white people. Another time this man spat in front of a store, and the white owner ran out and tried to make him clean it up. "No, you ain't gonna make me clean it up, because I ain't gonna clean it up." The white store owner pushed him, so the black man clobbered him and squashed his nose with one punch. There was blood all over and a crowd of white people gathered around. This black man just walked through the crowd and everyone was afraid to do anything to him.

Nate told another story about three black brothers who "didn't take anything from anyone." They were at a big party where everyone was having a good time; but, during the evening, a cop car nearby had its tires slashed, and the cops, hearing a party, came in and lined everyone up to search for knives. If a person had no knife, he was instructed to go outside. The brothers were searched but refused to leave. They insisted on sticking together, deciding that no one was going to push them around. Nate said they succeeded in defying the cops. (ET)

*   *   *

Some of the stories told do not relate to real events, but are no less revealing of migrant attitudes. Here are two by Slim.

Four little Negro boys were down by the train yard, playing in the mud, making little mud pies and things like that. A white engineer on a train stopped by the mud pool and called out: "What are you doing, boys?" The boys said, "Oh, we're just making little colored boys out of mud." The engineer laughed. "Why don't you make some little white boys?" One of the kids looked up and said, "Oh, no, my mama told me never to play in shit."

An elderly Negro man went out to a grave and prayed each night, "Dear Lord, please let me see my son once more, Oh Lord, just let me see my son once more." One night when he was standing out there praying, a white boy standing behind a tree overheard him. He said to himself, "Aha, if this nigger comes out here again tomorrow, I'll sure fix him." Sure enough, the old man came out and started praying, "Oh Lord, let me see my son once more, let me see my son just one more time." Meantime, the white boy had gone to get a white sheet and was behind the tombstone, and when the Negro made the prayer, he stood up with the white sheet on and started flapping his arms. The old man backed up and said, "Okay son, I done seen you. You can go down now, you can go back now." But the white boy kept waving his arms in the white sheet. Finally, the Negro said, "Dammit, that's why you should be dead today, cause you're so damn hard-headed." (GP)

*   *   *

Big Time told the following joke in the cherry orchard:

A white lady bet her husband that he could not get the colored field hand, John, to call him a son of a bitch. The white man said: "Yes, I can. I can get him to do it." His wife said: "No you can't. I betcha you can't." "Okay,

I'll show you." The white man got a jug of corn liquor from the still and he came up to the colored hand and said, "Hey, John, come on in and have a shot with me." John said, "No sir, I don't believe I should." The white man said, "Now, come on John, I want you to have a slug with me." John said, "No sir, I don't believe I should." The farmer said, more firmly, "Boy, I want you to drink some of this." John drank the liquor slowly. The white man then said, "John, I'm a son of a bitch, aren't I?" "No sir, you's a white man." This went on and on about seven or eight more times, with John refusing to drink the liquor or drinking very little and replying, "No sir, you're a white man." Finally, the eighth time, John was persuaded to have a real snort and he staggered around. The white man asked again, "I'm a son of a bitch, aren't I?" to which John answered, stuttering, "Yeah, yeah, yes sir, you's a son of a bitch . . . and a motherfucker, too!"

When Big Time finished, people laughed at the joke for five or ten minutes. They got out of the trees and sat on the ground laughing. This was apparently the funniest joke told all season, and the punch line was repeated for days. (MR)

*   *   *

Several stories were exchanged about a black farmhand called John.

One day, there was a panther down in the cornfield eating the boss's corn. The boss turned to John and said, "Something is down in my field eating up the corn. Go down there and get it." "Okay, boss, I'm going down to get it." So John went down to the cornfield, and the panther saw him and started running after him. John ran around the barn and then under it, leading the panther inside. Then he went up to the boss: "Boss, I've got him." The boss went down to the barn to kill the panther, but the panther was too much for him and he ran out of the barn, the panther following him. He ran across the field, right past the farmhouse, with the panther behind him. The Missus asked John, "How did you ever bring the panther out to the barn?" John said, "The same way the boss got him across the field."

John went up to the house to get a tool, and when he came back he told his friend Marcus, "I stuck my hand up the Missus' dress." Marcus wanted to do the same thing. He went up to the house, stuck his hand up the Missus' dress, and the Missus screamed. She told her boss, and they whipped Marcus to within an inch of his life. He went back and told John, "I ran my hand up the Missus' dress, and the boss tried to kill me. How come when you ran your hand up the dress nothing happened?" "The Missus' dress was hanging on the clothesline." (LP)

"Yas, suh"

The belligerence underlying many stories contrasts with the passive acceptance evident in others, especially among the older migrants, in-

cluding those who tell some of the most resentful tales. There are many people who dwell on the past: "Things were bad, but all that has changed." Others talk with deference of the help they have received and expect to receive from white bosses, indicating acceptance of a continuing paternalistic system. Even among those who are angry, the timidity and fear with which white people are approached contradict resentments expressed in the shelter of the camp. Attitudes of acceptance are related to how migrants perceive themselves. Regarding society as polarized, they accept dual standards as inevitable and, even, just. This is reflected in the dual façade exhibited by some migrants who are hostile and aggressive with other migrants while displaying deference and meekness with whites. People, accepting the system, "play the game," changing their character to behave as others expect.

Freddy says he likes white people and he likes colored people and he just likes to talk with everyone. He said there are some colored people who would beat on him for talking to a white man; but if he could have his way in this world for just a little while, he would put all the people who liked only whites in one place, and all the people who wanted just blacks together in another place. All the people who wanted to like everybody could then be left alone. He talked about the Ku Klux Klan. "Well, they're really terrible people. If they knew we were in here, they would kill both of us. They'll go into your home and make your mommy and daddy do it and make you watch them, and after that was all done, they'd take you all out, and they'd line you up against the wall, and they'd kill all of you. They might take you and nail your hands to a tree and set you on fire and cut off your pecker and put it in your mouth." I said, "I can't understand that." "Well, they're just sick, that's all, they're just sick. They can't stand to see white and colored together." (DR)

*   *   *

Shorty said he was going to tell some colored jokes. He looked over to me and said, "You're not prejudiced, are you?" I said, "No." I have gotten similar questions from others. Migrants assume that prejudice among whites runs so deep that even living with them and getting along with them for a month does not change anything. (IM)

*   *   *

Aaron said he used to drive a car for a Jew. One day he was drunk and smashed it up. A cop drove up and Aaron called his boss, who came by in five minutes in his daughter's car. The Jew said to the cop that he would take care of everything, and Aaron drove him off in the other car while the cop stood there, looking after them in confusion.

Cory told a similar story. He was driving the "man's" fancy car and decided to show it off to his girl. Later, trying to make up for lost time, he drove it into a telephone pole. When he finally got back, the man said, "Don't worry about the car. You'll have another one waiting for you on Monday." He told Cory to go home and see the present that was waiting for him. Cory figured it was a box of candy or something like that. He went home, opened the door, and his wife asked, "Do you see our Chevy?" Cory said, "No, I didn't see it. What happened to it?" "I gave it back. The car wasn't in very good shape." It was the only car, and Cory wondered why she did something as stupid as that. And then she said, "Do you see that new Olds parked out there? That's my car." The papers were made out in Cory's name, and the Man had paid the down payment. (DR)

*   *   *

Mr. Ed told me about his grandmother, who had been a slave, and what things were like under slavery. "You had to have a passport to go from one man's farm to another." "You mean a pass?" Mr. Ed said, "No, a passport. It has to be written down. You couldn't just tell the other man that this man sent you." He said if a slave started running away they would put dogs after him. The dogs would tear him apart. He claimed that even during the thirties, if a Negro went up to New York City they would find him and send him back to the farm in Georgia. Then Mr. Ed described how they used to make people breed, just like animals: "It's not in the history books either, but that's the way it is." Cory corrected him: "Well, it's not in the history books they give you at school, but if you read the right ones you'll find out." At that point Cory turned to me, "Do you know who the first slaves were?" Before I could answer, he said, "It was your race. The white people were the first slaves, and they were slaves to their own people—to white people—and they were treated just as bad as colored people. It took them fifty-six years to get out of their slavery. On the Fourth of July they were free. That's why the Fourth of July is so important to white people. It isn't important to colored people, because you got your freedom on the Fourth of July." He told how the pilgrims had brought slavery from Europe with them "across the water." Mr. Ed then resumed his story, telling how white people bought slaves in Africa and brought as many as two thousand over on a boat. "If the ship sank all the slaves would die because they were chained to it." (DR)

*   *   *

Some old men talked about how good the race situation is in Florida. "Colored people there can go anywhere that white people can go; there are no doors closed anymore." Tom said that at least two or three jobs in every store were held by Negroes. He described the white man he works for during the winter in the south. This man, he said, owns 1800 acres of corn and made a quarter of a million dollars last season. He owned a $60,000 house, but the government made him move out of that "because it didn't cost enough money" and he had to move into a $175,000 house. He gave his $60,000 house to his oldest son. His other son has a stable and race horses and a nice $8,000 car. Tom said that he could call up this boss any time and he would send him any money he needed. James said that his boss down in Florida would do the same thing for him. He and Tom agreed, "Colored people aren't afraid of white people any more." (DG)

                *   *   *

Albert was very anxious to work on the mechanical bean picker and wanted to see the farmer about it. We went up to the house together. A woman was there and told us to check in the office in back. We looked and he wasn't there, so she asked us in to telephone. We started in, but a dog barked, and Albert was afraid of dogs. He pushed me in front of him as if I could protect him and held onto me saying, "Keep that dog back, keep that dog back." I kept reassuring him that the dog is fine; he just barks; all dogs bark. He finally got on the phone with the grower after the dog calmed down; but he was very nervous on the phone and stammered a great deal. The grower did not understand what he was saying, and said he would come by in a couple of minutes. When he came, Albert merely asked when we would be working on the bean picker. The grower said, "I don't rightly know; maybe we'll start on Wednesday." Albert said, "Yas, suh," and walked nervously away, not asking anything further. Back at camp he told people that he would be running the bean picker on Monday. (IM)

                *   *   *

As we were driving home we saw a nice beach with a lot of white people on it. Longo said, "Those people have a nice place. Niggers can't have a place like that because we'd ruin it." He really meant this seriously because he continued in a little while, saying, "Niggers are motherfuckers. All this shit about civil rights, some of us don't even deserve it." (DG)

                *   *   *

Kelly argued with Emma. "Give me some coffee." She replied, "I ain't got none." "What the hell kind of a place is this anyhow, with no coffee?" "If you don't like it, go away." Kelly said, "I'm going to fuck you." "You come back here and try to touch this nigger." This shut him up for a few seconds, and then he looked at her and said in a very soft voice, "Don't call yourself a nigger. You ain't no nigger." She asked, "Well what am I?" He said, "A Negro." "What's the difference? They both got the same nig in them." (AK)

*　　　　*　　　　*

Ben has eight brothers. Except for him, they are all light-skinned because of Indian blood in his mother's family. He makes a big point of how he is the only dark one in the family. "I am the only one who was fucked up with the color of my skin." (AK)

*　　　　*　　　　*

Slim told a story about a monkey sitting beside the road:

A Jewish couple rode by. The woman said, "My God, dear, there's a monkey." So they stopped, patted the monkey, and gave it some food. "Oh, the poor creature must be sick or something, he's just sitting there." They set it back down and the woman gave it a kiss and they drove on. Then this Italian couple came by and did the same thing, picking the monkey up, petting it, giving it some food and a kiss, and setting it back down. A Chinese couple came by, petted it, gave it a kiss, gave it some food, and rode on down the road. And then you know who came by? Black people, and, of course, they had been drinking, and it just so happened they stopped right there in the road and got into an argument. All of a sudden the woman spotted the monkey and said, "Look at that goddamn monkey. Hit it, hit it, kill it." And the man rushed over, slapped the monkey, and they both beat it and pushed it into the ditch. They got in their car and drove on. The monkey up and shook his head and said, "My people, they just don't know how to act." (GP)

*　　　　*　　　　*

Brown told a joke about a little boy who had been given a quarter:

The boy went down to the corner grocery store and bought a box of popcorn, a soda, and had the rest changed into pennies. He went to a bridge and sat down. He started eating his popcorn, drinking his soda, beating his meat, and throwing his pennies off the bridge. An old man came along and asked the little boy what he was doing. The little boy replied that he was doing just like the grownups: eating, drinking, fucking, and throwing away his money. (CL)

*　　　　*　　　　*

People act differently in different contexts. They may act one way with family, another with peers or with an employer. With most people, this does not involve a complete change in personality. Many migrants, however, show a dual personality, one of which is evident when they are with whites, the other when with other migrants. These people change their behavior so much that they often seem to be different people. With whites they are meek, polite, understanding; they passively agree with everything and hide any feelings of aggression. In contrast, when the same people are with other migrants, they may become rude and aggressive.

Carl seems to have this sort of split personality. He is extremely polite in the presence of the white farmer. But, in contrast, when he is in camp or with other migrants he is one of the rudest and most inconsiderate people. For example, we were stacking hay and he was bitching because we needed a third man. He complained that the farmer knew we were shorthanded and should have sent somebody. Later, the farmer came up to help, saying, "You guys are short up here, let me help you," but Carl would not let him help. He told him to go down, "We can handle it, we don't need you up here. You're going to hurt yourself up here." He kept reminding the man about his health. The farmer, about fifty years old, looked very strong and was used to working hard. Carl spoke politely and intelligently, but once the farmer left, his language broke down and he started cursing again, almost as if he were a different person.

Red provided another example of this dual behavior. Red caught his hand in the grader one day and had to go to the hospital. When he returned, he claimed the grader almost took it off. He talked about his arm all day, showing it to everyone and pointing to where it had been cut. He did not think he would be able to work for a month. When the grower and foreman came around, he showed it to them also; but when they asked him how his arm felt, he said, "Oh, pretty good," although just a few minutes ago he had told us that it was terrible. The grower asked if he would be able to work tomorrow and he said, "Sure."

Similar duplicity was evident in the relationship between the crew and a group of white social workers who considered themselves "friends of the migrants." On the whole, relationships were smooth. Whenever there was an activity arranged by the social workers, the migrants followed all suggestions agreeably. However, when alone, they would criticize the way the entire program was run. For example, a basketball team was organized by a white social worker who announced that he knew little about basketball and was open to suggestions from the crew. None of the migrants said anything except that it made no difference because they were there to have fun. In private, however, they complained about the way he was running the team. Yet, the next day when he asked for suggestions again, everyone said that things were fine.

General migrant attitudes toward whites perpetuated this dual behavior even with well-regarded individuals. These attitudes are complex; they include not only perceptions of white society, but also beliefs as to what the white man expects of the Negro. The migrant adjusts his behavior in terms of these expectations: he goes along with the game. At a gas station, while waiting for repairs, members of my crew refused to go into the garage, knowing they were mistrusted. They preferred to remain on the truck to avoid suspicion. Another time, when the bus was in a white residential district, the driver was urged to hurry and get out of the area "before they think we are trying to rape somebody." Migrants also feel that whites regard them as stupid and lazy. When a farmer told us, "It's better to work for 75 cents an hour than to sit around doing nothing, waiting for better things to come," people argued whether the man really thought they were stupid enough to work for those wages. They concluded that "a person has a right to be lazy with wages like that."

Migrant perceptions of white people are similar to white attitudes toward migrants. White men are seen as dangerous. Afraid to enter a store, a person said, "They might beat us." I asked Sleepy to go to a farmer's door to ask directions, and he replied, "You go. I don't want to get shot," suggesting that the man was so dangerous he would shoot a Negro for simply knocking on his door and asking directions. White men are also talked about as lazy and unintelligent. Spaceman said that if it were up to him, the camp would be run entirely by colored people, that whites did not know enough to run a camp. Often in the work situation, when we were doing things that did not seem sensible, the crew leader would explain "the man wants it done." Although this was a way to exert pressure, comments suggested that the Man did not know as much as he thought he knew. Many stories are told about the promiscuity of whites. Sexual stories told about perverts, generally white, would often end with the phrase "There are a lot of white people like that around" or "And they talk about Negroes."

Nevertheless, the white man is regarded, unequivocally, as an authority figure who must be respected if not feared. "The man told me to tell you" was the most effective way to get a job done. This image is reinforced in all dealings the migrant has with white society. Police are usually white, farmers are white, social workers are white. (GP)

Poor Folks, Rich Folks

Just as society is polarized into black and white people, migrants contrast rich and poor and associate wealth with race. An ambiguity, however, is often revealed in conversations concerning money. On the one hand, it is widely believed that rich people are miserable and perpetually worried about their wealth. On the other hand, money is a contin-

ual preoccupation and the acquiring of sudden enormous wealth is a common fantasy.

Reverend says he doesn't want a lot of money; he only wants to live decently. The fat lady, who runs the store in the station wagon, agreed. "Rich people are unhappy, they don't sleep at night." Reverend claims he used to work for a rich man who never slept because he was always worrying about his stocks and bonds. People who had a million dollars were always trying to get two, and when they had two they were trying to get three. After talking about this unhappy rich man, Reverend went on to describe how his wife had almost inherited a couple of million dollars from some lady whom she had taken care of. The lady was an invalid with a lot of money, and she didn't like any of her relatives. She told Reverend's wife she was going to make out a will and give all her money to her. The old lady was too sick, however, to draw up the new papers in time, so they didn't get any of the money after all. (DG)

*   *   *

People talked about how rich James Brown and Jackie Wilson were. Punk noted that James Brown had his own airplane. Bertha wondered what it would be like to be rich. She said if she had a lot of money and was flying around with James Brown, she would not even recognize Punk. She would not even say "hello" to him. She would tell Brown to give Punk two or three thousand dollars and just ignore him. If she had all that money she wouldn't be out picking tomatoes. Punk said he didn't want to be rich; he just wanted to be comfortable. "If you are a millionaire you would have too many headaches." Bertha, still thinking of James Brown, said she had written a hit song and had sent it in and received five thousand dollars. She was not taken seriously. Then Punk told about a dream he had had of owning a brand new Caddy; but when he woke up and looked out of the window, the Caddy wasn't there. (DG)

*   *   *

A group of people were discussing how rich men caused all the problems in the world. "The rich men want to keep the poor men poor, not to give them a chance." "It's the rich people who run the country and they don't care nothing about the poor people." "The guy, Kennedy's brother, who got killed, he cared about poor people but he got killed." "Martin Luther King, he was getting two thousand dollars a week for doing what he was doing, but he gave it all away. His family didn't have a penny when they killed him because he was trying to help the poor people." (DR)

*   *   *

Out of a clear blue sky, a kid announced, "If I were a millionaire, I would help poor people." Hump said, "Me too. A working man just can't become rich. You work and you work and you still don't get nothing. You have to be a crook if you're going to be a millionaire. You have to be a crook and steal the money from the workers." (AK)

* * *

At about four o'clock Geech stood up in the bean field and said, "This is a hell of a way to make a living. Shit, you work all day in this heat and you get almost nothing. Us poor people should get together and have a poor people's organization. There are more poor people in the United States than there are rich people. All the poor people should get together, whether they are black or white or red." Aaron nodded his agreement, "Yes, that's right; yeah, yeah, yeah," in a quiet voice. Geech continued, "You may not know it, but the United States is run by about fifteen men and that's all, people like the Rockefellers and the Kennedys." Aaron didn't say much and Geech repeated, "It's just about fifteen men, whether you know it or not." Aaron said, "Well, I guess so." (DR)

* * *

Gail and her sister talked about their rich relatives. Gail bragged that she had a relative who owned four houses. Punk asked, "What do you mean by rich?" "He is a millionaire." Then there was an argument about how much a million dollars was. Gail said that a million dollars was ten thousand. Punk said it was more than that, that it was a hundred thousand. (DG)

* * *

People were waiting for the farmer so that they could be paid off. "God knows where he is. He may be drunk somewhere, lying in a ditch." "Maybe he's at the racetrack. He owns a lot of horses." Ernestine commented, "He owns a lot of everything," explaining how farmers were really rich, with more money than they knew what to do with. "But they don't give a damn about poor people." Freddy said that the only thing he liked about the army was that everybody got the same thing. "I got a uniform and a haircut, and the guy next to me may be real rich but he got a uniform and a haircut just the same as mine." (DR)

Prisons and Police

The extent to which migrants' experience with the larger society is dominated by police and jail cannot be estimated, but it is clearly the penal aspects of society that are perceived as the most relevant. From

the migrants' perspective, the government and the law are neither sup-
portive nor protective institutions; they are threatening and must be
avoided at all costs. Police are "out to get you" and must be outwitted.
There is a vast and often grim lore concerning jail. Loss of freedom is
dreaded, but people joke about the benefits of life in jail as contrasted
with the labor camp. Stories of jail experiences serve to make the
present situation more tolerable by contrast; or, they affirm that it is
possible to survive similar potential experiences in the future.

Bear told a story about driving at 80 miles an hour in a 50-mile zone. He
was stopped and given a ticket. The cop wanted his license and registration.
"Well, I gave him my license, but I didn't have my 'regimation' there, so I
had to go down and see the judge." When he went to pay his fine, the judge
was not there, and his wife told him to return in a few days. Bear, however,
paid her without waiting for the judge. "Shit, I don't want to see that judge;
he's a mean, mean bastard."

Bear also told about the time he was driving near the camp without a
license. The cop had stopped him once before and warned him to get a
permit or he'd be in trouble. This time, when he saw the same cop, Bear
circled around and went back to town, where he played hide-and-seek with
the cop. When he saw the cop going down one street, he would drive up
another. Finally, he parked his car, ran into the post office, and hid. When
the cop turned the corner he ran into the police station. Just as the cop came
back, Bear walked out of the police station with a stamped learner's permit,
which he had just that moment gotten, so the cop could not do anything.
(ET)

*　　　　*　　　　*

We were stopped on the road by a New York State policeman. The
policeman claimed that it was just a routine safety check, but people
mumbled that we had been stopped because we were a car full of black
people with Florida tags on the car. The cop wanted to know where we
were going and where we had come from. We gave him the name of the
grower. He opened the car door and shined the light around inside. The
only thing he checked in the "safety investigation" was the driver's license
and registration. He made no check of safety equipment in the car. (CL)

*　　　　*　　　　*

People seem to have definite ideas concerning the power of the police.
For example, Jessie mentioned that a black police officer from Lake Wells
can arrest only black people. Bubba added, "But, if you were a policeman,
you may have to arrest your own mother. You take a pledge and if your own

mother does wrong, you have to arrest her." Jessie tried to argue that since this officer could arrest only colored people, he didn't have to arrest *everyone* that had done wrong, and it would not be necessary for him to arrest his mother. Everyone agreed, however, that black officers take a pledge to arrest only black people. Jessie and Bubba then talked about the times they had been in jail. Once Bubba's "old lady" had also been arrested with him as "material witness." I asked him what a material witness was and he couldn't tell me. "No one wants their old lady in jail but all you can do is to beg the man not to put her in jail and maybe he won't." (MR)

*   *   *

J.L. runs a nearby camp and juke. He is reputed to be "very rich—worth a quarter million dollars." According to Tom, J.L. and our crew leader run a "slavery racket," trading workers. When J.L. is hard up for cash, he will "sell a man for fifty dollars." Then he'll send someone in to our camp to lure him back.

J.L. sells liquor and beer at high prices, and it is rumored that he deals in drugs. But now, Tom claims, things will get much tougher, for the local sheriff is retiring. It used to be that every Monday morning, J.L. made a big payoff at the sheriff's office. With the new sheriff, Tom predicts it will be cool for awhile. However, "This guy will be straight for a couple of years and then he'll learn and start taking money also." (ET)

*   *   *

Raymond told me that he has a son who got into trouble stealing a car, and, unlike most fathers, he refused to post bond. He felt that if he posted bond the kid would just go out and steal another car. He criticized the lawyers that you can hire for $1,000. "All they do is tell you to remember that you are colored, and that's how it is, you get your sentence anyway." (IM)

*   *   *

One of the teen-agers in the camp had been in prison when he was eleven years old. He described how he and a friend had been going through cars in a parking lot when the police caught them. Both ran and almost got away, when the policeman fired shots into the air. His friend froze and said, "I'm not going anyplace," and, afraid he would squeal, the boy stopped also. He told us how he was brought into the police station, thrown up against the wall, and beaten by the cops. "That cop hit me man, bam, bam, and I wouldn't tell him nothing, bam, bam, and I finally told him what he wanted to know and he asked me what I was doing. He hit me again, bam, bam." The boy went on to describe his stay in prison. When he first walked in, it wasn't too bad. There was a big sign that said, "The more work you do, the more food you eat." The first night he went to dinner and they had grilled cheese sandwiches and bacon and he was happy. He got up the next morning, figuring on a fine breakfast, only to find oatmeal with roach legs and heads swimming around in it. No one could eat the food and they dumped it out and never ate oatmeal again. There were microphones in every room, and one day when he was joking about how lousy the food was, the warden got on the microphone to ask, "Who is that in there talking about the food?" The boy got beaten up. "Man, I was crying, 'Don't hit me no more.' " (AK)

Our Town

The migrants' most immediate contacts with the outside world are through the local community: stores, gas stations, laundromats, and such service facilities. Never sure of social and physical boundaries in the north, migrants approach the local community with fear and ambivalence. Pressure is exerted on individuals who call attention to the group. The general assumption parallels the attitude toward the police: stores and other enterprises are "out to get you." And again, what is relevant is not the validity of this assumption, but that the migrants' perceptions are dominated by a nearly paranoid expectation of being exploited.

Driving down the road looking for the farm, the bus stopped at a road with a chain across it and a sign that read, "Posted." We stayed there for a while to wait for the other buses and trucks. In about twenty minutes, four vehicles arrived and we all stood on the road trying to figure where we were. One of the women said, "You see that sign, you better not be going on that man's property, you know it's posted." She pretended to read the sign. "All vehicles 60 miles per hour. Niggers on foot 210 miles per hour. We better not go in there cause I can only do 200." People laughed but someone said, "These fools better know what they're doing because they're not going to have me stretched by my neck in some tree up here a thousand miles from home." Then others began to worry that it would be dangerous to walk onto posted property; that the man could shoot them or have them put in jail. (GP)

*   *   *

I bought 50 cents worth of food at the grocery and laid a dollar on the table; then there was 50 cents on the table that I took as change. As soon as I reached for the change the guy said, "Wait a minute, that's what you're paying with." I didn't want to fight over it, so I walked out. When I mentioned what had happened, a woman said, "Yes, they try and cheat you." Once, she had given him a ten-dollar bill and he claimed it was only a five. She said, "If you don't give me my five-dollars change back, I'm going to wreck this store," and he gave her the money. Bull said that he lost a five-dollar bill in another store. He didn't try to get it back because, he said, the man would pretend that he didn't have it. Tom told a story about a Negro storekeeper who was cheated by a white customer. In another story a Puerto Rican went into a store, waving a bunch of twenties, but then paid for a purchase with a one. The lady, not thinking, gave him nineteen dollars in change and he walked out. The cheaters in all the stories were white or Puerto Rican and those cheated were black. (DG)

* * *

Roosevelt pulled the bus up at a supermarket, asking if anyone wanted to get out. There was no parking lot in front of the store so he had to pull up to the curb. Next door to the supermarket was a medical center and on the front lawn was a sign saying, "Parking in the rear," indicating a parking lot for patients. Those on the bus, however, took the sign to mean that our bus had to go round to the back of the store, which was impossible because we could not turn around. Roosevelt said that it would be really bad to park where we were and we would probably get into trouble, so we left without going in. (DG)

* * *

On the way back from the fields we had a flat tire and pulled into a garage. While waiting, the fellows on the truck stood around and would not go inside the garage. If they wanted something, they waited for the man to pass by and asked him to pick up a pack of cigarettes, potato chips, or cake, or whatever they wanted. The man would go inside to get the food, and when he came out they gave him the money. They never went inside with him. They were even afraid to ask him for the keys to the toilet. (GP)

National Crises

During the summers of research, an extraordinary number of dramatic events were taking place. The Vietnam war, the draft, assassinations, elections, riots in major cities in the United States, and the black power movement were subjects of public discussion and concern throughout the nation. Among migrants, however, the widespread lack of knowledge and interest in these events was striking. Relatively few migrants transcended the orbit of personal and immediate experience. Identification with civil rights issues, for example, was negligible: riots and other events, although satiating the mass media, were little discussed and seldom perceived as having any relevance. There were exceptions, particularly among the younger people, who were heard to speak bitterly against the Vietnam war and to relate it to civil rights questions: "The Negro should be fighting in Mississippi." But these views were also a source of dissension, for some apathetic migrants, on being probed, would support any national policy. Nevertheless, there is a pervasive ambiguity in perceptions of national events, dramatized by opinions concerning the popular hero, Cassius Clay. On the one hand, he was admired for his success in the white world; on the other, both admired and criticized for his defiance of the white world in refusing military induction.

"I don't know much about Vietnam except nobody wants to go." "It's bad, I don't like the army." "If the draft gets you, then it gets you; if I get killed, then I get killed." Most migrants are apathetic about the war and will never initiate discussion on this or other events, but if probed will comment as above. There were many migrants who were not even aware of the riots during the summer. When news programs came on television, this was a signal to start talking or to go get a drink. There was little interest in news of any kind. One evening a television show was interrupted by a speech by President Johnson on the riots then taking place all over the country. The five or six people watching all got up and went to sleep. All the lights were out and I was the only person left watching the speech. Completely out of touch with the urban ghetto, migrants see no identification between those riots and themselves. Another evening, during a special program on the riots, everyone was talking. Jessie said, "Everyone shut up, I want to hear it," but others replied, "We want to play whist, don't worry about it, what the hell do you care?" Jessie however, was interested in the riots. "You ought to listen to the news, you might learn something. Don't you ever want to know anything? You're going to be picking cherries all your damn life." The most apathetic people are generally the older and less educated migrants, and often, as in my camp, this includes almost everyone.

Another group, in some camps, were more interested in world events. They viewed the riots as destructive and the war and the draft as necessary. "Newark is a nice town. I don't know why them people want to mess it up." "If we don't fight communism over there, we'll have to fight it here." "We're fighting the dirty commies." "The war in Vietnam is just like Korea except there's more escalation now." As to the violence in the ghettos, this group, less apathetic than the others, talked as follows: "Black power is not the answer. I never went in for this racial stuff." "You know that Martin Luther King got a medal for what he did but Rap Brown sure ain't gonna get one." "Things are so good and quiet I don't know what people riot for up there in those cities." "Riots won't get them anywhere." "Colored folks want to go too fast. The North saved us from the South—the North is better than the South. These riots are just caused by young teen-agers." "Why can't we go along with these white folks no more. Why we gotta be fighting and shooting them and killing them and all?" This group, like the apathetic migrants, tend to be older people. They avoid associating any of the issues, the draft or the riots, with race. Race is discussed as a factor in the riots, not as a source, but only insofar as they will "give Negroes a bad name and slow down civil rights," which are "just around the corner." They feel themselves to be patriotic; it is "their" government that needs people to fight in Vietnam and they feel everyone should serve. A couple in one camp were very proud that their son was fighting in Vietnam.

In striking contrast, a small group of younger migrants perceive the war as between "white America and yellow Vietnam." They see the riots as an expression of black discontent and do not see integration as a path to equality. The very few migrants who talk this way, mostly young and personally preoccupied with the draft, rarely speak of riots without relating them to the draft, and tie all issues to racial sources. "The war in Vietnam is a mess, we don't belong there." "The black man is getting pushed around in Vietnam." "Why fight against someone who has never done anything to colored people, for the white man who has done so much against us." "I won't fight in Vietnam; if my brother was white, he wouldn't have had to fight. He got killed. I'll spend my time in the pen first." "Don't know what we're doing in Vietnam; we ought to get out of Vietnam and let them fight it out." "All the people in Vietnam should be fighting in Detroit. Those people (the Vietnamese) done nothing to us, but there are people here that have done a lot more to us and we should revenge ourselves on them." "This is hell on a colored man—he goes over there and fights and then comes back over here and fights these folks too." This group expressed approval of the riots. "They're raising hell and really kicking up some sand." "Negroes got the white man wondering what's coming next. This younger generation is not going to have to take what the last one did." In general, these people feel that "something good" will come of the riots.

Although this younger group of people took a line approximating a "black power" position, few ever used the term "black power," and few connected their verbal position with any possible action on their own part. The relative size of this group in the camps varied. In one camp with a young crew, about half could be placed in this group. In contrast, in my camp, "black power" types were nonexistent. By far the larger number of migrants were apathetic, and even those who took the more militant position were basically disinterested if the frequency of these events as topics of conversation is any indication.

There was one subject about which the people showed a great deal of interest: the affair of Cassius Clay. In the early part of the summer of 1967, Clay, who previously declared himself a Black Muslim, refused induction into the army. For this act he was stripped of his title as the heavyweight boxing champion and faced federal prosecution. This event was one of the most common topics of conversation in all camps, discussed only less often than the weather and the cherries that were being picked. People were constantly arguing whether Clay was right or wrong to refuse induction. If a man was against the war, more often than not he was influenced by Clay's action. The interesting thing about Clay was that nobody was apathetic about him: either he was a great hero or a great fool. He was a fool because he had a great chance to make it and blew it, "You just don't mess with Uncle Sam." "They had to burn his ass somehow." "Clay fucked himself up." He was a hero because no black man belonged in that war: "White preachers get out of the draft, why shouldn't Clay?" Some migrants even changed their estimates of Clay's fighting ability. "Clay's fight was fixed," or "He's dumb and couldn't fight anyway." He became either a "dumb nigger who blew his chance," or a "big hero and the government didn't know what it was doing." On this issue, only a few remained apathetic. (MR)

*   *   *

Flo said, "My cousins and brothers are over in Vietnam, fighting communism, so we can be free." Then she added, "They should have their asses over here, fighting in Alabama and Mississippi." Reece, however, thought they should be fighting both in Vietnam and in Mississippi and Alabama. "All the people in the country are one people and as one people we have to fight together." Flo replied, "We're not one people because if we were one people we wouldn't be in this camp and the man wouldn't try to cheat us. How can we be one people like that?" Another woman added, "You would think that they would try to help their own people before they help other people. Now they bring all the Cubans and Jamaicans in and give them jobs and let us suffer. That shows they don't care about us." Flo got belligerent, "Damn right, anybody messes with me and I'll mess them back, I'll mess them right back in Alabama or in Georgia. I'm not a nonviolent nigger. Let somebody mess with me and I'll kill 'em. I'm no Martin

Luther King: hit me on one cheek and then turn the other cheek and hit me on that." Reece said, "Well, I see you don't care for Martin Luther King." "No, I love him, I think he's a great man. I believe in what he says, but I don't want anybody to hit me. I'll kill 'em. My husband is a member of the NAACP back home and he goes to all that stuff. Martin Luther King's got an entire bodyguard with him . . . just like the president in this country, yet he wants to send other people out there on the streets and says not to hit back when you get hit. He must be crazy." Flo talked of a civil rights march in Florida. "We all went through and tore that town down." She hit her fists on the seat and said, "We rule that town. There ain't nobody gonna tell us what to do." Reece then asked sarcastically, "Why do you live on one side of town and they live on the other?" and she claimed, "No, you can live anywhere you want to. We Negroes run that town, they don't walk over us there." Reece answered, "Yeah, tell me another story, you run the town all right: you run out of it when they say run and that's about all the running in that town you do." Someone suggested that we all go back to Africa. Reece argued, "That's all wrong. You have to stay here in America because we are American citizens. We have to fight and keep this thing going and make it a better place." Flo argued, "How are we going to make it better when the white people control the thing? It's not up to us to make it a better place; it's up to them. As far as I'm concerned, we can just get out of here and leave it. I don't owe this country anything." The talk moved on to the gap between blacks and whites in America. Reece insisted we are gaining. "We're at the bottom. We started at the bottom, so there is only one way to go. Up." Flo, however, complained that we weren't progressing, but Reece said, "The trouble with most Negroes is they want this entire thing to happen overnight, boom; go to bed one night and wake up the next morning and everything's changed. Well it's not going to happen that way—you might as well get it out of your head." The women blamed the older people for the slow progress. "It's their fault, because when you have the voting drive and things like that, the old people look at you and say, 'Why should I go down and vote? Don't make no difference who gets in the chair.' They're the ones who stop everything. They got us afraid of white people." Then they blamed the school system. "I was going to school and it was always the kids with light skin and curly hair that they pushed, and if you were really black and had nappy hair you could be the brightest kid in the class and they didn't pay any attention to you." Finally, they blamed the Cubans and Jamaicans who were being brought in and given better jobs. "They keep us down so they don't have to worry about what we think." (GP)

*   *   *

Hart commented that he had heard a speech by Rap Brown on television about how "we're going to burn the town if they don't come around." He thought Rap Brown was okay, but he didn't like Stokely Carmichael and hoped they kept him over in Cuba and wouldn't let him come back to this country. "That damn nigger is too smart for anybody. He's just going around getting Negroes in trouble and not solving anything." He said, "You saw what happened in Newark, you saw what happened in Detroit, and you saw what happened in Maryland when Brown was there. This is the kind of stuff that doesn't accomplish anything. I just think they should keep him in Cuba and not let him come back. I hope they railroad him to the federal penitentiary forever."

Paul had heard Rap Brown tell people not to listen to this birth control business because Negroes should produce as many as they can. Paul agreed: "God put man on earth and said, 'reproduce and replenish the earth,' and if you let your wife take those pills and all those other things they have, you are really going against God's will. If he didn't want you to replenish the earth this would not be in the Bible." Paul also added another reason for being against birth control. "Once you release the seed from your body and you have something there to stop it, it's just like killing somebody." A young group sitting on the bench agreed with Rap Brown, "We should get together and produce more children so that when the time comes for us to fight, we can really do it because we will have the people to do it." (GW)

*   *   *

This morning we were talking about the way Negroes are treated in different southern states. Spaceman said, "They are still burning niggers in Alabama at the rate of one per week." Those listening took this very seriously and talked about burning Negroes as if it were true. Slim said it was a lie, that they were killing more Negroes in Florida than in Alabama, but Spaceman argued that in Alabama there are gangs of white boys who go around picking up people on the streets to beat them up and nothing happens to them. He said this would never happen in Florida because the Negroes in Florida tend to stick together. If a Negro was beaten in Florida, the next day a couple of white boys would be beaten in return. The subject turned to Mississippi, where everyone agreed "they still burn people." (GP)

*   *   *

Carl said a lot of guys are sick and tired of going to fight for freedom in Vietnam and coming home to find things the way they are here. He thought Cassius Clay was right not to go into the army. We discussed the number of Negroes in the army. One person said that one of the airborne divisions was 90 percent Negro, and 40 percent of the whole army was

Negro, at least on the front lines. Another had read that "half of the people who die are Negro, and yet when we get over here we don't have the same thing that the white guys have. We are dying fighting for someone else's freedom and we don't even have freedom ourselves." A young kid asked, "How many years will you have to spend in jail if you don't go into the army when they tell you that you have to go?" "Ten." The kid then said, "Ten years is a long time. Maybe it's better to go over and take your chances." Carl thought it was pretty stupid to go because you could get killed just walking around here. Why should you go over there and increase the chances of getting killed? "Jail might be a safe place around here after awhile." There was agreement. "If you're concerned about your safety, the safest place is in jail." This prompted others to air their grievances. "You go down there to vote and they won't let you vote; how are you supposed to get anything done for yourself if they won't even let you vote? Then we have a riot and they say you're acting like animals, or criminals, or something." "Yes, that's right. They put all the blame on you when actually they force people to do a lot of these things. They force people into violence." "How could King say to turn the other cheek?" "That's right, if you turn the other cheek the only thing that will happen is that you will get hit on that cheek." (GP)

*   *   *

Lonnie, Hart, and Red were playing cards and talking about the army and the draft. Red said he had been in the army once, but if it came time for him to go again he would not go. He didn't know exactly what was going on or why we were in Vietnam, but he didn't see any sense to it. Later on Hart and Red, both of whom had been in the army in 1961–1962, discussed World War II and the Korean conflict. They argued if it was a conflict or a war. Red explained that in order to have a war, it must be declared by Congress, and in the Korean conflict, Congress had nothing to do with it. He went on to tease others about their ignorance, asking them if they ever heard of "Pork Chop hill." "What is that, some hill?" "You never hear of that place they fought the famous battle?" Lonnie thought he was trying to tell some joke. Then Red asked about Iwo Jima, and Lonnie had never heard of that place either. He asked Red, "How do you know so much about American history when you only went so far as the ninth grade in school?" (GW)

*   *   *

Johnny asked me if I were going to vote next week. "There's a big election on August 6th and they're going to elect another president." I asked him whom he was going to vote for and he said, "Rockefeller. All the other guys want to take us back to slave times. There's that guy Nixon and he's real bad. He wants to take everyone back to slave times, and there's a guy from California and he's real bad. He wants to take everyone back to slave times." I asked, "Isn't there also a guy named Humphrey?" He said, "Yeah, he wants to take people back to slave times, too. I was raised in the south; I'm not going to vote for any Democrat." He talked of President Kennedy's assassination. He was working for a grower at the time and, he said, the grower laughed at the news and asked him what he thought. He had answered, "I don't think nothing about it." Referring to all three assassinations, Johnny commented, "Three good men were killed by foreigners. They bring those people from across the water and they treat them real good— they treat them better than the people who was born and raised here. They give them all good jobs, good money, and the foreigners kill three good men." Bean remarked that an awful lot of people were involved with these killings. "I bet if you looked into it you would find the same people behind those who killed President Kennedy, Martin Luther King, and the president's brother." There was some more talk and then someone said, "I wonder why Johnson hasn't been killed?" "He pays a real lot of money to keep himself safe." (DR)

*   *   *

Shorty said that three great men had been killed by guns lately and it was just no good. "Three really great men who tried to help other men have been shot. The only way for there to be any good in the world is for people to just stop making guns. They can settle all their problems with just these two [holding up his fists]. You don't have to kill a man to solve your problems." He then talked about the atomic bomb. "You can blow one of those things up and the air gets poisoned and nothing can grow, no people can live." He explained how a little tiny one had been exploded a long time ago, and for seventy-five years nothing had grown in the place where it was exploded. He was asked how many of these bombs there were in the world and he replied that there was only one. Shorty explained how it was surrounded by hundreds of guards, but he felt that wouldn't keep it safe. "All you have to do is have a third of those guards go out and get drunk, or have one guy call another a nasty name, and they'll start shooting and one of those bullets will hit the bomb and it's all over for the whole world. Those people won't even know they had lived and neither would you or I." (DR)

*   *   *

Pops and Joe have never filed an income tax form. Joe said, "If I don't file, I don't have anything to worry about. They will never know how much to take from me because they never know how much I make. They'll never catch me on income tax evasion." "Suppose you get a good job someday. Don't you plan to file then?" "No, I'll never file income tax." Pops said he had worked for forty years and had never paid income tax and never planned to either. He felt that if he started paying now they would catch up with him and make him pay for the last forty years. (GW)

The World of Television

Those who are apathetic about national issues are sometimes deeply involved in the fantasy world portrayed by television. A few migrants bring TV sets from the south and others pick up used sets in the north. Most camps, though not all, have at least one television set, and the owners usually allow others to watch. Where television is available, it is very popular. News programs are routinely rejected in favor of fictionalized programs, usually serials with which the viewers become closely involved. Literal interpretation of events on the television screen is common.

In the evening, the popular TV shows are the action shows, such as the *Invaders*, or *Combat*, or *Daniel Boone*—which is the favorite. In the afternoon, Jessamay often goes back to camp and watches soap operas. News programs or analysis programs are avoided. The migrants also avoid cartoon shows. When the *Lone Ranger* was a live western, it was watched, but now that it is a cartoon show, people complain, "We want to see the real Lone Ranger, not this stuff." The TV is in Jessamay's room and we watch through the open door, sitting on boxes and chairs. Occasionally the younger children go right in and sit on the floor in front of the screen.

Scrap knows the name of every TV actor, including the support actors, almost without exception. He and others have definite preferences. When *Star Trek* came on, everyone screamed that they didn't want to see it except for Jessie, who thought it was a good show. A Bette Davis movie in which she played a double role intrigued people, but they did not understand the plot because they kept confusing the characters. When the Thursday night movie played *Lilies of the Field*, people got very excited about Sidney Poitier. "That's some cat, he really can go; wow, the guy's great." People talk a great deal during the shows about what is happening, and it is necessary from time to time to shout for everyone to be quiet. Generally, they respond directly to whatever is occurring on the screen, listening very literally. In one scene in *Daniel Boone*, the men were talking about a pretty girl, and an older woman (as a part of the play) interrupted them saying,

"Can't we change the conversation and talk about something else. Let's not talk about this any more." All the migrants in the room watching this scene immediately got very quiet and responded as if this had really happened. (MR)

*   *   *

Junior asked me, after watching *Time Tunnel*, "If you could travel back in time, where would you want to go?" I asked what he meant and he described how you could go back any time in history. He wanted to see the Amazons because, "They sound real tough. They are women who used to fight in wars and stuff like that." He also wanted to see the animals in the Wild West. Then he asked if John Wayne was really at the Alamo. I said, "Hell no, man, he might have been in the movie picture or something like that but he wasn't at the Alamo. That was back in 1800." He said, "No, I read in the encyclopedia that John Wayne was at the Alamo." I argued that he was in a movie, but Junior stuck to his story. (DR)

*   *   *

Red and the group working near him in the field were talking about TV programs. They believe many of them are true stories of things that really happened, and they identify with the characters. Red remarked how Granny in the *Beverly Hillbillies* was spunky despite the fact that she was old. Checker Bill hollered over that she really wasn't that old but was made up to look that way. This started an argument as others said that she had to be as old as she was on the screen. Meanwhile, Pat, who wanted to go to college in California, was told seriously by Red that if she wrote to the Beverly Hillbillies and told them she wanted to come to California, they might send her the transportation money. No one contradicted Red. Many people in the crew believe that the Hillbillies have discovered oil and that they live out west in the manner portrayed on television.

Other shows are also interpreted literally. Pope, talking about the war in Vietnam, said, "Why don't they send some of the guys on *Combat* out to Vietnam? Those guys are good fighters." Another time, Willy Wine asked me seriously if *Star Trek* was real. I told him it was just made up, and he was relieved, because "it would be frightening if these things happened." He said that everything was happening too fast: the moon, the astronauts, under the sea. "Some day, monsters like Gargantua will be walking the earth." (LR)

10

The Search for Solutions

Migrant workers grope for solutions to their dissatisfactions. The efficacy of direct action for change is outside their experience. They express their malaise but perceive few means to change their way of life, for change involves dealing in some way with the outside world and this evokes anticipation of failure. Discontent, then, is likely to be expressed by vague complaints; demands are rare, and when made by individual migrants, seldom elicit group support. Cooperative and cohesive action in a migrant labor crew is impeded by mistrust. Although there are occasional moments of mutual support when a group is faced with external pressure, there is no experience in the utility of organization to achieve common goals.

This chapter is concerned with the gropings for solutions. One solution, an individual one, is to drop out of the migrant labor stream. Many discuss the possibility, but few actually try. Another form of groping is griping. Verbalizing irritations gives them incipient form and structure. These gropings represent the early stages of preorganization; out of them develop experiments with more concrete ways of expressing dissatisfaction: walkoffs, stoppages, and other forms of spontaneous strikes. These dissatisfactions might be utilized and built upon by organized labor, but several incidents involving migrants suggest the irrelevance of standard trade unionism. Finally, we turn to a single contrasting case of successful organization, a religious group that produced significant social gains for migrants.

Dropping Out

Unable to change their situation, migrants carry on a great deal of discussion about escaping from it. Some find jobs and leave the camps, but many soon return south to continue as agricultural workers.

Migrants learn about jobs and housing in town through occasional shopping trips or through the visits of ex-migrants to the camps. People seldom strike out alone, but wait until they can accumulate some money and get a friend to go with them. There is considerable uncertainty about leaving the camp, and many who talk constantly about leaving, never actually take the step. Those who leave have few concrete expectations concerning the future. They think only in terms of what they are escaping. They vaguely expect that "life will be better," but few have concrete plans, relying on acquaintances to pull them through an initial adjustment.

Dropouts confront such problems as jobs, housing, and loneliness, and often consider their stay in the north as temporary, even after finding jobs. They harbor plans of leaving, either to return south or to move on. Few have clear goals beyond making money. The common reliance on the grapevine rather than on institutional channels for finding jobs and housing, and the reluctance to use banks suggest a continued mistrust and fear of established institutions.

Some dropouts move into a growing number of permanent rural communities, known as "stagrant communities." These settlements, composed mainly of ex-migrants, differ from labor camps only in their permanence. Similarly isolated, they are also enclosed and insulated, with their own stores, jukes, bars, and barbershops. Migrants who move into these communities often continue in employment related to agriculture, such as packinghouse work. The following selections describe the visitors to the camp and the situation of several migrants who have attempted to establish a new pattern of living in a northern urban environment.

On Sundays there were many visitors in the camp from nearby communities. These were former migrants who had dropped out and settled in the area. They were better dressed than the rest of the people in the camp. Their children had lost much of their southern accent. Most drove in with new cars, immediately giving them prestige in the eyes of the migrants. Some came back to show off their cars and clothes. Others came to make money in the camp. There was one man who had become a pusher of "black market" (probably stolen) goods who approached me and asked if I wanted to buy a stereo set for $40.00. It was worth at least $250.00 on the market and could be delivered in two weeks. There was another fellow who came out regularly and became very chummy with a few migrants, giving them rides in his car. I rode around with him for a while, and his conversation focused on all the money he had and how little it meant to him. Then he talked about a friend who had money and wouldn't share it. He said guys like that were no good and he had no use for him; whenever he had money, he shared it. He always showed up at the camp on Friday night, after most people got paid. People like to hang around with him because he is a good dresser and has a new car. Rather than fall out with him, they will loan him money when he asks for it in the name of friendship.

Although ex-migrants were admired, there was hostility toward them as well. One of the visitors told Pinochle she had some shirts back home that he or someone else in the camp could have. He replied, "I have some shirts of my own in my room that maybe you could use." Although people accept old clothes from the Salvation Army and other organizations, they resent handouts from ex-migrants, whom they don't consider to be that far above them.

Visitors bring news into camp about job opportunities in town. Sometimes they will encourage people to leave, claiming to know about available jobs and promising to help with housing. Many migrants drop out to nearby cities by this route. An ex-migrant, in showing off his own success, will boast that he knows of available jobs, and someone will take him up on it and leave the camp, having some hope of assistance. One woman with seven children talked about going to a nearby town, getting on welfare immediately, and then trying to find a good job. She said she would know then that her children could go to a good school. People feel that in the north they may be able to get "a nice house, a refrigerator, a stove, a television, and a car." One woman said, "If I move north, my kids will learn to talk pretty like the people up here." I asked her what she meant. "Well, they pick their words better. Like someone from the north might say, 'I'm not going home' but someone from the south will say, 'I ain't going home.' They just pick their words better here." (GP)

*   *   *

A group of boys were laughing at a kid of about fourteen who had a map in his hand and was close to tears. He had gone downtown to buy a map of the eastern United States because he was planning to leave the camp that day. He was studying the map when someone discovered that it was a map of the county and not of the eastern United States. The guys were teasing him. He replied bitterly, "That's okay. You people had to lie to get me up in this wilderness. I don't know where I am, but I'm getting out of here sooner or later."

People over forty with families also talk of leaving, but seldom seriously. The older people say, "I'm getting out of here," but the younger boys are more specific and sometimes make definite plans. I was sitting up by the big house, and five young men from eighteen to twenty-three years old started to walk out of the camp. I asked them where they were going and the youngest, whom I knew well, said in a hushed voice, "We're cutting out for Syracuse. You wanna go?" "Well, I'll start that way, but I don't know if I'll make it all the way." We started down the road. As soon as we got on the main road, a hundred yards from the camp, one guy said, "I'm glad to leave that motherfucker," as if we were really away from the camp. They discussed how sick they were of having other people take money from them and how you can make more money in the south than in the north. They said they heard there was a big difference between people in the north and the south, but they couldn't see it. The people in the north are just as "hard" as the people in the south, only in a different way. "Everyone kicks you in the ass, no matter where you go; so there's really not that much difference."

We came to a house with a lot of dirt piled up on the lawn. One fellow said, "Why don't we go ask these people if they want to spread this dirt around? There's work there." Another replied, "Don't be such a damn fool. Come on, now. If we're gonna get to Syracuse, let's go." But the first man was stubborn and went to the house while the rest of us waited on the road. He knocked on the door and a dog barked in the yard. "Come on, man, before you get shot messing around here." There was no answer and he was getting ready to go to the back door, but the others said, "No, come on, you'll get us in trouble, if you go back there." Finally, he was persuaded and we continued walking. We asked the distance to Syracuse at a gas station and discovered it was 45 miles. We had walked only a mile, and one guy said, "I'll be goddamned if I can do that 45 times over again. Let's go back." There was a big discussion as to whether we should turn back or go ahead. Finally, someone said, "Look, man, there's nothing back there. We might as well keep on going. If we go back, we're gonna be stuck there for the rest of the summer. We either go now, or we don't go at all." Three decided to go, and finally the others followed. We walked down the road together another 2 miles, at which point I said I was going back. As I started back, one of the fellows ran and caught up with me and said he was going to go back too. We walked together about a quarter of a mile, and he changed his mind again. He turned around and ran to catch up with the others. Eventually, however, they all showed up back at the camp. The indecison was striking. They badly wanted to go but really didn't know what to do. (GP)

*   *   *

Moe has an apartment in town with a kitchen, a bathroom, and one bedroom (large enough to fit three beds), a table and a stove. He shares the apartment with two other ex-migrants who left the camp at the same time. They pay $60.00 a month rent. The building is in very bad condition. Moe originally came north because he wanted to get to New York City; he intended to drop out right away. He had $20.00 when he got to the camp but he did not leave immediately. He had met a couple of fellows on the way who said they wanted to leave too. He waited and worked until they were ready to go. That was a mistake because the crew leader, in order to keep him there, refused to pay him.

The first thing Moe noticed about the camp when he came was that it was a "nowhere place, out in the middle of nothing." He felt very lonely as soon as he got there and wanted to leave right away; but he had promised the others to wait and wanted company. He finally left the camp a month and a half after he arrived, alone, without the others, who were still reluctant to leave. He moved to Ithaca. He first went to an employment agency and found a job with a painter. He didn't have enough money for a room or apartment, so he stayed in an abandoned car for one week until he got his first pay check. His first room cost him $8.00 a week. He was able to make only $45.00 a week, so after getting settled in Ithaca, he started going to Elmira and Syracuse on weekends to look for a better job. Failing to find one, he then decided to try New York City. He quit his job and took his savings of $130.00 to New York. When he got there, he found a job in a record shop earning $37.00 a week. This was not enough, but he stayed, hoping to do better. When his money began to run out, he returned to Ithaca, using the last of his money for a bus ticket. He got a job in a grocery in which he works forty-five hours a week and earns $75.00. He is satisfied; the people that he works for are nice, but he still claims that this is only temporary. "It's O.K. for now."

His closest friends are the two people with whom he rooms. He doesn't do much for entertainment because he doesn't want to spend his money. His roommates often go to bars, and the women clip them as soon as they get drunk. This happened to him when he first came and he decided he wasn't going out drinking any more and is saving his money. I asked if he put it in a bank, and he said, no, he saves it "someplace else," suggesting that it is somewhere in his apartment. He sends no money south. His parents are able to take care of themselves and he has four brothers and sisters at home to help them. (GP)

*   *   *

Dickson shares a room with Moe. He had no notion of dropping out of the camp prior to coming north. He had heard about a crew coming through town, and he and two brothers got on the bus that very day. They wanted to make money to go back to school. When he got to the camp, however, his reaction was negative. He didn't make any money there; he didn't care about how bad or lonely it was, he was just there to make money. He decided that he had better do something, so he left the camp with one brother and came to Ithaca, where he heard there was work. He had no idea about any specific job or housing before leaving. His brother could not find work and went back home, but Dickson was told by a friend of a job at a cafeteria and he got the job right away. He washes dishes and picks up trays. His hours are "fairly short"; he works forty-five hours a week and earns $65.00. He likes the job and the people he works with but he still plans to leave town. He expects to make enough money before Christmas to go back and finish half a year of high school and then work his way through college. He is giving his savings to "someone downtown" to hold for him. (GP)

*   *   *

Jimmy is working as a hired hand on a farm. He once had a factory job in Florida, but got tired of that work. Things "went wrong" for him and he left a few years ago and came north on the season for several years. He had not planned to leave the camp, but things were so bad this summer that he decided he had to go. First he went to Syracuse. He could not find a steady job there, so he came back to the camp. A few days later he got a job with a farmer near Ithaca. He told the farmer that he would work for him all winter to get the job; but now he has decided that he will leave. The farmer treats him well but he doesn't like the cold weather and it is very lonely on the farm. There is nobody but the farmer, his wife, and his son. He gets only Sunday afternoons off, but all he can do is work, because when he finishes working, he has no way to get around. The only time he comes to town is when the farmer drives him in. He makes $40.00 a week plus his room and board. He now plans to go to Georgia, where he has a wife and three children whom he wants to see at Christmas. Then he will return to Florida and look for a steady job. (GP)

Preorganizational Gropings

From time to time, a few—and only a few—complaints develop into incidents that potentially could lead to incipient organization. The diffuse dissatisfaction described in Chapter 8 occasionally focuses, and possible courses of action are suggested. The few incidents witnessed suggest some of the obstacles to organization: the low level of trust, the reluctance to assume or recognize leadership, the debilitating sense of dependence, inefficacy, and impotence. Protest is feeble, and demands soon dissolve into the usual generalized complaints.

Protest, as it takes form, manifests itself typically in two ways: often it is the women who become the spokesmen of resentment over conditions and who refuse to work; in other cases, the response tends to be focused on the younger men, with two or three people complaining and possibly stopping work but finding little or no support. On the contrary, there is often considerable group pressure, particularly from the older people, to bring those who protest back to work. Those who keep working feel that protest by a few individuals is far from helpful: indeed, they consider it threatening.

Attempts at change by mobilizing the group for overt action are rare and seldom successful. In one case an individual demanding a wage increase for the group failed when the crew leader did not cooperate and the group did not support him. In another, an attempt to stage a walkout was doomed by lack of support. Slowdowns are a common group response to dissatisfaction, but they are not so much an act of organized protest as a symptom of discouragement. The final selection is a record of an abortive attempt by a social worker to organize crews in a large camp. Inexperienced groping and lack of confidence precluded the success of this effort. In terms of the potential for organizational attempts in the future, it is important to note that presently organized industrial workers passed through similar failures due to the same kinds of mistrust, lack of leadership, social dependence, and feelings of impotence vis-à-vis change.

The twenty-three people in the bus were expecting to get a full day's work. No one realized we were going for a mop-up operation on the same field we had picked the day before. When we got to the field, another crew was already picking. We refused to get out of the bus. Several people said the beans were wet, and they would not move. Spaceman, the field walker, said, "Come on now, get out, because the bus has to go back." Eventually, people began to leave the bus. There were five women, however, who remained for a while, but they, too, soon followed reluctantly and joined the group pulling bushel baskets off the back of the truck. Then, when the baskets were down, people turned them over and sat on them. We noticed that the crew at the other end of the field had a bonfire and we walked toward it, still not ready to work. We stood by the bonfire for a while, but when it died down and the other crew began to work again, our crew walked back to our section of the field and settled down quietly to work. We tied bags around us to stay dry in the wet field.

Everyone complained, "It was stupid to come back here and try to pick these beans because no one can make any money." "What do you mean, nobody can make any money? The crew leader can make money. You think when you pick a bushel for 60 cents that the crew leader is getting 60 cents for it? He gets more than that. If you are getting 60 cents, chances are he is getting 20 cents from each bushel you pick. Count the number of people out there, and then think how many bushels they are going to bring in." Then a lady talked bitterly about why people come to our camp. She said there is free rent, there are no gas and electricity bills to pay, you can always eat as long as the crew leaders are there, and there's really no work to do. There are plenty of games every night, adventures, and fights. It is really "one big rest home." She kept a very serious expression and everyone started laughing. Then she said she was going to leave. She couldn't take any more of it, and as soon as she got some more money together, she was leaving the camp.

The complaining continued all morning, and the most anyone picked was 2 bushels, worth $1.20. Around 11:00, Flo said, "This is stupid, I'm not picking any goddamn more," and she turned one of her baskets upside down, sat down, took a wad of snuff and started chewing on it. That was that. Others began to gradually follow. We got on the bus and finally, at the end of the morning, they took us back to camp. No one said anything to Spaceman about the day except Flo, who said, "If you ever bring me out into another field like this, you son of a bitch, I'll cut your goddamn throat." Everybody laughed, including Spaceman, so it was not really considered a threat. (GP)

*   *   *

The crew was glad to go to work, but when we got there everyone was sore because it was a field that had been picked twice before. The field walker said, "Just get out there in the field, there are beans out there." Some people got off the bus, but kept repeating, "Where are the beans? Where are the beans?" Tussy remarked, "These beans are just like me—no damn good." There just weren't any beans out there. Then a dispute started. Six women remained on the bus and said they were not going to pick any beans and they wanted Spaceman to take them back to camp. "What the hell does he think we are anyway—dogs, or something?" Spaceman passed the responsibility to the crew leader, "Look, it's not me; it's the crew leader. Emmett tells me what to do. I have to do what he says. That's how I get paid. If you don't want to pick, don't pick. I think he's foolish myself, but he said for me to bring you out here so what can I do? He's the boss, not me." A woman replied, "Well, you son of a bitch, you should have told us that when we were back in the camp. I'm not picking." All the women now climbed back on the bus, but the men remained in the field. Spaceman shouted, "Well, you can stay on the bus, but you know what Emmet's going to say if he comes and finds you here. Get off." The women got off and started to walk back to camp, with Spaceman yelling after them, "Yeah, you're cussing me out now, aren't you? Mad as hell at me, aren't you? It's not me, it's the crew leader. He decides what's done around here, not me. Why do you pick on me all the time? I don't do any of this stuff." Just then, the crew leader's wife showed up in her car. Spaceman told her what happened and she said, "Yeah, I seen them walking down the road. You get work for them and they don't want to work. Yet when they don't have work they sit around and complain that there's no work. A pack of damn fools. You can't do anything to please them." (GP)

* * *

Five of us were working well ahead of the other people in the field. The field walker told us to go back and help others because the grower likes everyone to work together. He doesn't want some people to get ahead of the rest of the group. Curtis and Checker Bill refused and we kept working where we were. Then the grower walked over and asked, "Why aren't these people helping the others?" The field walker told him we didn't want to, and the grower said, "If you don't want to go back and help the other people, put your hoe in the truck and get out of the field." Checker Bill immediately dropped his hoe and walked off and we followed. When we passed the older people, they made remarks about "the boys walking off." They didn't know how Frank was going to get the celery in with such a bunch of lazy bums. "These kids better wise up or they're gonna be killed, or get hurt real bad." Later, the grower walked over to the bus and asked for the names of the five people who left the field. He got four names right off, since four of us were there, but the fifth person, Pope, wasn't on the bus at the time. No one wanted to give his name. Each person gave his own name, but even the older people who disapproved of the walkoff did not want to rat on him. While the grower was standing on the steps of the bus, Pope walked up behind him. Then Willy Wine pointed to him and said, "Isn't that him?" The grower turned to Pope, took his name, and left. One of the girls on the bus yelled after him, "This is the last time I'm coming to this place." The grower replied, "Don't blame me, blame your crew leader." "I don't care, this is the last time you'll ever catch me near here." At that point the grower said sarcastically, "Thank you, people, for helping me out," and walked off. As we were leaving, Pope's sister yelled to Willy Wine that he had better keep his mouth shut because the next time he rats she's gonna kill him. Willy Wine said that he wasn't trying to rat, he just wanted to get out of there. Everyone was really cutting down Willy, "You've got a big mouth; why don't you just use it for wine?" (LR)

*   *   *

We finished the field early but there was no checker to weigh in the beans. About a half hour after everyone had quit work, he finally came and we could move to another field. This new field seemed to be worse than the previous one. We got off the bus slowly, went down to the rows, and sat down on bushel baskets looking at the beans. Only four people got right to work. "Reverend sure can find the shit beans. There's nothing here." But people gradually began to work.

Later a white man drove up in a car, and Tom, one of the pickers, started arguing with him. "There's no beans here. Do you expect us to pick scrap beans for 90 cents?" The man said, "What do you mean there are no beans here? There are plenty of beans here." He bent down and picked up a vine to show how many beans there were. He was lucky and got a pretty good one. Tom pointed to another area, but the man would not look at that. Tom insisted we wanted more money for this field, since it would take longer to fill our baskets. Finally the man agreed to go back and get the boss. Meanwhile, Tom wandered around among the people complaining about how bad the beans were. He said he wouldn't pick such a field for 90 cents. Several people stopped working, and he asked them if they'd pick for $1.25. They said they would and Tom said, "Well, that's the price I'm going to try to get." Soon another white man appeared in a truck, and Tom told him that unless we got $1.25, we would just go home. The man said, "Okay, if that's what you want, you'll get it." But he told Tom not to tell the other crew working at the other end of the field because they lived on the farm and were getting only 90 cents a bushel.

Many people still working in the field did not pay much attention to the argument, apparently unaware that it was going on. The only people who participated were Honey and her daughter, who happened to come back at the time Tom was talking to the man, and they added their support.

Later in the day, on our way home, we stopped at a market. We had already been paid for the first field of beans at 90 cents, but now Reverend was supposed to pay us for the second field at $1.25. It turned out after all there had been some misunderstanding. Reverend claimed that we were to get only 90 cents, that the man was paying the regulation price, that is, $1.25 to the crew leader and 90 cents to the crew. Reverend denied he was at fault; the farmer had mistaken Tom for some kind of foreman. He placed all the blame on Tom, claiming he did not know anything about how prices worked and had gotten us into this mixup. He had no business trying to change the price when the crew leader was not around. After we got back to camp, Tom got drunk. He was bitter and discouraged. He came over to the bullpen during the afternoon and complained about what Reverend had done to him. He tried to justify himself for misleading us. All he knew was that the grower agreed to pay $1.25. He was sure the man must have realized this was going to the picker, not just to the crew leader, and that this would mean an increase in the total cost that he would have to pay. The crew leader eventually compromised, to keep people happy, and we were paid $1.00. People grumbled but there was no tendency to do anything further. (DG)

*   *   *

After turning in a bucket of cherries, I looked at the top of my ticket and noticed it said 55 cents per pail. The crew had expected to receive 60 cents. I mentioned to several people that we were getting only "55 goddamn cents a pail" and they took out their tickets and noticed the same thing written on theirs as well. Complaints spread across the field. "You can't live on 55 cents." "I ain't picking for 55 cents. I'm going to get my ass off here." Most people stopped picking when they heard and sat down at the bottom of their ladders. Ann said she would never get a car for 55 cents a bucket and she was damned if she was going to pick. Her husband, Coonie, however, seemed less concerned. He explained the drop in price by the fact that, "Well, they pick easier," but everyone else was in an uproar. Then Bubba suggested that if everyone just walked out of the field, the man would have to raise his price. People seemed to agree; "Yes, Bubba's right, we shouldn't pick. We should all get out of the field." However, in five minutes, they began very slowly to resume work, mostly walking around the trees, picking the cherries from the bottom rather than climbing the ladders. They continued to talk about how the man would have to raise the price if they walked out of the field, but it was apparent that no one was actually going to try it. Bubba stopped picking for himself and began picking for Jessamay, who promised to buy him a beer if he helped her. Jessamay talked about how she was going to pick only three buckets instead of five, although later this also changed. There was a general slowdown, but no one stopped working entirely. Ann, after walking several times around the tree, picked up a couple of cherries haphazardly and said, "Damn, this sure has cut my spirit, but I guess I gotta keep going," and she began to pick seriously again.

When it became clear that no one was going to walk out of the field, I was curious to see if they would if I tried to agitate. I began to complain that "no one can make money for a shitty 55 cents." I directed my comments mostly to Bubba, attempting to get him started again. He was likely to be interested in walking out because he had a hangover and was not particularly anxious to pick anyway. After talking about a walkout and sitting down on the ground, I soon realized that this would not cause anyone to leave the field, so I stopped. Soon, everyone started talking about how they hoped it would rain. (MR)

*   *   *

The social workers knocked on doors to get people to a meeting "to bring about change in the camp." About sixty people showed up—a low turnout considering there were over three hundred adults in the camp. There were also some people at the meeting from OEO, from a regional health center, and from a church group. A social worker began the meeting with a speech, "We gather here tonight because you must do something to help yourselves." He continued, "I can't do it for you; these people over here can't do it for you; I can't even tell these people over here about your problems. You must tell them yourselves. It sounds better coming from you and they'll believe it coming from you. Now we came here tonight so that you could tell these people what's wrong here. It's time for you to speak; we are here to hear you speak, so if you have any complaints let's hear them now. I can't talk about your complaints because if I do the man up there [pointing to the grower's office] would say I am a troublemaker and tell me to go down the road; so if you have any complaints now is the time to hear them." Several people stood up and voiced complaints. Some were very articulate, others had a great deal of difficulty expressing themselves and constantly reached out to the audience for reinforcement. If they were unable to get support, they shuffled back to their seats.

The complaints were on the following: "We have no warm water to take showers. All the water is cold." "When it rains, water runs into the room." "There are no screens on the doors to keep the flies and bugs out, so we can't open the door and the place has to stay stuffy all the time." "The damn bedbugs drive me crazy." "There is no place to cook. Some of the kitchens do not have stoves that work." "The stove is dangerous because the gas leaks and the man won't do anything about it." One woman said she had seen the man about the stove and he said to call the gasman. Then the gasman said he couldn't do anything until the grower called him, "so, what do I do?" "The dust in the place, why can't they wet the place down and get rid of all the dust that's in the air?" There were no complaints against the crew leaders, although several people griped about the food, without specifying any one kitchen. The social worker kept interrupting, "All right, we're going to change things around here." He wanted to get two "captains" from each crew to go together, in a group, to see the camp manager. He said this was the way to bring about change.

Then one of the migrants got up and made a speech. He had been to see everyone and nothing gets done. "They all tell me that there is nothing they can do, 'If you don't like it, you can get off the camp.' Now how are we supposed to handle something like this?" The social worker replied, "I don't want to talk to you because you're the man saying, 'Let's die already.' You have to try things before you say, 'Let's die.' " The migrant responded, "I'm just telling you that I have already tried. What can we do if the grower refuses again?" Then the social worker said, "Well, we'll cross that bridge when we come to it. First, you have to get organized. Get all the people organized and let the grower know you want these things. Chances are you'll get them."

The son of one of the crew leaders asked, "What happens when the man tells us to get down the road? What happens when we send the twelve men up there and he tells them, 'Okay, I don't need you; you are on my property; get off,' then what happens? We're in a worse position than you are. If a man tells you to go down the road, he can tell us to go down the road also, but we probably need the money more than you do." Again the social worker said, "Don't worry about it; we'll cross that bridge when we get to it," and he went on with the meeting. People started to drift out, and the social worker said to them, "Yeah, you can leave now if you want to, but the bedbugs are going to be biting just as hard tonight as they were last night. Beans are going to be jumping next week, and now is the time to organize," but he never said how or what to do beyond appointing captains. He didn't realize that the people have no experience in organization and no one really knew what he meant.

Outside, Jones and Reece, both crew leader's sons, were talking. "All that stuff is a lot of bullshit. This guy is just a big talker. Who does he think he is? Why doesn't he let the people talk?" "I would like to talk a little bit myself. I couldn't get a word in edgewise because he was doing all the talking." The social worker did not want people to talk too long and would cut them off. Reece also noted, "We don't need any recreation or better conditions. What we need is work, higher wages, and more money. As far as I'm concerned, they can take all the social workers off the camp and the place might be just the same." They agreed that no one came to the meeting but the "jitterbugs." Those who were working did not go, because they were home sleeping. "You know that these meetings aren't going to do anything and aren't going to bring about any changes." Jones suggested that if he really wanted change, he should have brought in the crew leaders, "That's where the power is and they didn't even talk to them. He'd get a lot more done if he had them go to the grower because they're the ones who can go in and talk. If all of them go down together, the man couldn't tell them to go down the road."

A little later we returned to the meeting, and there was a man speaking who had not been around before. He was saying that what we needed was higher wages and not better living conditions . . . essentially the same thing Reece had said outside. "The farmers don't give a damn about you. What you have to do is demand higher wages, and once you get higher wages, the contractor will make more money and it will mean more money will trickle down to you." But he added, "You can't do this by just getting the contractors together and having them demand more money. You have to get together yourselves. That's the only way you're going to get it." He was a professional organizer and said he was going to be in Florida. "How many of you are interested?" Everyone liked him and the enthusiasm picked up, but after the meeting there were mixed feelings. "Well, this is a lot of foolishness. We wait all year to work and now that the work is here and the beans are here, we're going to go on strike. What happens? After we get the raise there are no more beans to pick. What good will it do us? It's nonsense to go on strike because once the crop spoils we'll have nothing to pick. It's better to go out and pick them for 60 cents a bushel than to take a chance." "Yes, but in other parts of the state, they are getting more for a bushel of beans." Then Tina said, "The whole thing is a lot of nonsense anyway. So if he is going to give you 75 cents, he'll give it to you; if he's not, he's not going to give it to you. What can we do to make him give us the extra money for picking the beans? The man said what he was going to pay, and if we don't want to take it then we have to go. That's all there is to it." Most people pessimistically agreed; yet many, especially the young people, said they would go on a strike if the crew leader asked them to. The older people were willing to go along because they didn't have much to lose, but their attitude was "better take what we can get."

One of the results of the meeting was a decision by the crew leaders to ask the boss for more money for the workers. Thursday evening was considered a propitious time because the crop was beginning to peak. But on

Thursday, one of the crew leaders backed down. He wanted to send some-one in the crew in his place. He would not participate because he felt the contractors would make "goddamn fools of themselves." It was silly for men like him to go up and ask for a raise for their bean pickers and not for themselves. Then another contractor, who had previously said he would go along with the strike, refused to go and sent his son instead. He was reluctant to ask for more money because, "No matter how much I pay my people, they won't pick any more beans. I know my people—they pulled as many beans today as they're ever going to pull." Then a third crew leader showed signs of concern. He could not bring himself to threaten to strike. He was new in this business, "This is the first time I have ever owned any-thing." He did not want to risk losing everything. (GP)

Unionization

The incipient attempts at structuring dissatisfaction indicate that there exists some potentiality for organization. Despite several efforts at unionization of migrant workers in the east, there has been little significant union organization except among some packinghouse work-ers. Indeed, knowledge about unions and strikes is limited and is rarely the subject of discussion in the camps. When our researchers, attempt-ing to discover what unionism meant to migrants, specifically talked about it, the response suggested that unions had little relevance to the situation of migrant workers. References to actual attempts at organi-zation among migrants in Florida were sometimes favorable but, more often, the attempts were regarded negatively or, fearfully, as a some-what threatening development.

I stimulated a conversation with Jessie about unions by making up a story about a walkout in a tomato field when the price was too low. Jessie mentioned some small walkouts that had taken place at an orange company in Florida. Other strikes had taken place in the orange grove, but he said there were always people who stayed behind and worked in the field. "They were all ladies and there wasn't much we could really do about it. But some cats tried to walk by us and go to work while we were walking around outside, telling everybody not to work until they raised the price. This cat came along whistling his way in, thinking he's going to go to work, but we really put something on him. He couldn't stand up when we were finished with him." Jessamay told a story about working in a field where they were paying only $2.00 a day, and everybody started to walk out. The farmer ran over and said, "Okay, I'll pay you $3.00." Everybody kept walking, and the farmer said, "Okay, I'll pay you $4.00." They went back to work. (MR)

*   *   *

A new sign was put up on the wall in the juke. This was an announcement about the celery season: a farm labor registration form listing the crew leader, the number of people in the crew, the crop, and the rates to be paid for the various jobs. It said that there were sixty-six workers in the crew, and that the room rate was $3.50 per person per week. If two men were staying in a single room, they each must pay $3.50 per week. This figure raised a lot of anger. People complained that they had better places in Florida for less money. This conversation led to talk about strikes. Sam talked about a strike in Belle Glade. There were AFL–CIO organizers down there who did not want the crew to go out in celery for a day. "When the people were on the bus, the organizers started shaking it, tipping the bus, until finally everyone had to get out. We didn't work that day." Sam said that nothing much came after that. "People just wanted to get out to work; they needed the money." (LR)

*   *   *

On Thursday, people were complaining about the 55 cent price, for they had found out there was a man up the road paying 75 cents. St. Louis, our crew leader, said, "Well, that man's got a small place. He hasn't got any damn cherries. He has to pay 75 cents just to get someone to come up and mess with him." Everyone believed this. Even after St. Louis left, Bubba, who had earlier suggested we go to work for the man paying the higher price, changed his mind. "There's got to be something wrong there. The guy's paying 75 cents, so there must be something wrong, something funny going on." I tried to get a conversation started about unions and mentioned that auto workers were getting something like $4.00 an hour, just because they happened to strike. However, there was no reaction to this, one way or another. The only response came from Bubba, "That's pretty good pay, $4.00 an hour." Everyone else was just quiet about it. (MR)

*   *   *

Nate, who works in the packing house, is a member of a union. He said, "Well, you gotta join. I don't know what it's going to do for me. I don't care much. I had to keep my job, so I joined." He doesn't know the name of the union. Junior commented, "I don't need no union. I'm a pieceworker. The difference between you and me is that I go out and get the money whenever I've picked a bucket. In the packinghouse, if you don't do what the man tells you he can send you on the road. If you've got a union, they might be able to help you. But I don't need no union. If they aren't giving the price here, I'll go up the road where they are paying the price." (ET)

*   *   *

Bear was complaining about the hours we had to work. I asked if there are any unions around here, and he replied, "There are unions for everyone except the farmworkers. It would be great to have a union. Then we wouldn't have to work so long. We could quit at 5:00 P.M. like we should." I asked if he thought we could get one. Tee, who works for the grower by the hour, said, "Sometime we'll get one because everyone else is getting a union. These pieceworkers won't get it because they don't really want it. They're making the money. But us hourly workers, we should get one. This money ain't bad. It's just that we gotta work so goddamn long to get it." Junior interrupted, "Shit, there ain't nothing you can do. The man's got all the money." Bear added, "Yeah, it looks that way. I don't think there's anything we can do because, you know, there's always people who need work, and if we didn't go to work the man would get someone else." (ET)

A Successful Organization

One group was able to overcome the difficulties intrinsic to organiza- tion among migrant workers. Although the goals of this group had little to do with social change (it was a religious organization), the group faced and resolved problems of leadership, participation, and stability common to all organizations. In the process of mobilizing a constituency, the church had significant influence on the crew and operated as an agent of change in that it fostered leadership, aspira- tions, and organizational skills among its members. It is significant, however, that the religious focus of the group represents a further with- drawal from society rather than the kind of confrontation and in- creased participation usually envisioned in talking about "social change." Nevertheless, in its success, this organization provides an interesting contrast to the failures previously described.

The Church of A to Z was a stable and successful organization that played a pervasive role in the camp. Although not organized for the purpose of social change, the church shared many of the problems of organizing faced by all groups. Although goals may differ, all organizations share the need to develop social and leadership skills and to attract and maintain adherents. The history of the church, and the source of its appeal to migrants—its organization and leadership and its payoff for the membership—contributed to its success.

The history of A to Z is the story of the Elder, a story that comes entirely from his own statements and is perpetuated by the members. True or not, it is the basis for his legitimacy, since his followers believe it. The Elder, a white man, had at various times in his life been a vagrant, a criminal, a mechanic, and a soldier. After a period in the army, both he and his wife became ill. His wife developed breast cancer and he had a disease described as "one lung gone and the other filled with water." The Elder knew of miraculous cures but assumed they were a "pack of lies." In his incapacitated state, he challenged God "to prove that either all of it [the Bible] was true or none of it." In a few days, the Elder's disease was cured, "although he was certified dead by the doctor." His wife also recovered and "she generated a breast where there was none before."

After a period of study, meditation, and communication with God, the Elder arrived at a theology and began to teach.[1] He felt that most races had been given their chance to attain the "power of the universe," but had not accepted the gift. He, a white man, chose, therefore, to teach among the blacks in Florida. The Elder's theology contrasts with that of other religions on two points: (1) The Elder, himself, is a "living Christ," and others may attain this state if they persevere. (2) Jesus, the man, died to grant the spiritual powers of the universe to men and these powers are available if man only learns how to use them. They include the power to make and stop rain, to walk on the water, to heal the sick and raise the dead, and, finally, to make the natural body immortal.

The early meetings of the group were small, but attracted the attention of local clergy and the local police. According to this history, local ministers entered his home with rifles, beat him, and attempted to rape his wife. Then for twenty-seven days and nights he was beaten by the police in the local jail. After these trials, the Elder returned to teach the message again. His support and the church began to grow until today he claims there are five churches in Florida and others in Alabama, North and South Carolina, Georgia, Michigan, and the Bahamas.

This history, as related by the Elder, includes several important features. The Elder teaches both from "experience" and from the Bible. Although aspects of the religion, in particular the powers of the Elder, are unusual, they exist within a framework of Christianity based on the Bible and contain many familiar elements. A more important feature, however, is the persecu-

---

[1] See Chapter 5 for further details.

tion of the Elder at the hands of white ministers. Although the Elder is himself white, his black constituents tell of the trials he went through for "us," which help to legitimize him among black people. Moreover, the Elder's message is strongly anti-established religion.

Besides this history, stories are related by his followers concerning his miracles performed "in the early days." Miracles were always in the past and are no longer performed, but there are a few long-standing members willing to testify to their authenticity. The common myth explaining why these miracles are no longer performed is straightforward: people today aren't spiritual enough to understand these feats. They would worship the acts and not see the Lord behind it. These stories were believed by the migrants in my camp, most of whom became adherents of the Church of A to Z. When challenged, especially on the issues of immortality and miracles, his followers would say, "What reason does he have to lie? He doesn't get anything from it."

The Elder's dramatic entrance into the black community would serve to support an organization for only a brief time if it were not reinforced by continuous activity. Events in the camp during the summer illustrate the process of development and reinforcement of the organization. Within the camp, there was a polarization between the A to Z people and the others, who knew about the religion but did not believe in it. Separate working and living patterns in the camp served to reinforce this polarization. Most of the time antagonism between the two groups was latent, but when the crew leader invited the Elder to come from Florida to look after a woman who was ill, the polarization became more apparent. Ten days before the actual arrival of the Elder, conversation focused on the religious differences in the camp. Women gossiped about the religious girls, saying that they were "just a bunch of whores shacking up around every dark corner." The religious men, it was said, "are a bunch of holier-than-thou hypocrites who wouldn't even take you to a doctor if you were dying." (Medicine is against A to Z doctrine.) The A to Z people spoke against the nonreligious people but took great pride in the fact that they were "fair" in their criticism: "We try to tell them of the evil way they are living, drinking, going to doctors, and talking those corner conversations, but they just won't listen, so we gotta turn our backs on them and just walk away." This sort of talk irritated the others.

Leadership roles for the two groups were well established. Cliff, a young minister, assumed the religious leadership, while an eighty-year-old matriarch was the most articulate spokesman for the rest of the camp. By the time the Elder arrived, there were several things accomplished by the polarization. An aura of absolute godliness surrounded him. Among his people, he was a "living Christ," and among the opposition, he was to be avoided at all costs. The nonreligious people were superstitious and feared the Elder; this fear was encouraged by the A to Z members. It was said, and they believed, that if the Elder touched you, he would know your whole life and all your past sins and would tell what you were right to your face. Before the Elder even arrived, his reputation as a man of power was established. Conflict with the nonreligious group served to strengthen the solidarity of the members, and the Elder was further legitimized through the resulting "publicity." Agree with him or not, the Elder was known and respected by all.

Although the Elder was visible during his stay, the actual process of organizing the religious group fell to three assistants: Deacon, the crew leader; Cliff, the young minister; and Big Betty, a heavy girl with a loud voice. The crew leader was an indispensable support to the organization. Although he did not readily mingle with the people, his physical presence was always felt. A recent convert to A to Z, Deacon would use himself as an example of how religion could change a person. Because of his age (56), his size (6'6"), and his authority as crew leader, his views demanded respect and attention. Cliff essentially served as a teacher. A quiet person, he was constantly present in the fields. Whenever the occasion arose, he would illustrate how some mundane event related to what the Elder had been teaching. One day there was an automobile accident near the field and people rushed over to find that, although the truck involved had been smashed, the driver was unhurt. Someone commented that the driver was lucky to be alive, but Cliff responded, "Ain't no luck about it. It was God's will. Imagine people taking God's will for luck." Cliff was able to lend special significance to each event and relate it to the church's authority, and this gave him a position of leadership in this group. Betty's role was much more direct. Physically large, Betty had a loud voice and easily intimidated people. Her targets were usually females in her age group, sixteen to twenty years old. If she heard a four-letter word or a fight, she would immediately interfere, "That's not Christlike." One time, I was standing near the juke-box and noticed some A to Z people giving me strange looks. No one said anything. It was Betty who explained, "We're all trying to live holy; listening to the blues is a natural world. When we make music, it's singing the praises of the Lord." It is Betty who voices the norms and is careful to see that they conform to those of Cliff and the Elder.

From an organizational standpoint, these three leaders are interesting. With Deacon, the Elder has plugged directly into an existing power structure. Betty's role has developed from her naturally forceful talents, already in evidence in the migrant situation. Cliff's leadership potential, however, had not been previously evident. Through his role as minister, he has acquired skills in handling people and speaking effectively. There were others who developed skills through their involvement in A to Z. The participatory nature of the services, in which there were pressures to stand and give testimony, encouraged the development of skills of expression. Furthermore, it gave the Elder a chance to spot potential leaders to carry the faith in his absence. Cliff had shown some promise in this context and was taught and encouraged. It was a point of great pride to Cliff that he was part of a new group of ministers, "There are a lot of young ministers in this thing. We're pleased with all of them, and they're coming up fast." The Elder himself would joke with Deacon. "You know, you had better keep on your toes or these young ones are learning so fast they'll shoot right past you."

The final problem is that of "payoff." What gives the members a feeling that they are getting something from the organization? One important product for the membership is the solidarity from common religious beliefs. In a migrant context, however, spiritual development and the resulting sense of community are not sufficient to stabilize most attempts at organization. Other religious groups visited the camp, for example, and people attended their services. Yet as soon as the outsiders left, the structure collapsed. The well-defined polarization between the A to Z group and the other group in the camp helped to stabilize the organization, but the greatest payoff for the members and the most effective in cementing the group was a confrontation with a group outside the camp. A service run in the camp by the members of the Assembly of God Church, a local sect in a nearby town, provided just such an opportunity for a confrontation.

The Elder was well versed in the behavior and the sensitivities of other groups and learned to exploit them to his advantage. During the services, the Elder made constant and colorful references to the rest of the church world, "Slop-sided, knock-kneed, blubber-lipped hypocrites who are so busy preparing you for heaven way out there that they are missing the heaven right here now. Methodists worship methods; Baptists worship baptism; Lutherans worship Luther; but none of them worship the God in themselves. They create division, when Christ taught brotherhood. Look at the churches and see if the preacher doesn't have a D.D. after his name. You know what that stands for? Dead dog. 'Cause he's just looking for God out there in heaven, when the kingdom of God is at hand." Such accusations were always greeted with amusement and agreement from his followers. And, when the people from the Assembly of God Church challenged the Elder, the results were foregone. With their message of sin in this world and only the slightest hope of salvation after death, how could this group hope to compete with the Elder's message of "divinity now"? The Elder's suspicion that the Assembly of God people would not resist attempting to "expose the Elder in front of his own people" played into what he told his followers: "You see they just want to cause division. They came here to the camp. I didn't meddle with them." A debate between the two groups took place and centered around the Elder's claim to immortality. Assembly of God people asked the followers if they believed the Elder. The followers reply was so forceful and so affirmative that the Assembly of God people did not remain long. Before leaving they were heard to say, "That man's got them hypnotized. We will have to put a stop to this. They don't know what he's doing to them." The Elder used the incident to further reinforce his message. They behaved according to script and the A to Z group was strengthened by their assault.

There have been attempts by unionists and others to organize migrants. Most fail to stabilize, blocked by the reluctance of migrants to participate and by their mobility along the east coast. The A to Z Church, however, has succeeded in stabilizing itself within a mobile group and in developing a high degree of migrant participation. (CL)

11

The Children

If migrants find themselves trapped in the system of migratory labor, and if this entrapment is so thorough that escape is difficult for most and impossible for many, then the entrapment of their children is even more devastating. Often those concerned with obtaining social change suggest that the focus should be upon the children and that the adults will have to be "written off" as a loss. Such an approach fails to recognize the near impossibility of helping the children without bringing some kind of change to their parents. More significantly, examination of the migrant labor situation reveals that very little is being done to reach even the children, who are trapped in a situation for which they are in no way responsible. To "write them off" is to force them into the same kind of life that their parents live. Not only do the children believe that they will remain migrants, their parents and other adults— although maintaining aspirations for the children—are often realistic in their appraisal about the future of the children.

While it is illegal for children under fourteen to work or for those between fourteen and sixteen to work without a permit, many do, adding their pickings to those of their parents. Children have learned to scatter when warned of the arrival of any stranger—lest they be caught by an inspector and the crew leader get "in trouble." Since the crew leader's "troubles" are always followed by sanctions against parents, an effective system for the avoidance of detection of legal violations has been established.

In the larger camps and in areas where large numbers of migrants are concentrated, there now exist various possibilities for children to participate in educational and other programs. This is another world outside the camp, but there is little discussion of it when the children return each day. Although useful, its meaning to migrant children in terms of helping to escape the system is extremely limited.

This chapter is concerned with migrant children and adolescents. Children ten years old or younger are commonly considered by migrants to be children, "kids." If there are attempts to protect children or isolate them from adult activities, they are seldom relevant beyond the age of ten or eleven. Between the ages of eleven and fourteen, children are regarded by migrants as adolescent—too old to be "kids," but not old enough to be adult, "grown-up." Beyond fourteen or fifteen, adolescents cannot be discussed as distinct from the adults, although children up to about eighteen are regarded as a distinct social category, frequently called "jitterbugs." The general orientations and values of migrants to child-rearing practices are also discussed. The chapter concludes with a consideration of migrant attitudes toward education.

Kids

Children adapt themselves well to the migrant camp environment. Even when parents try to protect or isolate their children, the physical setting does not permit it. Each day, they are exposed to conditions and experiences similar to the adults', whose reactions they closely observe. Like the adults, they have learned to "play the game," that is, to survive camp life by being tough and clever and, with their peer group, aggressive.

As I approached the camp, there were about twelve little kids under ten years old who came out to look at me. I was carrying my duffel bag over my back, and some of the kids yelled, "Santa Claus." They came up and waited for me to hand out presents. (DG)

*　　　　　*　　　　　*

The younger children stick to themselves. There are many of them and they keep busy hunting frogs and throwing stones. Only occasionally do the kids hang around the adults, and when they do, they usually go about their own activities. The kids often mimic the adults. Once I saw Geech showing some kids how to shoot dice. Today a little girl picked up a cigar someone threw down and smoked it. The kids curse as well as the adults. Contrary to what I had expected, their speech is faster and has a heavier dialect than most adults. (DR)

*   *   *

The kids have a very good idea of everything that goes on around them, including the sexual relations between the adults. Even the two-year-old girl shows, from time to time, evidence of being aware of which couples are going together, who has broken up, and similar aspects of people's personal lives. The children, in fact, are amazingly sensitive to everything that happens in camp. However, they do not imitate the adults, and their mothers really slap them if they are heard swearing. (MR)

*   *   *

When I got home, I went into my room to take a nap. There were two little kids, a boy and a girl around seven years old, running around the corridor trying to bum money from people returning from work. I have seen the same kids often begging change in the jukes. The little boy said, "Give me a dime," but I refused. This did not faze him at all and he asked, "Well, can I have a quarter?" The little girl was more subtle. She was trying to get money out of Roosevelt by telling him about some friends who needed money. After a while, I went to sleep. As I was lying there, I felt a hand in my right hip pocket. It was the little boy, looking for my wallet. (DG)

*   *   *

The children spend most of the day playing on the large trucks parked in the lot near the juke. There are crates on the back of the trucks, which they use for stacking and playing war. Another common pastime is for the children to take a stick and whip up some soap bubbles in a soda can. They smear the bubbles all over their faces and bodies. Similarly, they like to write all over each other with chalk. (LR)

*   *   *

Junior told me about his father, who was a big man, "6' 3", 225 pounds, and a real mean motherfucker. He always treated me right. He only beat me three times in my whole life. Beating a kid does no good. If I go out and do something and my mama beats me, as soon as she's done beating me, I go out and do it all over again. But if you talk to me and explain what I did was wrong, and tell me never to do it again, then I listen."

He says he used to be a real mean little kid and described how badly he treated his sister. One day he was playing with her, chasing her around, and she refused to chase him back. He got angry and accidently pushed her downstairs and she got cut up. She ran and picked up the baby, since she was afraid that Junior would try to hit her again. "Well, I grabbed that motherfucking quart mayonnaise jar, and I bashed it over that brat's head. She got all cut up and the baby got cut too. When my daddy got home, that was one of the times he whipped me." Then Junior told another story of when his sister told him to get some ice for lemonade. He had complained, "Why should I go into the house and get some ice for your motherfucking lemonade?" She replied that if he didn't go, he wouldn't get any lemonade, and this started another fight. This time, he grabbed a big pin and "poked it right into her head and blood came gushing out." He described all this was "fooling around, cause that's the way brothers and sisters do." (DR)

*   *   *

One nine-year-old boy was called a "Mamma's boy." He is being brought up by his grandmother and runs to her for protection when the other children pick on him. Kids are expected to be tough and to beat up anyone who is younger. I heard a five-year-old disdainfully comment about his five-year-old friend, "He couldn't even beat up that four-year-old, he's such a baby." Although kids learn to be aggressive with each other, overly aggressive children are a problem difficult to avoid. There is a highly aggressive seven-year-old girl who is always fighting. The women speak of her as a "bad child" and warn their children to avoid her. (AK)

*   *   *

A ten-year-old boy was sitting in a chair that his sister wanted. She called a friend over and whispered something in his ear. They giggled, and then she called her brother over, telling him that she had something to whisper in his ear. When he got up, the other child jumped into the chair and started laughing. Both kids tried to get a foothold on the chair, squeezing each other over to the sides. Suddenly, the three children got up and forgot about it. A few minutes later, the same ten-year-old had a fight with his sister. He threw a rock at her and she came back waving a broom. The boy was near tears, and an adult saw them and tried to separate them. Meanwhile the adults at the whist table laughed at the kid, who retired into one corner and played cards by himself, looking very forlorn with his head turned away. (IM)

*   *   *

Neither social workers nor health inspectors have come to our camp, but we did have one enforcement man come to the fields to check if any of the children were working illegally. At the time, the children weren't picking on their own, but were helping their parents fill their buckets. As soon as someone spotted the state license plate on the car, their mother said, "The man's here, go get out of here," and they all scattered. They ran off into the apple orchard behind the cherry trees in which we were working. A few kids started playing ball in a clearing in the apple orchard. They didn't move out of sight, but stayed away from where people were picking and appeared preoccupied with other activities. (MR)

Adolescents

Above the age of ten or eleven, children are no longer merely observers of the adult scene, but very much a part of it. They become actively disinterested in the younger children and begin to hang around the older adolescents. At this age, this group is usually expected to contribute to family income by picking regularly.

Roger was eleven and said he was going into the second grade. He told me exaggerated stories about Florida. He also lied about his age, his grade, and his strength. He said he could beat up anyone in his class, even the biggest ones, and to prove his point, he ran over and hit his twelve-year-old brother and then ran. There are eight boys in Roger's family. One of them had quit school in the eleventh grade, joined the Job Corps and quit that, failed a post office exam, and now was in the camp. Another brother was planning to be an actor since, Roger said, "he's a long-haired nigger." I asked Roger what he planned to do, and a younger brother commented, "He's going to be a dick-sucker because he's already had enough practice." His brother claims that he, himself, wants to stay in school. He didn't want to come north, preferring to go to summer school, but his mother made him. He is in the fifth grade and received all A's and one B on his report card. (AK)

*   *   *

Scarlet's mother asked her to pick another hamper but she was very reluctant. She played down her ability to pick, saying she just couldn't pick beans. Peanutman said he knew she could pick if she wanted to but it is good tactics to play down picking ability to your mother. If she thinks you can pick well, she will expect you to pick more in the fields each day. (IM)

*   *   *

Gail's mother was pushing her to pick faster, pointing to her sister, "who has picked three hampers while you've just been sitting around." She complains that her mother has told her that if she wants any money for clothes and for school, she had better work hard. She threatened to drop out of school when she got home. (DG)

*　　　　*　　　　*

A father told his son, "Don't do anything where you might get a record before you are twenty-one, because the juvenile courts are the ones that are really tough. After that they might give you a break, but if you don't have a record before you're twenty-one, I'll be very proud of you." (HG)

*　　　　*　　　　*

Curtis said he never did anything to stop his mother and father from fighting. He described a scene when he was in the next room and overheard a violent battle. He did not interfere. "Whoever fights, whoever they are, you let them fight it out." (LR)

*　　　　*　　　　*

A ten-year-old was fighting with his older sister, Scarlet. He was swinging a bat at her and she was screaming and running away. People watched the scene and laughed; no one interfered. Eventually, Scarlet got the bat away from the kid and was swinging it at him while the group around them encouraged him to "do something about it." He began to wrestle with her but he was very small and could only hang on. The kids soon lost interest in the fight and began playing again. (IM)

*　　　　*　　　　*

In the juke, there were kids from twelve to fourteen watching the adults play pool. The boys were trying to goose the girls and the girls were giggling. There was a little baby, scarcely able to walk, trying to dance to the music. Gail, age fourteen, was leaning over Emma's chair, watching a card game. She was "hustling," hoping to beg a quarter so that she could play pool. She was leaning over provocatively, with one hand on her hip, and one of the boys of about the same age made a grab at her and they started wrestling. (DG)

*　　　　*　　　　*

Sara told us how she had to stop school in the eighth grade because she had gotten pregnant. All of her sisters had stopped school before they finished high school for the same reason. "If a girl in the muck can get past thirteen or fourteen without getting pregnant, then she is doing all right. The way the boys are down in the muck, that's all they want." (LR)

Child-Rearing Practices

Children in migrant labor camps are raised by many people. The group living pattern affects child-rearing practices as it does every other aspect of life. Men and women work, and children wander around in the camp or in the fields with relatively little parental supervision. They are protected and disciplined by whoever is around at the moment. This is a point of confusion, both for adults and children. On the one hand, there is a tendency to discipline other people's children since they are underfoot much more than in other circumstances. On the other hand, this is often considered by parents to be interference and is resented. Similarly, children waver between defying and accepting the supervision of adults other than their parents. This is an ambiguous area with few normative rules.

There are other ambiguities in child-rearing practices. The model of comportment held by many mothers includes a gentility out of place in the migrant setting. Should one encourage children to display the toughness requisite in migrant society, or does this include behavior that is upsetting to other, more middle-class, values? Parents often despair of the language used by their young and the difficulties in controlling them. They complain that the camp is ruining their children, but at the same time are proud of demonstrations of toughness and precocity. This ambiguity leads to alternating approval and harsh, spontaneous discipline. For the most part, however, attitudes are permissive. The following selections focus on these ambiguities: first, with respect to the problem of authority, and second, in the definitions of appropriate behavior.

Everybody in our camp tends to correct the children. If there has been a conflict with a child's parents, however, this becomes a point of sensitivity. Larry had an argument with Spaceman and his wife. The next day Spaceman's kids were around our side of the building, playing in front of Larry's door. When the little boy put his bottles and trash up by the door, Larry asked me to tell the kid to leave—although in the past he has never hesitated to correct the children. I asked why he didn't tell the child to go away himself. "He's playing in front of your door not mine." Larry replied, "No, I don't want any trouble from his mother." People who are married and have children of their own discipline other children more than those who are single. The older women, also, give the children the most attention.

When women go out to work, they leave their babies in the nursery if it is open. Otherwise a group of children from many families will be left with one adult in the camp, or the children will be brought to the field. The bus often waits for the nursery to open; otherwise I have seen women just leave, telling whoever is around to see to it that the child gets to the nursery later in the morning. (GP)

*　　　　　*　　　　　*

J.B. was sitting on a bench, and several little children came up to him to ask favors. One had a pair of shoes tied together and asked him to cut the string. Another had a toy plastic cow needing repair. When J.B. handed it back, the child twisted it again and J.B. yelled at her, "You little bitch, why do you always have to mess up anything I do?" Another six-year-old girl came by and asked him for a dime. He told her to ask her mother, at which point she took away his sunglasses, put them on her nose, and made faces. He asked her to return them several times and when she did not respond, he ignored her. Eventually she gave them back.

Kindness alternates with exasperation. In the fields one day, three children were waiting in the truck while their parents were picking. One of them began to cry, and the driver, Mr. Ed, shouted out to Ernestine, "Little Timmy here wants your titty. He's crying." Ernestine laughed, and the driver told the boy to shut up. Then a two-year-old girl started to cry and asked to get down. When he lifted her off she cried harder. He brought her back in the truck saying, "Stop jiving me or I'll beat your ass." (DR)

*　　　　　*　　　　　*

Early one morning, a three-year-old was sitting outside, eating a hot dog on a slice of bread. Raymond, one of the older men, noticed that she was just licking it and told her to eat it up. She ate the bread and defiantly tossed the hot dog over the fence. Adults often tell children who are not their own what to do. They scold children for making too much noise. Sometimes, as in this case, the children ignore or defy adults other than their parents, but at other times, they accept the word of any adult at all. (IM)

*　　　　　*　　　　　*

A little boy, age three, threw some tomatoes at Bertha, so she gave him a slap. When he cried, his father came in and said, "You leave this boy alone. When he cries I have to come in and see what's wrong. Don't touch him." Bertha said that the father was stupid. The boy ought to be punished when he does something wrong or he'll grow up to be a hoodlum. Sugarmama then told a story about a man convicted to die. His final wish was to see his mother. When she came, he said to her, "If you had spanked me when I was little, I wouldn't be here. Now I'm about to lose my life."

Then he leaned over as if to whisper something in his mother's ear and he bit her ear off. Bertha and Honey agreed, "If you don't spank them now, you'll be sorry later." (DG)

*   *   *

When we go out picking, two little children, about three years old, come regularly to the fields. They are objects of community attention. They know all the adults well. When Sugarmama said, "I'm going to hit you, I'll wop you on the head," they laughed, knowing that she didn't mean it. The kids are looked after by the entire crew. Longo warned them to get off the road. Sugarmama gave them some food and Bertha gave them water and wiped their noses. Longo and his wife often bring along their three young boys, all under ten. The family works together, although the boys are often more interested in running around. Once in a while, Longo yells at one of them to get busy, but they don't pay much attention. (DG)

*   *   *

The women talked about a children's summer school program near the camp. They said that even the parents couldn't control the children from the camp, and they could hardly blame teachers for not wanting to teach the kids. "They'll do anything and say anything to you." One of the women, a mother of seven children, criticized them for swearing; although she curses a great deal herself, she did not connect this with the children cursing. She talked about a little girl who stood in the back of the bus "just twisting her behind." She had "never seen anything like it before," again ignoring the activities observed by the children in the jukes each day. The women agreed and thought the children's behavior was terrible. "It seems to me that those kids are around white people enough so that they would learn how to act decent. I don't know why they do the things they do. It seems that kids just don't want to learn today." (GP)

*   *   *

Roy was playing with his baby son. He spotted an older kid playing with a knife and shouted at him to put it down. Then, holding the baby out precariously at arms' length as he often does while playing with him, Roy looked him in the face and said, "When you grow up, you're not going to have a knife to play with are you? If someone messes with you, you're gonna get a motherfucking pistol and shoot him. This boy's not gonna be a knife man, he's going to have a gun." Roy's wife said something about getting their baby off to a wrong start, but she was smiling and both she, Roy, and the baby enjoyed the scene. (CL)

*   *   *

Honey and her grandchild are very close. The baby calls her "Mumma" and is always coming up to her and punching her affectionately. Honey says she loves the baby more than her own child. She talked about how children must learn to fight. She claims she forced the child to "get out there and fight," but then she had to pay a lot of money in hospital bills. "She is always getting messed up." Honey said all this seriously, but was exaggerating. The baby will be only three years old in October. (DG)

*   *   *

When the kids are playing, they often fall hard, but they seldom cry. One day, Bo saw a little boy crash into a wall while jumping. It seemed as if he hurt himself, but Bo said, "Let's see you do that again." The child acted as if his fall had not hurt at all and had been part of the trick. He got up and tried again. Another time, a baby girl fell on her face and her mother responded by immediately laughing. This stopped the baby before she could even think of crying. (IM)

*   *   *

There is usually little adult supervision over the children, but if a parent sees his child do something wrong, he will often take off his belt or shoe and hit him. Yesterday, Checker Bill saw his little boy standing at the ballgame when he was supposed to be doing a job for him. Saying nothing, he took off his shoe and slapped the kid on the leg. This prompted a discussion among those who saw the incident concerning how to raise children. Someone had seen Checker Bill's little girl drinking leftover beer in the juke that morning, and Checker Bill went into a tirade about how the camp was ruining his children. People felt the children were spoiled by having so many people around so that the kids didn't listen any more. Checker Bill's children are afraid of him; he feels the only way to handle them is to hit them. Sara told a story about her ten-year-old. One day in the barbershop, the barber accidently nipped the boy with the scissors. The kid turned around and said, "If you do that again, I'm going to break your black ass." His mother thought this was funny, but Miss Bea said it was bad to have them use that language when they're so young. (LR)

Education

Education, though valued by most migrants, is another area of ambivalence. On the one hand, it is felt that education is the only way to free one's children from the migrant situation; intelligent, responsive children are a source of pride. Similarly, among the children, there are many who enjoy school and aspire to continue. On the other hand, the desire for education often conflicts with the economic needs of the moment; children in school cannot be supplementing family income and they are a constraint on the necessary mobility of their parents. Furthermore, although education is associated with long-range future success, for many people it is a symbol of past failures and unfortunate experiences. Thus, children with educational aspirations are often discouraged. In some cases the source of discouragement is merely the inconsistencies between values emphasized in school and realities at home. In others, aspirations are squelched deliberately by the more bitter and possibly more realistic adults.

The most important activity on Sunday was washing, and cleaning the children and their clothes. All the little girls were washing their hair and having it neatly braided. There were a lot of children trying on fancy clothing. At first I thought this was for church or for some sort of meeting, but discovered that this was all in preparation for school, which was to begin the next day. (DR)

*   *   *

I asked Ann what she wanted her three youngest children to be, and she said that she hoped the boy would be a doctor and the girls, teachers. A little later in the conversation I phrased my question a little differently: "What do you think they will be?" Her answer was quite matter-of-fact— "Cherry pickers." Later in the week I asked the little boy what he wanted to be when he grew up. He told me he already was "growed up" and that he wanted to be a cherry picker like his old man. (MR)

*   *   *

Sara has a little eight-year-old girl who says she wants to be a lawyer. She is pleased that the child has a career in mind so early and saves all the money she can for her child's education. Sara often talks about education. She regrets having left school in the eleventh grade and hopes someday to return to school herself. (LR)

*   *   *

Roy's oldest daughter, who is in the sixth grade, spends much of her time taking care of the baby. This girl's development is considerably advanced for her age. She is an eager student in summer school and is generally very capable. She is a source of pride to Roy's wife, who talks about helping her continue her education, although the child is not hers but Roy's by a previous relationship. (CL)

*   *   *

One of the women in the juke began a long tirade: "If you're a Negro you have to go all the way. There's no in-between. If you have no education, you're on the bottom; if you have a high school education, you're still on the bottom. To make it, if you're a Negro, you have to go all the way through college. Now, with white people, it's different. They take those white girls that only go to twelfth grade and make them tellers in a bank. How many Negroes do they do that for? Go down and tell them that you have a twelfth-grade education and they tell you to go away, that you don't have enough. The thing is, you have to go all the way through four years of college, you can't think of stopping at high school. But, most people can't even stand to make it through high school, and to think that they have four years after that just discourages them." (GP)

*　　　　　*　　　　　*

Gail is fourteen years old and going into the ninth grade. She wants to be an artist. Yesterday, taking a break from picking cucumbers, she was sitting with her sisters, drawing a house in the sand and bragging that she was the best artist in her class. She said if she didn't become an artist she would want to be a schoolteacher or a secretary. She heard a woman on TV say that if colored people didn't get what they wanted, then white people wouldn't get what they wanted either. She added that colored people had to get an education if they wanted to get ahead in this country. This was her second year on the season and, she claimed, her last; she much prefers Florida. I asked what she would do if her family came north again next summer. How would she stay without them? She shrugged off the question and did not want to consider it. (DG)

*　　　　　*　　　　　*

Junior had eleven years of schooling. He claims to have been very good in school, but had lots of trouble because his family was always traveling. He was told, "You're not in one place long enough to graduate." One year he did both the fourth and fifth grades at once. But then they made him go through the sixth grade twice. "I remember that motherfucking blue-covered book that we had to read about some runaway boys. I had to read them damn books twice." He explained how he finally quit school. "I was in the bathroom. I had asked the teacher to leave and went out to take a leak. Afterwards, I was combing my hair. There was a bunch of boys in the bathroom and they were all beating their meat [masturbating] over in a corner. I didn't care; they could do what they wanted, but I didn't do that kind of shit. Well, as I was combing my hair, suddenly the principal walked in asking what all the noise was about. The boys were laughing, and I started to walk out the door back to class when suddenly he grabbed me and said, 'You were doing what those boys were doing too, weren't you?' I denied it, telling him I never did that. 'Yes, you were, you were doing it just like them.' 'I wasn't, I wasn't, I don't do that kind of stuff, sir,' and I put my hand up to his face and said, 'Smell my hand. I wasn't doing that.' He replied, 'That's three months, boy, for trying to hit me.' I said, 'Bitch,' so he said, 'three months more.' Every time I tried to explain anything he docked me for more time. So I was suspended for something I never did, and, hell, I never went back.

"That was my last year at school. Principals are like that. They never hit you or anything like that, but as soon as they don't like the way you are doing, they say, 'That's three months; you get three months, boy.'" Junior felt they should have considered his record. He said the teachers thought he was a very good student and sometimes had him look after the class when they had a meeting. "Shit, I'd go into that room and I'd say, 'Where are you at? Where are you reading now?' And those motherfuckers in the seventh-grade class, they were big and they'd say it was none of my business." Then he told me about a Spanish teacher whom he had "made," and an Algebra teacher who always gave him an A. "I would look her right in the eye, and lie to her and she would know it, but she still gave me A's." He didn't like Algebra, "all the p's and c's and x's and q's and shit like that. Those teachers in the south can't teach. I'll tell you that. Ask anybody who has been to school in the south. They just don't want to teach us. They don't care." (DR)

*   *   *

Shorty was originally from South Carolina before his parents moved to Florida. He went to school in South Carolina but dropped out during the eighth grade. "School could make a good boy turn bad. The teachers would come in all drunk and beat you for no reason at all, saying, 'I haven't beaten you in a long time, so today I'm going to get you.'" Now he claims that he doesn't care at all about school. He likes to learn and he also likes to talk. One of his favorite pastimes is to get some beer and to get some friends together and just sit around and talk and talk. Whatever he could learn at school, he could learn better in the world. "Whatever a person is going to learn at school, he's gonna have to tell it to someone in the outside world. Sooner or later it's all gonna get back to me just through talking." (DR)

*   *   *

Curtis was working on a tree and someone called over to tease him about walking around at night. They said he was always "looking for some cock." Curtis is teased a great deal, especially for his aspirations to go to college.

He replies, "You do what you want to do and I'll do what I want to do; my business is mine and your business is yours." Pat also has ambitions to leave the migrant labor stream. She wants to continue in school and to go to college someday. But when she was talking about this in the fields, someone put her down, saying, "You'll always be in the fields, so don't even think about it." (LR)

Appendix

OUTSIDERS IN THE SYSTEM

The migrant labor system includes a network of government agencies—such as the employment service, health departments, and police—and social service organizations, as well as private organizations, church groups, and individuals concerned with the migrant worker. To provide perspective on the complexity of this network, migrant services in several different areas were studied.

The network of auxiliary services and organizations was very substantial in some agricultural areas, and almost nonexistent in others. In one county with less than 500 migrants, for example, a considerable number of agencies and volunteer groups operated; in a second county, despite the presence of approximately 3000 migrants, there were only a few control agencies (police, for example) and practically no voluntary organizations or service agencies.

In every case observed, those involved in migrant services often found themselves frustrated by their inability to come to grips with the offensive and distasteful aspects of the system. The problems these organizations confront stem in part from the intrinsic difficulties of working with temporary social groups; in part, from internal difficulties within the agencies themselves. Coordination is absent among diverse agencies, all of which have different interpretations of the nature of the problems and varying strategies as to what should be done to deal with them. Thus, there is little possibility for the long-range planning necessary to establish efficient and comprehensive programs. Worse still, the structure of the migrant labor system supports those who do not upset the existing balance of priorities—priorities in which the migrants al-

*most invariably are placed last. The migrant labor system is a battle-
ground of conflicting interests, in which those of the growers (as the
providers of employment) and of the crew leaders (as the coordinators, recruiters, and controllers) tend to dominate. Those groups seeking access to migrants, either to change the system minimally or
fundamentally, must find entry through these two controlling groups.
Most groups seek change by working unaggressively; yet even "Band-
Aid" approaches prove hazardous, since many growers regard them as
threatening.*

*The migrant, ostensibly the focus of concern, is often the most
inconspicuous part of the entire system. To most northerners, the
migrant represents a "temporary" problem (although he may remain
in the community for four or five months of each year). In any
case, many argue, mechanization will ultimately make him "disappear." Although it is certain that the numbers of migrants are dimin-
ishing gradually, there are no indications that migrancy will completely
disappear. The question is rarely dealt with as to what will happen to
the thousands of unskilled workers who presently operate in the system. Meanwhile, it is hoped to keep the migrant as content and, therefore, as harmless as possible and to get the harvest work done with
minimal involvement.*

The External Network

*There is considerable variation in migrant labor programs, depend-
ing on state law and the energy and concern of the local population.
The situation in one county in south central New Jersey has been
selected for description. This county had one of the largest and best-
coordinated migrant programs that we could find in the field or described in the literature. The external system, seen in its best light,
provides a comparative perspective on less satisfactory conditions
elsewhere.*

Education

Preschool day care

Day-care programs for migrant children up to three years of age originally
were handled by the County Child Welfare Department. Later, when the
local Office of Economic Opportunity (OEO) organization came into
existence, it assumed responsibility for the program. Two large camps have

Migrant Programs in a South Central New Jersey County

Service Provided	Operating Agencies	Source of Funds
Education		
preschool	CAP organization	Federal OEO
school	Local school board	Federal and state education
adult education		
prevocational	Adult education service	Federal OEO grant
vocational	Manpower training center	Federal MDTA (U.S. Dept. of Labor)
Health	County Public Health Dept.	Federal (U.S. Public Health Service) and state grant
Employee recruitment	Farm Labor Service	State Employment Service and U.S. Dept. of Labor
Enforcement		
wages	Wage and Hour Bureau	State Dept. of Labor
housing, crew leader registration	Migrant Labor Bureau	State Dept. of Labor
Puerto Rican wages, housing	Community Service Association	State Farm Bureau
police protection	State (primarily), county, and local police	State, county, local
Legal services		
major issues	NAACP	Private
everyday issues	County Legal Services	Federal OEO
Social Security	Social Security Administration	Federal
	CAP fieldworkers	Federal OEO
Voluntary services (recreation, clothes)	Local migrant ministry committees	Church, private
Coordination	CAP	Federal OEO
(referrals)	Migrant Ministry, NAACP	Private
	Migrant Task Force	State

day-care centers held in a trailer, each large enough for twenty children. A third center is operated in a church basement in a local town and serves the other camps. The three centers are open from 7:00 A.M. to 7:00 P.M., serve breakfast and lunch, and have a full-time staff working in two shifts. There are also a part-time nurse, cook, and physician. The service provided is competent, but only 60 out of an estimated 230 eligible children are included in the program.

School (ages four to twelve)

The first migrant school was started by the State Department of Labor and Industry, using state-certified teachers. As the program grew, it was handed over to the State Department of Education. There are now [1968] three migrant schools in the county. Of the two visited, one had an enrollment of 96 children, the other 121. Each school had six teachers, six aides, plus special teachers. The aim of the program—social, cultural, and academic enrichment in an informal setting—includes trips, art, and similar activities. Both principals used the term 'readiness" in describing their goals for the children. Readiness is conceived of as teaching "social living," that is, how to work with others and be dependable, rather than formal learning. The principals also stressed the value of "cultural enrichment."

Recruitment for the schools begins during the first week in July, when teachers and aides go door knocking in the camps to explain the program to parents. The success of the six-week program varied with the quality of each teacher: in some classes observed, there seemed to be more emphasis on discipline than enrichment.

Adult education (prevocational)

The Community Action Program (CAP) organization funded by the OEO operated several prevocational and enrichment programs. CAP functioned in the camps, providing consumer education, dispensing Social Security information, and teaching black culture. The biggest prevocational program was a federally funded county adult education program where practical skills such as driving, English, and consumer education were taught.

HEALTH

In 1961, a state law was passed requiring each municipality to have full-time licensed public health personnel to make certain services available to the public. In 1962, the state contracted with the U.S. Public Health Service for support of migrant health services and passed the funds to the county to establish field clinics in the camps. After this service was established, the state recommended that the county apply for its own federal support, and the first grant was awarded in 1966.

As the services currently operate, when a migrant needs help he contacts his crew leader or grower, who provides identification and notifies the

Health Department. If the worker cannot find transportation, a health aide is supposed to provide this service. In case of sickness, the migrant can be referred either to a private physician, the local hospital emergency room, or to the migrant health clinic, which is held twice a week at the hospital. Under the current program there are no field clinics, and the hospital clinic is intended only for those actually sick. The clinic operates during the months of June, July, and August; at other times, the worker must find his way to a doctor or use the hospital emergency room. In case of acute (rather than remedial) dental problems, appointments are made by the Health Department after notification by the crew leader or grower. Physicians are reimbursed for their services: private doctors at $5.00 a visit, clinic doctors at $20.00 an hour, and dentists at $8.00 a visit.

Employee recruitment

In February, the Farm Labor representative contacts those local growers with labor requirements. Clearance orders specifying the period for which labor is needed, the wages to be paid, the crops to be worked, the character of housing, and so on, are prepared and mailed to the state office of the Farm Employment Service and then forwarded to Tallahassee, Florida. There they are dispersed to local Florida Farm Labor representatives, who recruit the crew leaders, who, in turn, recruit the migrants. Under federal law, workers must be informed of the contractual terms. In the county studied, the orders request specific crews. If a crew leader does not perform satisfactorily, he is effectively "blackballed" and eliminated from the area by the Farm Labor officers, either by getting the farmer to fire him or by informal collusion with other Farm Labor representatives to keep him from returning. The Farm Labor Office has field representatives who go to the fields occasionally to observe. The Office also helps crew leaders with paperwork on insurance, Social Security, taxes, and medical certificates.

Enforcement

Wages

The Wage and Hour Bureau of the State Department of Labor and Industry is the agency responsible for policing the state minimum wage of $1.40 an hour, as well as child labor and female hours laws. Violations are discovered by direct complaints and occasional checks of records. Although the Bureau has power of prosecution, this is usually a last resort. If a violation is discovered, the employer is contacted and given the opportunity to correct his mistakes.

Several problems arise in enforcing wage and hour laws. It is difficult to find accurate bookkeeping records and to keep up with mobile people. Thus, accusations or observed violations are rarely followed through. In addition, migrants often do not know the channels through which to make their complaints and rely on social agencies to protect them. The enforcement of child labor laws poses particular problems, since many parents feel they need the income of their children. Indeed, the head of one important state agency felt that it was more important for a child to be with his mother than to spend the day in a day-care center: "No mother will let her child be exploited in the field." With many other state labor problems to occupy them, and a limited staff, little attention is given to migrant wage problems by the Wage and Hour Bureau. Since migrants are usually paid on a piecework basis and work is irregular, the hours can be "adjusted" by crew leaders to meet minimum wage laws.

Housing and crew leader registration

In 1945, the State Migrant Labor Act created a Bureau of Migrant Labor, the only such bureau in the United States. This was an attempt to protect the worker by consolidating crew leader registration and housing enforcement into a single agency with enforcement powers. The activities of the Bureau are controlled by its chief and the Commissioner of Labor. There has been a tendency each year for increasingly stiffer enforcement; in 1968 the staff of inspectors was increased from eight to twenty. Crackdowns on day haul crew leader registration and vehicle insurance took place following a bus accident in 1968 in which nine day haul workers were killed. The Bureau cooperates with the Wage and Hour Bureau, and when a crew leader violates payments to his crew, the Migrant Labor Bureau can revoke his license. As noted before, however, enforcement is difficult and revocations are rare.

Puerto Rican wages and housing

There are two groups responsible for contract Puerto Ricans: the Service Association, which acts as employer, and the Commonwealth of Puerto Rico Department of Labor, which is the employees' representative. Representing all growers who have requested Puerto Rican workers, the Association negotiates a contract with the Commonwealth Department of Labor. 1968's contract stipulated a guaranteed 160 hours of work per month, a minimum hourly wage of $1.45 for picking and $1.50 for nursery work. Each worker signs a contract accepting the conditions of employment. The Association also provides travel arrangements, medical facilities, and guaranteed housing conditions. It is legally liable for violations, and the farmer can be sued only as a second party. It is the Commonwealth that presses enforcement for the worker. It can also refuse to contract with a particular grower. There is no similar program for southern Negro migrants.

Police protection

Depending on the location of incidents, state, county, or local police are involved. Since most camps are in rural areas, it is usually the state police who handle problems in the camps; if a problem occurs in town, local police are involved. The county is called only when additional assistance is required. It is rarely migrants who call the police, and when an officer is called into the camp for a fight, it is usually after the incident is over. The county sheriff felt that most troubles stem from liquor. When asked why illegal liquor continues to be sold in the camps although it is a matter of public knowledge, he replied, "You can't make a raid without a complaint; to have a complaint you have to have a buy; you can't make a buy because they won't sell it to you because they don't know you."

Social security

The main concern of the Social Security Administration office is to see that people are registered and their earnings reported. Several approaches are used to register migrants. Two field representatives visit the camps, often with CAP field representatives. They show a short film, distribute a comic book explaining how Social Security works, and hand out earnings books for keeping records. There are problems in making this program effective, and many migrants fail to register. The director attributed this to several factors. A general suspicion of the white bureaucracy often precludes cooperation. Also, many migrants hesitate to register, fearing they may be identified for some crime that they may commit or have already committed. Some want to avoid paying taxes and do not want their earnings recorded; some do not want to be found holding two jobs. A major problem is the failure to see the importance of planning for the future and investing now for old age or disability. Others register but lose their cards or move before cards reach them. Growers and crew leaders also compound the problem by failing to report earnings through negligence or cheating. Some plead confusion as to who is to serve as the actual employer, the grower or crew leader, although material is circulated defining legal responsibilities. Finally, despite the presence of two field representatives in the area, many camps were never visited by anyone from the Social Security office.

LEGAL SERVICES

Legal services are scant. Only in the last few years has the National Association for the Advancement of Colored People (NAACP) taken an interest in the rural migrant. The state president and the director of the local chapter have become increasingly aware of legal abuses, but the organization is moved to action only after crises such as accidents or fires.

The Public Defense Office has had no migrant cases although its services can be used by anyone involved in a crime in the State, whether he is a resident or not. The County Legal Service is part of a state chain of OEO-funded legal services. Although not specifically designed for migrants, it is available to them. This service is new; as a professional organization, it is not allowed to advertise so that few people knew about it in 1968.

VOLUNTEERS

Two community Migrant Ministry Committees originated when parishioners of a Presbyterian Church group visited some local camps in 1964. There are presently twenty-five churches involved in the two committees. They engage in a variety of activities: recreation, clothing distribution, worship, and transportation. They also refer migrants to medical officials. Recreation includes games, movies, stories, and trips. The committees are involved in a small way with the location of several families who decided to stay in the area and were, in 1968, negotiating to rent or buy a "halfway house" to serve as a center for relocation. However, the committees specifically avoid urging migrants to change their way of life, fearing the resentment of growers.

COORDINATORS

The main function of the CAP organization is referral and coordination of various service agencies. Field representatives visit the camps to find out what needs to be done and to develop awareness among the workers about their rights and the available services. Although some field representatives are sufficiently involved in some camps to know who has problems, internal dissension in the group—and the often antagonistic response of other agencies and local communities—have greatly reduced their effectiveness. With only fifteen field representatives and three coordinators, their program is limited.

The Migrant Task Force, established by New Jersey's Governor to investigate living conditions, earnings, and other problems of migrants, is another coordinating group. It includes representatives of other agencies as well as state officials and civil rights workers. It is a temporary organization.

In general, coordination between the many agencies involved with migrant labor is weak and ineffective. There are both formal working relationships and informal or actual working relationships. The distinction is important, since formal relationships are often quite different from those actually implemented.

Formal relationships between agencies are implemented through either planned contacts between individuals or referral processes. At the state level, formal ties exist between the Migrant Labor Bureau and the Wage and Hour Bureau to deal with crew leaders who violate the minimum wage law. The Migrant Labor Bureau also has formal relationships with the State Police when investigating a crew leader. Other formal ties exist between the state migrant education program and the CAP day-care center. Sharing specialized teachers, the two programs must cooperate in hiring and planning schedules. Referrals are made by several agencies. The adult education program refers its students to the Manpower Training Center and to CAP. CAP formally is the main referral agency for the other organizations.

In discussing informal relationships, we can only indicate contacts observed or discussed during the research period. Except for one incident where the State Police assisted the Migrant Labor Bureau in setting up a roadblock, most relationships observed between the Bureau and other groups were through the personal activities of the director. CAP has informal contacts with the district coordinator of the NAACP, who shares an office with some CAP administrators. Similarly, there are contacts between CAP and the Migrant Ministry Committees through an old-clothes distribution program. The clearest instance of an informal but regular working relationship between agencies was that of the Social Security officers and CAP field representatives who brought the Social Security people into the camps, helping them with registration. In contrast, there was no evidence of similar cooperation between CAP and the Migrant Health Services. CAP workers avoided calling the medical social worker in several cases where his presence might have been useful. On one occasion, a public health nurse assumed that a Negro CAP worker was a migrant. After a whole summer of working in the same camp, the nurse had no idea who the woman was and had no contact with her. There exists a general potential for cooperation among agencies—with CAP or its equivalent as a central coordinator—but, to date, this potential has developed unsystematically and irregularly. The system remains diffuse, and actual working relations often differ from those formally specified.

This became painfully evident in the opinions expressed by those involved in each agency concerning the work of other groups. A medical social worker felt that the Health Department had more access to camps than CAP because its activities were better understood and "less political."

He felt that CAP workers did not want to chauffeur people to the services they needed. The director of an important state bureau involved with migrants felt that the director of CAP was a "good man to work with," but the president of the state NAACP felt that he was negligent: "CAP isn't doing one single thing and should be gotten rid of. It's a waste of time and money." The Migrant Ministry Committees were criticized by the NAACP and CAP as trying to make the migrants' "degradation a little more bearable." Comments on their plans for a halfway house indicated begrudging approval; at the same time, the plan was criticized by an NAACP leader who doubted that the Migrant Ministry would ever follow though. In any case, he was concerned that the people who moved into the house might never leave, which would put the Migrant Ministry in a difficult position. On the other hand, a migrant minister criticized the other groups: "People in the NAACP are concerned with getting people higher wages and better housing but that is not the real problem. The real problem is to teach people how to keep clean, how to have concern for themselves and their children, and to value education."

An official of the Farm Employment Office criticized the emphasis on housing, remarking on the good conditions that prevailed in the area. "The housing is fifty or a hundred times better than what they have to pay for in Florida and there are no complaints from the crew leaders in this area." He noted how much the government does for the migrants "even if they don't want it." He claimed that migrants did not want money taken out for Social Security and should be able to decide that sort of thing themselves. On the other hand, all other groups regarded the Farm Employment Office as grower-oriented and unconcerned with the well-being of the migrants. Finally, Senator Harrison Williams from New Jersey, a major spokesman for reform legislation on migrant labor, was criticized by the director of a state agency as "a big source of the injustices going on in the agricultural field."

Each agency had ideas, not only about their own activities, but about those of other groups; and there was an underlying sentiment that the interests of one group conflicted or threatened those of another. Thus, avoidance, rather than cooperation, was often the pattern. Part of this may be attributed to the personalities and interests of many individuals involved in the system. Growers, for example, frequently hold political positions in the community. One of the most prosperous and influential growers was mayor of a township and a member of the now defunct Migrant Labor Board, a state group with close contact with the Migrant Labor Bureau. He is thus influential at both the community level and the state government level. A relative of another large family of growers is a policeman. A migrant minister lives with his brother-in-law, who is a minister of a non-migrant church in one of the local towns. His mother works at a food stamp office and his fiancée is the daughter of a county welfare official. In small rural communities, these interlocking personal relationships may greatly affect the work in a sensitive area such as farm labor.

In conclusion, most groups and organizations auxiliary to the migrant labor system work relatively independently. Although there is some contact and coordination, there is no overall unity, integration, or comprehensive planning to provide for the efficient handling of migrant problems to identify and meet migrant needs. (SGK, JP, and LT)

Government Services

Although visits by representatives of government agencies were by no means frequent (indeed, in several camps studied, no contact with government personnel was had during the summer), a few were observed as they brought their services to the migrant labor camps. When the rare visits occurred, migrants often reacted with mistrust and resentment even when the visitors tried to establish rapport. Some government officials appeared to be more concerned with the protection of their own position than with protecting the rights of others. This led them to avoid problems within their jurisdiction.

The Social Security man came into camp in a blue Rambler. He was dressed in a suit and tie. He talked to Robert for five minutes and then walked over to Peanutman and asked if his Social Security check had come through. Peanutman said he couldn't get the check because he had been told that he didn't qualify. The man was annoyed, since it should have gone through. He told Peanutman that they would have to start all over from the beginning again. Peanutman replied he would probably never get it, but the Social Security man said he shouldn't be such a pessimist. Referring to the "system," he said, "It's like half a glass of beer. The pessimist says it is half empty, while the optimist says it is half full. The system is like a mule. If you kick it long enough, it will move." He then turned to Raymond to find out if he was getting his checks. Raymond was receiving them in the south but had not gotten one since he came north. The man said he would look into it, but Raymond had lost his number. Looking annoyed, the man commented that was the problem he always ran into. "The crew leader should keep track of Social Security numbers. It is very important." Just before he left, he suggested to Robert, who was sitting by the garbage fire, that he better move to the other side away from the smoke. Robert's reaction was to get up and move. As soon as the man turned around, he deliberately went back and sat down where he had been before: he didn't want a white man telling him what to do, no matter how friendly his intentions. (IM)

* * *

Monday morning, at 10:00 A.M., a camp inspector woke me up. He opened the door and asked if I was sick. I jumped out of bed and joined the others, who were sitting in the front. The inspector was checking through the cabins, sticking his head inside each room and jotting things in a notebook. The yard was in bad shape, cluttered with Tiger Rose bottles, beer bottles, and scrap paper. He pointed to the bottles, saying we ought to put them in the trash can. He asked how many of the houses were empty and Hart said, "Eight." After checking the toilets, he told Hart, who was supposed to be the yardman, that there was a pile of trash in the john and that was the place to start cleaning up. Hart said he would get to it soon. Inquiring whether the yard would be cleaned today, he was told it would be cleaned tomorrow since "things are sort of slow on Mondays." He accepted this without questioning and left. Someone quietly commented that the inspector understood how Monday mornings were because he drinks too. Hart then complained that he was not getting paid for cleaning up the yard and it wasn't his job. Then Raymond, the crew leader, who had been chastised by the farmer for the condition of the camp, said, referring to the inspector, "You know those people. All they do is cause trouble but they never bring us nothing. They ride around here and find things wrong and cause a whole lot of trouble and then they are able to get a good office job." There was no response and, after a while, he continued about inspectors, "They think we are stupid and uneducated and that we can't do anything else; but we want to do this work here. It's not like working on the farm, you can work a while and then lay off when you want to." No one seemed to be taking Raymond up on this conversation and he left for his cabin. (LP)

* * *

The sheriff was in the camp in his patrol car. He was talking about how he dislikes to intervene in "family quarrels." He had been called into the camp because of an incident the previous evening involving Albert and a schoolteacher who came to the camp regularly. Because of the incident, the teacher left, threatening not to return. The people in the camp were furious at Albert and, afraid of being hurt, he fled to some houses nearby. Concerned about someone coming to their door at night, the people in the houses called the sheriff to investigate the incident. Now he was in the camp, making a big effort to gain the confidence of the migrants by talking about what a "regular guy" he was, how he had a family with five children, and how he understood migrant problems. He said he did not want to interfere in "family" incidents and described, humorously, his experience with a family quarrel in another camp. A woman whose husband had been beating her filed a complaint. He went to the camp and talked to this woman "who was covered with blood," and she got so emotionally involved in telling him her problems that she got a pan and hit her husband on the head. The sheriff thought it was funny that the husband finally got his due. The people listening to the story smiled politely, and he went on to talk about the problems of being a sheriff and how hard it is not to take sides on issues. He also mentioned how he played horseshoes with migrant workers and how once one of them won a game. He carried on a monologue for at least fifteen minutes while the people just stood around, listening very quietly. Slim, however, was angry that the sheriff was not taking any action about the incident with Albert, although he did not express his annoyance directly. He just kept asking him what he was going to do about Albert, whenever he could interrupt the sheriff's monologue. The sheriff finally replied that he had a deputy, who, he pointed out, was Negro; the deputy would speak to Albert. Then he left the camp. The incident was not followed up. (IM)

*   *   *

I talked to a police officer involved in a knife incident in a migrant labor camp where a migrant had been arrested. The officer claimed he did not like to "make a big thing out of these incidents," and that he does not like to arrest migrants "because they will just be out of work." He was forced, however, to intervene in this case. I asked what the grower's reaction was to the incident and he did not know, never having talked with him. He said he had heard a number of bad things about the man and didn't really care to know him. During the investigation of the incident, his contacts were only with the crew leader and the migrants involved. During the summer, he has had to interfere in only one other incident with migrants in the county. Some people had been drinking in town and caused a disturbance on the street. He was called over and instructed a group of Negroes in the crowd to take care of the problem. "I told them it was their problem because these were their people. They should take care of them." They did; they drove them back to the camp. He felt that migrants can solve their own problems and that his job was just to enforce the law. "We can't bring people in and lay them down on a bed and solve their mental problems, but we do want to help them if we can." He claims that when he spends time talking to migrants, his superior tells him to stop wasting so much time, that his job is simply to enforce the law. (JA)

*   *   *

The state troopers came this morning, looking for one of the men. They asked the crew leader's wife if she knew of a guy from some other camp who had come to her crew to work about three days ago and they described him. She said to the trooper, "Well, I don't like telling on nobody, and anyhow, people just give me their first names and I don't know their last names." Discussing the incident later, her response was lauded by the crew. "That's right, you shouldn't tell on him. If a man is in tight, I'd help him out. I don't want anyone to get caught by the law." (HH)

*   *   *

The welfare services in this area are slow to act on emergency problems. There is one camp that is so constructed that it is located in three counties whose borders happen to meet at that point. The camp consists of an old rambling house that is said to have been part of the underground railroad during the Civil War. It is said that the purpose of its unique location was to enable slaves to move to different parts of the house when pursued and thus to avoid capture by a county posse. Now, as a migrant labor camp, ironically, the situation works in reverse. During the summer, a forty-five-year-old migrant suffered an epileptic attack in the camp and required hospitalization. A social worker brought her to three county hospitals before she was finally admitted, each claiming that the camp was in another county.

In another case, the welfare department was asked to investigate the need for welfare food in a camp where, because of the late crop, there was a critical food shortage. Work was expected in several days, and there would then be money to buy food; until then, food was needed to hold them over. The director of the welfare department, skeptical of reports, made a personal investigation and agreed that the need was indeed critical. He said he would file a report and food would come in fifteen days. The social worker argued the immediacy of the problem, but the director pleaded red tape. He was reminded that in a critical situation it was possible to obtain food within a day. Provisions were made for an immediate order, but it still did not arrive for four days. (MCS)

Social Work Services

Many federal, state, and locally supported social work organizations attempt to ameliorate conditions and provide opportunities for migrants through social and welfare services and educational programs.

Hampered by inadequate personnel, these programs focus mainly on the largest camps. Many social workers get discouraged with the results of their work, feeling they are doing no more than "wiping noses." Those who attempt to go beyond the limited activities expected of them find themselves in a precarious position. A dynamic worker in one CAP organization was well liked by the migrants, provided them with much useful information, and injected a positive spirit into the camps he visited. He was, however, constrained by the central leadership of his organization. As a militant black, he was described by others in the organization as "not very well liked." He was subjected to continual pressures and eventually left the program. As in other "action" programs, this agency had to gear its activities more to please established community interests than the migrant, who makes few conspicuous demands. In doing so, organizations lose many of their most talented and potentially most effective personnel. The following selections describe the migrants' experience and reactions to adult education programs and recreational activities brought to the camps by social workers.

Several people drove into the camp, walked around, and asked people if they wanted to go to school. I was standing outside with a group of men when a well-dressed Negro woman walked up to me and asked me if I wanted to go to school. I expressed reluctance and she remarked tartly that, rather than wasting my time picking, I should get interested in a trade. She wouldn't leave me alone, so I finally agreed and she handed me a sheet to fill out. That evening seven people from the camp went to the school, including the wife and two children of the crew leader. The lady who recruited me came on the bus with us. She didn't want to sit down on the seat, claiming it was too dirty. One of the men had to go and get a piece of brown paper for her to sit on. When we arrived at the school, there were two programs, one for automobile repair, the other for reading and writing. I went to the reading clinic and was given a mimeographed booklet of exercises to do as a preliminary test. This included reading comprehension exercises and sentence construction problems and was very tedious. Few people could understand the questions, and those who seemed to be having the most trouble were sent next door to the other program despite the fact they had come to this class voluntarily with the desire of learning to read. On the way home, people said they came after a full day's work to learn a trade. Several women wanted to learn to type, and the men wanted to learn to drive. They resented what they called "second-grade tests" in the reading school. (LR)

*   *   *

Social workers have been coming into the camp in the evenings to urge people to go back to school. There was a program available whereby people could get paid $40.00 a week just for going to school. The women said they would like to go back to school for this money, but the men said it was not worth it because they could earn that much working in a week. The talk was completely on the present. No one looked far enough ahead to project that, after they finished school, they might be able to earn more than $40.00 a week. (AK)

*   *   *

On Wednesday, the social worker came in around 9:00 P.M. and set up a projector. There were twenty-five adults and seven children in the juke. He introduced the movie by talking briefly about how parents should tell their children about sex and said the movie dealt with this topic. The audience showed little reaction to this announcement, and actually, there were few people present for whom the subject was relevant. The movie described problems a parent faces in telling the facts of life to his children. It started with an example of how a child should be informed as to where the baby comes from and how it got there. Then it edged into a discussion of how little children masturbate, conveying the message that it should not be frowned upon or regarded as evil. There were some graphic displays of little girls and boys with their hands in their pants, which had the audience—adults and children alike—in hysterical laughter. The movie went on to describe subtle social pressures concerning sex at school and at various white middle-class social events. This was a movie designed for a health class or a P.T.A. meeting in a white middle-class suburban high school. (LR)

*   *   *

Some social workers brought a movie in to show. It is usually the younger people who attend the movies; except for a few old winos who wander in at odd times, the older people seldom come. This evening there were about forty people in the audience. The film was called *What Makes This Country Great*, and it was about the American farmer. It began with a big husky blond man driving his tractor through the fields, pulling it up to the barn, and hopping off. His two little kids were on the back of the tractor and his wife was in a very modern kitchen. An oil truck drove up and it became clear that the film was made as an advertisement for an oil company. The narrator than talked about all the progress, the greatness, and the great agricultural production in America. "What helped make the farmer so great? Nothing but hard labor. This man arrived by the sweat of his brow and by the use of fuel . . . but it took a long time to do this." Then the movie took us back to the stone age. An animated cartoon showed how the caveman spent all his time hunting for food. The caveman was depicted pulling on the tail of a monstrous animal, which turned around and faced him. He ran and just as he got to a cliff, he ducked behind a big rock and the animal went over the cliff. The next scene showed his family gnawing on huge bones. Moving through time, the film showed how man used his brains to get food, and eventually showed the farmer pushing west to conquer new land. It continued making the point that it was the American farmers who made the country great because they used their heads, worked hard, and of course, had fuel. The reaction throughout the evening was complete and impassive silence. (GP)

*   *   *

A young white social worker drove up to the camp in a convertible with some athletic equipment: a softball, a basketball, a bat, and jump ropes. He tried to sign up children between the ages of nine and twelve to go to camp for a week. A local Catholic camp had volunteered to take migrant children. No one was interested until he announced they would get swimsuits and a sleeping bag; then eight girls and three boys signed up. There were other boys of the appropriate age, but one of them with a lot of prestige among the children decided he did not want to go because it would prevent him from working and earning money. The others followed his example.

Several days later, we got back from work about 1:00 P.M., and the social worker was at the camp again, unloading athletic equipment. There was a hassle trying to get a basketball net up. The hoop was first put up upside down and as soon as it was hit by the ball, everything fell. Someone climbed on the roof, balancing on top of garbage cans, and got it up correctly. Nails, rescued from the ashes where some siding boards had been burned the night before, were used to put the net up. Finally, things were in order and the social worker unsuccessfully tried to get a game going. He called a bunch of kids over and suggested choosing sides. They reluctantly did so and started a game but kept switching sides. They just wanted to toss the ball around and weren't interested in playing sides.

Another evening the social worker came to show some movies. It turned out that he did not know how to use the projector. I got up and threaded it for him. While I was working on it, he hovered over me and explained things very slowly, distinctly, and condescendingly. When the machine was ready, the sound was not working well, and with the usual screaming of the children, we couldn't hear much of the film. It was a Laurel and Hardy comedy and everyone enjoyed it. (DR)

*   *   *

After I interviewed the social worker, he offered to show me around a camp. We walked over to one of the shacks where two men were shooting dice on a bed. He asked if he could show their rooms and they didn't respond. He walked in anyhow. When we entered, the men asked us if we wanted to shoot craps. The social worker said he didn't but I said, "Yes." At that point, the social worker quickly pulled me aside and said, "Let's get out of here." He told me that the object of his bringing movies to the camp was to keep people from drinking and gambling, and if I joined them it would set a bad example. He quickly took me to the room of a married couple. The woman was standing in front of her door and he asked if he could show me her room. Before she could answer, he opened the door and walked in. She looked surprised but said nothing. As he showed me the cabin, he said, "It is really beautiful, isn't it?" She glanced at him and asked, "Are you crazy, man? This is beautiful? I bet you live in a nicer place." We thanked the lady and left. As we walked away, the social worker commented that this was his favorite camp; the people here were very friendly and there was never any violence or threat of trouble. "They work hard and are good people." (LR)

*   *   *

A photographer from a community social work program came to the camp. He took pictures of the camp and the garbage disposal area. When he asked Lamb if he could take a picture of his room, Lamb refused. I later asked him why. "These people are just out here to get the crew leader in trouble." I asked him what he meant. "Just look around for yourself. This isn't a decent place for anyone to live. If these conditions are reported and these pictures are put in the paper like the photographer said they might be, then there will be a whole lot of talk about this camp and it might be closed." (GW)

The Church and Its Volunteers

Many churches have taken an active interest in migrant labor problems. Religious and recreational activities are brought to camps by ministers and volunteer laymen associated with a church parish or with the Migrant Ministry. Often ministers are the initiators of programs within their parishes. In a number of cases, ministers of conservative rural parishes, consisting largely of growers, find their humanitarian interests in conflict with that of the parish and are constrained by their own vulnerability. Not one of the ministers we met considered the possibility of having migrants come to his church.

The proverbial "do-gooders" and the "bringers of old clothes" are usually volunteers, often women, from local parishes. For many volunteers, welfare work is an occasion for church suppers and meetings with a heavy social component. But there are also many genuinely involved people, some of whom find themselves sorely constrained by community and grower pressures. Those who try to publicize conditions or openly encourage and help migrants to find better employment are criticized and delegated to innocuous and harmless tasks. However, depending on their energy and initiative, volunteers provide many useful services. In particular, transportation to day-care centers and hospitals is offered in many isolated camps where other agencies have not penetrated.

Reverend Black had organized a group from his church to bring films and athletic equipment to migrants in the evenings. The reception was so poor that the effort had been discontinued. He felt that migrants were too tired after a day's work to participate in athletics and that the films were not interesting to them. He described their attitude as apathetic. There are no Negroes in Reverend Black's church. His parish brings old clothes to him for distribution to the migrants, but they feel, "Migrants do better in their own situation and should have their own church." The Reverend, himself, felt that no migrants would want to attend his service. His parish includes successful growers, small marginal farmers, and local merchants. The successful farmers, he claimed, cannot get along without migrants and give them good camps and good wages. They keep their workers well employed and, "while they don't see migrants as equals, you can't knock the way they are treated." He gave several examples of the attitudes of marginal farmers. One man retired early from farming because his area was building up as a stagrant community and he was afraid to live there. His wife bought a pistol but they soon moved to another area. The third group, the local merchants, do a lot of business with migrants but scorn them. Reverend Black claims to be personally sympathetic both to the migrant and to the attitudes of his parish. He feels that the migrant worker will not be needed much longer and he waits for machinery to develop and the stream to "dry up." (CL)

*   *   *

The minister was concerned about potential cancellation of the child-care program. The school that had been housing the day-care center could no longer be used because the academic year was about to begin. An alternative location had to be found quickly or the program would have to be dropped. I asked about the possibility of holding it in the meeting house of his church. He replied that the vestry was in favor of such a move; but it couldn't be done because the church has a very small septic tank and the use of the toilets by too many people would ruin the system. He also claimed that the vestry was more liberal than the parishioners and he had to be careful. The parishioners said nothing about his migrant activities; indeed, many people donated money and clothes, but there were some who did not like what he was doing. He felt guilty during the summer when he spent considerable time with migrants and neglected some of his church duties. He felt himself torn by conflicting allegiances. No migrants come to his church and he is certain that, even if they came, they would not like the service. Furthermore, there was little or no direct social contact between any member of his parish and migrants. He sees himself as a radical in the community. (LR)

*   *   *

At 6:30, Reverend Tom arrived in the camp, wearing a neatly pressed dark business suit with black rosary beads around his neck and carrying an attaché case of synthetic leather. On the dance platform where he usually holds Sunday services, Shorty was trying to get a penny crap game going. He shook the dice and screamed, "No craps, no craps. Got to get a penny game going, penny game, any takers." Someone came over and said he'd be willing to play for nickels but not pennies. Meanwhile, there was a "coon" game going on between Whiskers and Aaron on another part of the dance platform. Still another card game was going on in the corner and a whist game was being played in the middle. The jukebox was blaring through it all.

Into this secular scene walked the minister, and he stood there for a moment, taking it all in. Shorty was elated because he had found a taker for his game and was rolling the dice. He won quite a few nickels and proceeded to challenge his partner to another game. At this point, Aaron said to Whiskers, "I think we should stop playing. We have to show some respect for the Reverend." But Shorty continued shaking his dice, showering them with kisses. The Reverend walked quietly over and stood next to Shorty, who was on his knees. He stood there conspicuously staring, and Shorty looked up and said, "You don't mind, do you?" The minister mumbled, "Well, I think I'd like to get services going. Please, could we get a service going here?" Shorty shouted, "No crap," and threw the dice. They bounced off the minister's shoe and turned up a seven. Shorty collected from his partner while Reverend Tom stared down incredulously. "Could we please get a service going?" Shorty yelled, "Crap," and got four. "Shooting for four, baby, shooting for four, let's go four," and shot the dice. He lost when seven came up and the crap game broke up. The two card games continued.

The minister walked to one end of the platform and produced a paperbound copy of the New Testament from his attaché case. Just then, someone in the coon game near the minister shouted, "Motherfucker, I've lost." The minister opened his Bible, a contemporary language edition, and suddenly Geech, wearing his purple paisley basketball hat, a red cotton knit shirt with white stripes down the sleeves, and a pair of gray, very worn pants, walked up to the minister and said, "You call yourself a Reverend?" The minister looked at him and said, "Yes, I'm Reverend Tom." "You're no Reverend. You sold me a pair of pants that didn't even have a zipper on them. Cost me 50 cents, them pants." A hush came over the platform. Geech leaned against the post and said, "You ain't no minister. You just come here to line your pocket. That's all you do. You're like those rich men. They can't go through the camel's eye. You're going to burn in the wake of fire. Do you hear that? With all the sinners and everyone else, you're going to burn in that wake of fire, too."

The minister stood through this dumbstruck, put his attaché case down, closed his book and stood there. Geech began to speak of Moses as a leader of the Hebrew children. Suddenly the minister began to laugh defensively. He laughed harder and harder, until finally Geech walked away, whereupon the minister opened his Bible and began reading from Matthew. As several appropriate points, Geech very loudly made relevant biblical comments. The noise in the area surrounding the platform began to increase, and the minister finally closed the book, saying, "These people just aren't ready to hear God's words today. I'll have to come back some time when there's less money. Then, maybe they'll listen." After he left, I went to the store with Cory and we discussed what Geech had done. Cory laughed a little and said, "Well, it wasn't very respectful the way he treated the minister, but I guess it was a good idea that somebody finally said that to him. Some people just say whatever comes into their minds." I said, "Yeah, that's kind of like little children." He replied, "Yeah, but Jesus always said to be like little children." (DR)

*   *   *

A man came around and said he was a preacher out to help people save their souls. In response to that, Raymond, the crew leader, told him a story about a man who went to a service. At the service the preacher told him that if he gave money to Jesus, tomorrow Jesus would give it back to him twicefold. The man did and the next day he was sitting beneath a tree and said, "Jesus, I know you're here. The preacher said you're everywhere. Could you give me back my money twicefold? I gave you five dollars last night. I want ten dollars now." Nothing happened. So he raised his hand and tried again. Just then a load of shit appeared in the man's hand and he said, "Jesus, I asked for money. I don't want to take this shit from you."

The visiting preacher was visibly upset and left. Wolf chided Raymond for saying something like that to a minister, but Raymond replied, "That's a big hustle. Look at that car he's driving. Shit, what a great hustle being a preacher is." Raymond said he hadn't been to church since 1949 and every time he goes near one he gets scared. "I mean I'm not jiving, man, people hitting me and singing those songs. Man, it really scares me." Then he moved back to the subject of ministers. "Man, ministers are the biggest hustle going these days." He told a story about one in Texas who got a new Cadillac every six months. "Man, I'd like to get into one of those churches and sit in the back when the plate comes around with all those tens and twenties on it. Man, I just think I could do it; I mean they always say the Devil sits at the back of the church. I'd just take off. There's only one thing, man, you gotta believe it. I'm not jiving you. There's only this one thing; that's all that's important. All you got to believe is that there's one God and everything else ain't important. Just that there's one God." (LP)

*   *   *

The church committee was discussing migrants who had asked for help in leaving the migrant labor stream. They were concerned about encouraging them to leave because of the grower complaints. One woman was recently criticized by a grower when she handed out surplus food, which the grower claimed reduced people's desire to work. The minister heading the group noted that the grower had contracted for the labor and he did not want to help violate a contract by pulling people out of camps during the season. Someone in the group commented that, after all, migrants were free to come and go. The minister acknowledged this but the church had to think of its own situation, which could be jeopardized by taking labor away from growers. (LR)

*   *   *

Bobo was critical of the secondhand clothes often brought to the camp. He said no secondhand clothes could match store-bought clothes. There is much more status to new clothes, regardless of the quality of the seconds. At about 5:30 P.M. one Sunday, five church cars came into the camp together, selling used clothes at a low price. There were at least twenty white people in the group. I heard a white teen-age girl describe how she gave away a cap to a child because he wanted it so badly; but most of the clothes were sold. Slim bought a pair of shoes for 40 cents, and some suits were sold for $2.00. I would estimate that about $50.00 was spent during the evening. Although they prefer new clothes, people feel it is all right to buy secondhand stuff to work in the fields. After the group left, we talked about them. Bobo said, "They're good people, these Catholics; they mean well." He then observed how the excitement of the evening had worn away and he went to bed. (IM)

*   *   *

A visitor to the camp came over and tried to engage me in a conversation about how poorly migrants work, wondering why they pick so slowly, are lazy, and have such low motivation. I tried to avoid her, and after a while she began to talk to Tee about motivation. She had a difficult time trying to express her questions in terms he could understand. She finally said, "Well, why do you think it is, son, that colored people just don't seem to want to work hard; that they have such low motivation?" Tee brightened up and replied, "No, Ma'am, we ain't got no low motivation. We came up here on a big bus." (MR)

Bibliography

The following list of readily available books on migrant labor is offered for the reader who would like to pursue the problem further. Some of the books deal with migrant labor in general, while others are concerned with the more specific topics that their titles suggest.

ALLEN, STEVE, 1966, *The Ground Is Our Table.* Garden City, N. Y.: Doubleday.

BISHOP, C. E., ed., 1967, *Farm Labor in the United States.* New York: Columbia University Press.

FISHER, LLOYD, 1953, *The Harvest Labor Market in California.* Cambridge, Mass.: Harvard University Press.

HILL, HERBERT, 1959, *No Harvest for the Reaper.* New York: National Association for the Advancement of Colored People.

MACGILLIVRAY, JOHN H., AND ROBERT A. STEVENS, 1964, *Agricultural Labor and Its Effective Use.* Palo Alto, Calif.: The National Press.

MADSEN, WILLIAM, 1964, *Mexican-Americans of South Texas.* New York: Holt.

MCWILLIAMS, CAREY, 1942, *Ill Fares the Land: Migrants and Migratory Labor in the United States.* Boston: Little, Brown.

MOORE, TRUMAN E., 1965, *The Slaves We Rent.* New York: Random House.

NELKIN, DOROTHY, 1970, *On the Season: Aspects of the Migrant Labor System.* Ithaca, N. Y.: New York State School of Industrial and Labor Relations, Cornell University. ILR Paperback No. 8.

NELSON, EUGENE, 1966, *Huelga: The First Hundred Days of the Great Delano Grape Strike.* Delano, Calif.: Farm Worker Press.

PADFIELD, HARLAND, AND WILLIAM EDWIN MARTIN, 1965, *Farmers, Workers and Machines.* Tucson: University of Arizona Press.

RUBEL, ARTHUR, 1966, *Across the Tracks.* Austin: University of Texas Press.

SHOTWELL, LOUISA ROSSITER, 1961, *The Harvesters: Story of the Migrant People.* Garden City, N. Y.: Doubleday.

WRIGHT, DALE, 1965, *They Harvest Despair.* Boston: Beacon Press.

The following bibliography provides a comprehensive and up-to-date listing of most of the relevant books, periodicals, United States government documents, dissertations, bibliographies, bulletins, and unpublished materials on the subject of migrant labor.

RUESINK, DAVID C., AND T. BRICE BATSON, 1969, *Bibliography Relating to Agricultural Labor.* College Station, Texas: Texas Agricultural Experiment Station. (Departmental Information Report Number 69–1.)

LIBRARY
SOLANO COMMUNITY COLLEGE
P. O. BOX 246
SUISUN CITY, CALIFORNIA 94585
(707) 864-7000